Preventing Child Maltreatment in the U.S.

The Black Community Perspective

Violence against Women and Children

Series editor, Judy L. Postmus

Millions of women and children are affected by violence across the globe. Gender-based violence affects individuals, families, communities, and policies. Our new series includes books written by experts from a wide range of disciplines, including social work, sociology, health, criminal justice, education, history, and women's studies. A unique feature of the series is the collaboration between academics and community practitioners. The primary author of each book in most cases is a scholar, but at least one chapter is written by a practitioner, who draws out the practical implications of the academic research. Topics will include physical and sexual violence; psychological, emotional, and economic abuse; stalking; trafficking; and childhood maltreatment, and will incorporate a gendered, feminist, or womanist analysis. Books in the series are addressed to an audience of academics and students, as well as to practitioners and policymakers.

Hilary Botein and Andrea Hetling, *Home Safe Home: Housing Solutions for Survivors of Intimate Partner Violence*

Preventing Child Maltreatment miniseries:

Milton A. Fuentes, Rachel R. Singer, and Renee L. DeBoard-Lucas, *Preventing Child Maltreatment: Multicultural Considerations in the U.S.*

Esther J. Calzada, Monica Faulkner, Catherine A. LaBrenz, and Milton A. Fuentes, *Preventing Child Maltreatment in the U.S.: The Latinx Community Perspective*

Melissa Phillips, Shavonne J. Moore-Lobban, and Milton A. Fuentes, *Preventing Child Maltreatment in the U.S.: The Black Community Perspective*

Royleen J. Ross, Julii M. Green, and Milton A. Fuentes, *Preventing Child Maltreatment in the U.S.: American Indian and Alaska Native Perspectives*

Preventing Child Maltreatment in the U.S.

The Black Community Perspective

MELISSA PHILLIPS, SHAVONNE J. MOORE-LOBBAN,
AND MILTON A. FUENTES

Rutgers University Press
New Brunswick, Camden, and Newark, New Jersey, and London

Library of Congress Cataloging-in-Publication Data

Names: Jordan, Melissa Phillips, author. | Moore-Lobban, Shavonne J., author. | Fuentes, Milton A., author.
Title: Preventing child maltreatment in the U.S.: the Black community perspective / Melissa Phillips, Shavonne Moore-Lobban, Milton A. Fuentes.
Description: New Brunswick, NJ : Rutgers University Press, [2022] | Series: Violence against women and children | Includes bibliographical references and index.
Identifiers: LCCN 2021055691 | ISBN 9781978820630 (paperback) | ISBN 9781978820647 (hardback) | ISBN 9781978820654 (epub) | ISBN 9781978820661 (mobi) | ISBN 9781978820678 (pdf)
Subjects: LCSH: Child abuse—United States. | Child abuse—United States—Prevention. | Child welfare—United States. | African American children—Social conditions. | African Americans—Social conditions.
Classification: LCC HV6626.52 .J67 2022 | DDC 362.760973—dc23/eng/20220512
LC record available at https://lccn.loc.gov/2021055691

A British Cataloging-in-Publication record for this book is available from the British Library.

www.rutgersuniversitypress.org

Manufactured in the United States of America

Contents

Preventing Child Maltreatment in the U.S.

The Black Community Perspective

Introduction

> Today we begin in earnest the work of making sure that the world we leave our children is just a little bit better than the one we inhabit today.
>
> —Barack Obama, 44th president of the United States

Overview

The prevention of child maltreatment is a multifaceted public health issue requiring focused attention and concerted efforts to protect children adequately. In this chapter, we provide the context for understanding the information presented throughout this book. We define maltreatment and introduce prominent issues surrounding maltreatment such as prevalence and disparities, particularly concerning Black children. We highlight relevant associations between women and children. Lastly, we introduce three cases that will be discussed and given further context throughout each chapter of this book.

Maltreatment of Black Children Matters

Violence against children has been an important human rights issue across the world's continents. A number of efforts have been developed as a response to the growing recognition of this issue. For example, the World Day for the Prevention of Child Abuse was established in 2000 to foster a global culture of prevention and proactive protection against child maltreatment (American Psychological Association, 2019; National Institute of Health, 2006). The World Health Organization (WHO) also spearheaded several initiatives to protect children, such as the United Nations (UN) and Child Rights International Network, helping to build global networks to prevent child abuse. At least sixty countries have banned the corporal punishment of children, and an additional twenty-eight countries have made committed efforts to reform laws to prohibit corporal punishment (Burns, Stein Helland, Kriz, Sanchez-Cabezudo, Skivenes, & Strompl, 2021). These are important steps in the reduction of child abuse. In the United States (U.S.), child maltreatment continues to be an important focus for prominent national organizations. The American Psychological Association (APA), for example, in the past five years, has taken a strong stance against physical punishment (American Psychological Association, 2019). The APA has also established major initiatives to fight against child abuse, such as the Adults and Children Together (ACT) Against Violence, which is a national APA program that provides education and resources focused on the early years of a child's life and establishing protective environments around children. This is one of many programs designed to tackle the problem of child maltreatment.

Nurturing the growth and well-being of children is a cornerstone of a humane society. Yet, the rates at which children are abused and neglected are alarming. In 2019, Child Protection Service agencies received approximately 4.4 million referrals of alleged child maltreatment, of which 656,000 children are found to be victims of abuse and/or neglect (U.S. Department of Health & Human Services, Administration for Children and Families, Administration on Children, Youth and Families, Children's Bureau, 2021). In 2018, there were 1,800 children whose deaths were attributed to child maltreatment (Administration for Children & Families, 2020). The magnitude of this problem is vast, and the negative outcomes associated with child maltreatment are expansive (Corley & Crenshaw, 2018; Feletti et al., 1998; Norman et al., 2012; Vidal et al., 2017). The harming and endangering of children is not only concerning for children, but is also a public health issue that has pervasive effects at the family, school, community, and societal levels. Consequences of maltreatment can include physical health problems, mental health conditions, juvenile justice involvement, and child fatality. The impact of maltreatment on society is also evident in several ways; for example, through increased rates of healthcare utilization for child maltreatment victims, which has implications for overall U.S. healthcare costs (Kuang, Aratani, & Li, 2018). Ultimately, the ecological impact of child maltreatment reaches all citizens of a society.

In 2008, the Centers for Disease Control and Prevention (CDC) defined child maltreatment as, "any act or series of acts of commission or omission by a parent or other caregiver that results in harm, potential for harm, or threat of harm to a child" (Leeb et al., 2008). The CDC has defined acts of commission as physical, sexual, and/or psychological abuse, and acts of omission as failure to provide for a child's basic physical, emotional, or educational needs or to protect a child from harm or potential harm. Thus, acts of omission include physical, emotional, medical/dental, and educational neglect, as well as inadequate supervision and exposure to violent environments. Child maltreatment takes on many forms, from what can happen in the home or community such as physical, emotional or sexual abuse, neglect, and harsh discipline methods, to commercial exploitation including child sex trafficking and child pornography.

There is uncertainty regarding the number of children who experience maltreatment, which speaks to the difficulty of identifying these children (Gonzalez, Bethencourt Mirabal, & McCall, 2021; Norman et al., 2012). There are some clear cases that can be readily identified. However, there are other cases that are more difficult to discern, which poses a danger to abused and neglected children who continue to be hidden in plain sight. Further, some cases are hard to discern because they have to be understood within the cultural and family context of the individual. The need for ongoing identification and monitoring methods of child maltreatment, prevention tools, and effective interventions is clear. It is the pervasive nature of the effects of child maltreatment that deems it a public health crisis that needs to be continually addressed. Notably, given the clear influence of culture and behavior, child maltreatment should also be cautiously addressed.

By virtue of various characteristics including age, size, physical strength, development and maturity, susceptibility, and legal stature, children do not have adequate capability to ensure their own well-being. The limited ability to self-protect and the lack of power within the hierarchical, patriarchal societal structure leaves children particularly vulnerable to being taken advantage of. It is the inherent responsibility of the adults in a society to care for and protect the children among them. Through policy, legislation, resources, and supportive services, societal structures seek to protect children as well as equip adults with adequate knowledge, boundaries, and resources to protect children. The discussion about groups within a society who cannot protect themselves extends beyond children to those individuals that are marginalized and oppressed, which is the case for people of color. It is in this regard that Black children are the particular focus of this book. There is notable research indicating differences in the severity of outcomes of child maltreatment along racial lines (Child Welfare Information Gateway, 2017a; Fluke et al., 2011; Kohl et al., 2011; Sedlak et al., 2010). Child maltreatment occurs to Black children at higher rates than any other racial group (Child Welfare Information Gateway, 2017a). For the purposes of this book, Black is used as a broad racial category to refer to U.S. or foreign-born individuals of African descent. Specific subgroups of ethnicities within the Black category includes African Americans and individuals of African descent born in countries in the Caribbean, South and Central America, and Africa. Most of the literature on child maltreatment is focused specifically on African Americans, with a few studies and articles including other Black ethnic groups as well. As a result, this book has a similar distribution of focus, but particular effort has been made to highlight other Black ethnic groups, when possible, to broaden the understanding of the impact of child maltreatment within Black families and communities.

Research has shown that there is a disproportionate number of Black children experiencing maltreatment (Raz, Dettlaff, & Edwards, 2021). Although there is not consensus about the cause of this race-related disparity, there are factors that are thought to be likely contributory factors to the disproportionate number of Black children being maltreated. For example, the children of poor mothers and/or in low-income families are more likely to experience maltreatment (Child Welfare Information Gateway, 2017a; Dixon, 2008). Given that African American children are three times more likely to live in poverty than other racial groups, this factor points to their being at higher risk of maltreatment (Dixon, 2008; Drake et al., 2008). Children of single parents are also at higher risk of maltreatment, and there are higher rates of single parents in the Black community (Fluke et al. 2011). There are disproportional numbers of Black children in the child welfare system (Fluke et al., 2011; Kohl et al., 2011; National Conference of State Legislatures, 2021). This adds another layer of negative outcomes for Black children to face; from increased juvenile justice involvement to the potential of additional maltreatment being suffered in the child welfare system. This is further compounded by Black families tending to have less access to services, including legal representation, a lack of which was found to be associated with high rates of entry into foster care (Kohl et al., 2011). Thus, Black children are at significant risk of maltreatment and related negative outcomes. This warrants targeted prevention and intervention methods in order to protect them effectively.

There is a distinction to be made when categorizing the disparities impacting children in the child welfare system. That is, there are population-based disparities that are apparent as particular sub-groups such as Black children are examined, and there are disparities associated with decision making related to child welfare (Antwi-Boasiako et al., 2020). For example, it is notable that population-based factors such as social, economic, and cultural differences can impact racial groups differently. As delineated above, there are many population-based reasons that are likely contributing to the disparate amount of Black children experiencing maltreatment compared to other races. There are also disparities that are likely related to decision-based factors, which can occur at various stages of child welfare involvement. For example, the decisions made by referrers such as healthcare providers regarding whether to report that a child may be maltreated, or decisions made once a child is in the child welfare system such as determining need for out-of-home placement and the length of stay in foster care (Antwi-Boasiako et al., 2020). Distinguishing between population-based versus decision-based factors can be important as the disproportionate number of Black children in the child welfare system is examined and as prevention and intervention methods are discussed later in this book.

Relevant Associations between Women and Children

Examining the circumstances surrounding child abuse reveals notable associations between women and children. Research has noted that mothers are the most common perpetrators of child maltreatment (Santhosh, 2016; World Health Organization, 2002). Certainly, there are individual factors that can be examined, but delving beyond the individualist acts of child maltreatment to examine the context in which it occurs offers a deeper understanding of underlining associations. Women are often the primary caregiver for children and in that regard, children are impacted directly and indirectly by the ills affecting women. For example, there are high rates of co-occurrence between intimate partner violence against women and violence against children, as high as 40 percent (Nami, et al, 2017). This degree of overlapping violence points to the contextual factors as key in understanding how to reduce maltreatment.

Broadening the discussion from mothers to parents reveals other factors associated with child maltreatment. Parenting approaches, which can differ across racial groups, can be a contributing factor to suspected or alleged child abuse. One prominent challenge to unpacking child maltreatment within the Black community is the use of discipline. It has been established that Black parents endorse physical discipline methods at a higher rate than White parents (Horn et al., 2004; Patton, 2017). The commonplace nature of physical discipline methods within the Black community creates inherent difficulty in identifying where the demarcation falls between discipline and abuse. Consider, for example, a Black mother who repeatedly spanks her seven-year-old son with her hand, and another mother who lets her twelve-year-old son babysit his five-year-old brother while she works a night shift. These examples are common occurrences in Black communities and reflect the interplay between cultural, socioeconomic status, and child rearing choices. Understanding the individual, cultural, and contextual systemic factors associated with child maltreatment is key to developing targeted and effective ways to protect children.

Chapter Content

Each chapter of this book will methodically delve into various aspects of child maltreatment in the Black community from definitions to outcomes, prevalence to prevention, and public examples to redacted case studies. This introductory chapter frames the context for understanding the information presented in the other chapters of this book.

Notably, this Introduction includes three cases, discussed below, which will be briefly presented and then expanded upon throughout each chapter of this book. Chapters 1 through 3 lay the foundation for understanding child maltreatment, child maltreatment specific to Black families, and the disproportionate rate of Black children in the system. Specifically, chapter 1 describes cultural considerations surrounding Black families in order to provide a contextual understanding of the child-rearing practices within the Black community. There is specific attention to the strengths and positive attributes of Black families, and the challenges they face being an ethnic-minority group within society. Chapter 2 provides definitions of child maltreatment, epidemiological data including laws protecting children and prevalence rates, types of child maltreatment, statistics about child abuse perpetrators and fatalities, and data on maltreatment outcomes. Chapter 3 explores the disproportionality of Black children in the child welfare system. Factors that are likely contributors to the overrepresentation of Black children in child welfare are also explored, including racial bias, lack of access to resources of Black mothers, and the intersection of intimate partner violence and child abuse in the Black community.

Chapters 4 through 6 address prevention, intervention, and advocacy interventions to help. Specifically, chapter 4 discusses current prevention methods and effective interventions for the individual, family, school and agency levels. The two most widespread forms of child abuse prevention methods of offender management and school-based educational programs are delineated. The role of public policy in prevention and intervention is discussed, with particular exploration of the implication for Black children. Chapter 5 focuses on ways to improve the well-being and health outcomes for Black children and families affected by child maltreatment. The importance of empowering women, given that they are frequently the primary caregiver of children is discussed as an important means of protecting the well-being of children. Chapter 6 explores advocacy and child welfare reform by highlighting actionable steps that are possible from the micro to macro levels of a social ecological model. This chapter is largely based on a proposal that was put forth in a journal article in 2008 for a law, the African American Child Welfare Act, that would specifically address the needs and circumstances related to Black children in the child welfare system and the maltreatment they experience. The impact that this law could have at the various level of influence will be discussed, including at the point of child maltreatment identification, investigation, substantiation standards, foster care placement, exit from foster care, and family reunification.

Chapter 7 is about application. Specifically, this chapter includes a fourth, more detailed case that can be viewed in a complete form, from beginning to conclusion. This case will be presented in four parts, cover the main topics of each chapter, and include discussion questions that can be used in a college classroom setting, or other group discussion formats, such as professional trainings. Finally, chapter 8 provides a conclusion to what has been discussed in this book and discusses an image of what the future should include to protect Black children and reform the child welfare system. Final thoughts on the four cases discussed throughout this book will be provided in the context of future efforts that can be made for them. The impact of the Me Too Movement and the Black Lives Matter Movement on child maltreatment will be discussed, as will the potential future directions of agencies that promote and include child protection. Finally, we will cover the future direction of child protection from a global standpoint, including international trends for child protection laws and policies.

Case Studies: Madison, Daniel, and Oni

The following three case vignettes are presented to facilitate the reader's exploration of child maltreatment within Black families. Each case offers a view into the life and circumstances of a child who has potentially experienced child maltreatment. Notably, all identifying information in these cases has been redacted and fictitious names have been used to protect the identity of the individuals the cases are based on. The first case discusses a two-year-old Black girl whose daycare provider found a bruise on her leg. The second case is of a fifteen-year-old second generation Jamaican boy whose younger sibling ingested pills when left unattended when he was supposed to be babysitting. Child Protective Services (CPS) was alerted when she was taken to a hospital emergency room. The third case discusses a ten-year-old Ghanaian girl who immigrated to the U.S. with her family and entered the foster care system when CPS determined her home was inadequate. For each case, the factors to be considered and the implications for child maltreatment and well-being are discussed. Subsequent chapters further discuss these cases as is relevant to chapter content.

Madison

Madison is a two-year-old Black girl. She was born three weeks premature and was initially hospitalized in the neonatal intensive care unit for one week due to breathing difficulties before she was released to go home with her parents. Until she was six months old, she had recurring respiratory infections requiring visits to urgent care for treatment and monitoring on three different occasions. Madison started walking at thirteen months and talking at fifteen months. She has had occasional earaches and has an allergy to nuts, but she was generally considered a healthy child. Madison was in a middle-class family who lived in a suburban neighborhood in a Northeastern state in the U.S. Her family included her twenty-seven-year-old mother, father aged thirty-three, and her ten-year-old brother. Her mother worked as a human resources assistant and had earned an associate's degree. Madison's father worked as a large-chain supermarket store manager. He also took online and evening college classes toward attaining his bachelor's degree in business administration. Her brother was a fifth grader in a public elementary school. He sometimes helped his parents with changing and feeding Madison. Her mother previously attended psychotherapy intermittently related to grieving the loss of her father and the resulting distress of two miscarriages.

Madison's mother stayed at home for the first three months of her life. Then Madison began attending daycare and her mother returned to work. Both of her parents were actively involved in raising her. They shared childcare responsibilities, including drop-offs and pickups from daycare, diaper changes and baths, meal prep and bedtime routine. Her family was Catholic and attended church services two to three Sundays a month. Madison had a cousin who was approximately her age, whom she played with at least once a month. There was also a neighbor who had a son around Madison's age that she played with occasionally. Madison attended her first daycare for three months, but after she developed recurring diaper rashes, her parents changed her to a different daycare due to concerns that the daycare staff were not changing her diapers as much as needed. Madison has remained at the subsequent daycare for approximately a year and a half. Reports from that daycare staff consistently noted that Madison was generally a mild-mannered, happy child who tended to be fussy about taking naps. She seemed to get along well with other children. She enjoyed playing with baby dolls and LEGOs, and hearing nursery rhymes. On typical days, Madison was taken to daycare by her mother and picked up in the afternoons by her father. Once at home, she had a snack, took a nap, played and watched TV, then was put to bed in the crib in her bedroom at 8:00 P.M. She sometimes spent the night with her grandmother, who lived ten minutes away, and had play dates every few weeks. She occasionally awoke crying during the night. Her parents would typically let her cry until she fell back to sleep, provided that her crying did not last longer than five to ten minutes, in which case they would go into her room to help soothe her.

One day while Madison was at daycare, one of the daycare staff noticed what appeared to be bruising on Madison's inner right thigh. The staffer was initially unsure it was a bruise as the coloring of the bruise was difficult to distinguish against Madison's medium brown complexion. But upon inspection in bright light, the area in question appeared to be one inch long, oval shaped, reddish, and raised. This was the first time the bruise had been observed. No other bruising was found on her. The staffer shared her observation of the bruise to the daycare owner's attention. The owner checked with all staff to inquire if there were any observed incidents at daycare with other children or staff that may have caused the bruise. The daycare owner then spoke with Madison's father about it when he picked her up from daycare that afternoon. Madison's father was initially confused about the bruise, stating that he had not noticed it and supposed that maybe she fell while playing or maybe there was an incident that happened at the daycare that caused the bruise. The daycare owner assured him that while the children could not be observed 100 percent of the time, they were well supervised and that he would have been informed if there was an incident that caused bruising. Madison's father, visibly irritated, said that he would follow up once he talked with his wife about the issue.

The next day, Madison's mother and father went to the daycare with Madison and had a meeting with the daycare owner. Her parents explained that they do not use any form of physical punishment with Madison, and they believed the bruise resulted from "something that happened at daycare." The daycare owner let the parents know she had to report this bruise to CPS. The parents left the daycare center irate that it was "being suggested that [they] could hurt her." They also contacted CPS to report that they believed their child was likely hurt while at daycare. Two days later, a caseworker from CPS came to their residence at 4:00 P.M. Both parents were interviewed together, then separately; Madison's brother was also interviewed. Additionally, a neighbor and Madison's grandmother were interviewed as they have babysat her previously. Madison's parents were informed that the daycare workers were being questioned as a part of the investigation as well. Two days later, another bruise appeared that partially overlapped the original bruise. They insisted to the caseworker that they had not caused the bruise. The worker advised them to pay careful attention to her behavior day and night. Madison's parents watched carefully as she played at home, but noticed nothing that would explain the bruises. The next night, Madison's father slept in her bedroom on the floor where she could not see him. At approximately 11:30 P.M., Madison's father watched as she awoke and whimpered. Within minutes, she attempted to climb out of her crib by lifting one leg over the wooden crib rail. She rocked her body on the rail a few times but could not hoist herself over the rail. She then laid back down and shortly after, fell asleep. In the morning, Madison's parents called the case worker to let her know of this observation. The caseworker expressed that this behavior was a likely cause of the bruising. The caseworker advised them to sleep in the same room with Madison and give her encouragement to stay in bed when she tries to get out. She also advised them to mount crib rail covers to soften the edges of the crib so that if Madison attempted to climb out again, it would be less likely to create bruising. The caseworker determined that child abuse or neglect was not substantiated, and the case was closed. The worker had no further contact with the family. No further bruises appeared and no further incidents that raised suspicion of maltreatment occurred. Madison's parents decided to have her attend a different daycare. They were already concerned with how various daycare providers viewed them. Not because they anticipated doing anything wrong, but because Madison's parents understood the views that some people in society have toward Black people. Although there was another daycare ten minutes from their home, they preferred to drive twenty minutes to another daycare that was run by a family of color. They perceived they would be better understood and given the "benefit of the doubt" about their parenting.

Daniel

Daniel is a fifteen-year-old Black young man who lived with his mother, father, nine-year-old brother, and five-year-old sister in a Midwestern state. He was a ninth grader at a public high school. He generally performed well in school and participated in a Japanese animation club after school once a week. He had no history of behavioral problems in school and had never been suspended. His parents, who were in their late thirties, were Caribbean immigrants from Jamaica who came to the U.S. in their early twenties and became naturalized U.S. citizens. Daniel was being raised in a low-income family. His mother worked for a large retail chain and sometimes worked late night shifts. His father was a truck driver and was gone from the home for two to three weeks every month. His mother was the primary caregiver of the children and carried out most parenting responsibilities. She made sure they were on the school bus in the mornings, had them call her when they get home in the evenings, prepared meals, planned their social activities, and carried out discipline. When their father was home in between truck driving tours, he was often tired and slept long hours. He struggled to become reincorporated into the family routine. Daniel helped with chores at home, including cooking simple meals, cleaning, and watching his younger siblings at night when his mother worked a late shift. His mother would leave him in charge of his siblings once or twice a week. Daniel usually helped his brother with homework, let his brother and sister watch TV, then sent his brother to bed and put his sister to sleep.

Daniel had several friends with whom he attended school that lived in his neighborhood. He enjoyed playing video games, making gaming videos to put on YouTube, and drawing comic book characters. Some days after school, he socialized at friends' houses if he did not have to babysit, or a friend came over to play video games. On days when he babysat, he would sometimes have friends come over as well. One night when left in charge, Daniel snuck out to go to a friend's house and left his siblings home alone after they had gone to sleep. He was gone for approximately two hours. Unknown to him, his five-year-old sister woke up crying and vomiting. She went to Daniel's room, then to her other brother's room. His brother ran through the house looking for Daniel, and when he did not find Daniel, he called both Daniel and their mother's cell phone. When neither of the calls were answered, the youngest brother called his grandmother. The grandmother told him to give his sister a tablespoon of Nauzene, a children's over-the-counter medication for nausea and upset stomach. She immediately drove over to the home from a neighboring state. Daniel returned home a few minutes before his grandmother arrived. Seeing that her granddaughter was still vomiting when she arrived, she took her to the emergency room (ER) of a nearby hospital. After several hours in the ER, toxicology tests showed that Daniel's sister ingested pills that were prescribed to her mother. The ER staff contacted CPS, and a case was opened to investigate the circumstances under which Daniel's sister ingested the medication.

A CPS caseworker came to the home the next morning. All family members were interviewed separately. The caseworker raised concerns about the pills being accessible to the children, as the medication bottles were on the sink counter in the master bedroom. There were also concerns raised about Daniel having babysitting duties given that he left the home, leaving the younger children unsupervised. Daniel's parents were assigned a continuing-care caseworker who visited the home weekly. During the second visit, Daniel's grandmother told the caseworker that one of her granddaughters, who is Daniel's cousin, had recently said she was "touched" by Daniel while they were "playing around" on more than one occasion. This claim was investigated by the caseworker, who then conducted additional interviews with Daniel and his cousin.

When Daniel was questioned about this, he said that he did not touch his cousin inappropriately. His parents spent the next few days asking him questions about why his cousin would say so if it did not happen and why she would be uncomfortable coming to their house. He described what they do when hanging out, including playing video games and social games, sometimes with his friends included. One of the games involved pushing each other off a seat akin to musical chairs. He was asked to describe the game in detail. He then described that when pushing his cousin, he sometimes did not pay attention to where his hands were on her body. When his cousin was questioned, she explained that he never grabbed her body, but that he did push her and, in doing so, touched various parts of her body, then "cracked up" about it.

The caseworker found that neglect was substantiated regarding Daniel's sister, and sexual abuse was not substantiated regarding Daniel. CPS recommendations to the family included keeping medication secured from a child's reach by keeping medication bottles in a locked box or cabinet. It was also recommended that the family attend therapy and have more reliable babysitting options for Daniel's siblings. His parents hired an adult babysitter for the nights when their mother had to work late. Daniel's parents had several subsequent conversations with him about being careful with how he conducts himself around other children and being more aware of what behaviors are appropriate versus those that could make someone feel uncomfortable. Daniel and his father argued with increased frequency after CPS involvement occurred. Daniel attended psychotherapy for approximately four months, during which time his parents attended some of his sessions. Tensions occurring between Daniel and his father were discussed in therapy. His father expressed frustrations over all that the "family had to deal with" because of Daniel. His father expressed anger about the "family name being dragged through the mud because [Daniel] is being a knucklehead." The tensions within the family reduced over time; however, the father continued to express frustration that he could not "teach" his son responsibility in the same way that he learned responsibility during his childhood—by watching his siblings while his parents worked. The father noted that he always cared for his siblings and his cousins when any member of the family needed him to. He learned responsibility that way and although his son made a horrible mistake by leaving his siblings home alone, he believed that Daniel should learn from that mistake and continue the lesson in responsibility. To him, that felt culturally congruent.

Oni

Oni was a ten-year-old girl who migrated to the U.S. from Ghana with her family when she was five years old. Her parents immigrated to the U.S. for job opportunities. Oni has three biological siblings, including an older brother and two younger sisters. She and her family first stayed with an aunt and her children who immigrated to the U.S. many years before them. What was meant to be a temporary stay with relatives for a few months became permanent when Oni's parents were hit by a drunk driver and unexpectedly died in that car accident. Oni and her siblings remained with her aunt for two years. Also living in the home was the aunt's boyfriend, a male family friend referred to as an uncle, and two older cousins. Her aunt worked as a house cleaner and at a dry cleaner. She received public assistance services, including Medicaid and food stamps. There were frequent financial struggles and periods when health insurance coverage lapsed. Oni and her siblings attended public school. She and one of her younger sisters had learning challenges during their first year after immigrating, namely, trouble with math calculations and written English. Oni experienced teasing from peers about her accent, which negatively impacted her self-esteem. She stopped asking questions in class or seeking help from teachers when she did not understand what was being taught. Oni was in danger of failing two subjects during the first semester of school. Oni's aunt advocated on her behalf with school staff. As a result, Oni began receiving after-school peer tutoring, and tutoring at home by an older cousin. Within a few months, Oni was back to performing as well in school as she did when in Ghana. Shortly after, there was a fire in her aunt's apartment due to the use of an electric heater in a bedroom. No one was hurt, but when firefighters and police officers responded to the fire, it was discovered that there were ten people living in the two-bedroom apartment. This was reported to CPS. It was deemed to be inadequate housing, and Oni and her siblings were placed in foster care. Oni's aunt made several attempts to have Oni and her siblings return to her home, but her aunt could not meet the stipulations made by CPS for the children to return based on financial limitations. Oni moved to at least three foster homes over the next year until she was placed in a foster home with a family that eventually wanted to adopt her. This family consisted of foster parents who themselves had migrated to the U.S. as children from Ghana and became U.S. citizens. They lost their biological son to cancer when he was twelve and decided to help foster children. Oni has remained with this foster family, along with an older foster sister from Liberia, for the past three years.

Oni recently revealed to her foster mother that she was molested in previous foster homes. When asked details about what happened, she explained that a previous foster father rubbed his body against her several times when hugging her. She also explained that a foster brother in another foster home kissed her while she was sleeping, then touched her breasts. He later told her she "wanted it to happen." She shared that she has had nightmares about these situations. Her foster mother reported the incidents to CPS and has been told the allegations are being investigated. Two months later, Oni's foster mother was told that the foster parents denied Oni's allegations. In each of the cases, there was not enough evidence to substantiate abuse. The cases were closed by CPS. Oni was eventually adopted by her foster parents. No further indications of abuse occurred. Oni has attended ongoing psychotherapy. She tended to feel uncomfortable around men and prefers to interact with females, although she has said that she felt at ease around her adopted father. She sometimes would become anxious and overwhelmed and would withdraw from social contact. She also had migraines that could last for up to two days. Oni continued to perform generally well in school and has had opportunities to see her biological siblings and aunt regularly.

Case Discussion

These cases provide a humanistic context for discussing and understanding the abuse and neglect that a child can suffer. In each case, there is information that raises the question of whether child maltreatment occurred. Madison, Daniel, and Oni each have had CPS involvement, and in Oni's case, involvement with the child welfare system. Oni also experienced maltreatment while in the child welfare system. Along with the question of whether maltreatment occurred, are questions about the role of race, maltreatment reporting, and prevention and intervention opportunities. How does the race of these children and families intersect with the other factors in these cases? In Madison's case, is it meaningful that the daycare owner did not report the suspected abuse immediately? What preventative efforts would have been beneficial in these cases? What interventions are appropriate? How can the well-being of these children be promoted? How can the cultural expectations and norms of the families be respected? In each chapter of this book, we will discuss aspects of these cases to expound upon the impact of maltreatment on the child with the hope of identifying all related factors and illuminating the various pathways available to help these children and prevent other children from being subjected to maltreatment.

Closing Summary

Violence against children is inhumane and is associated with short-term and long-term consequences for the child, their family and community, and society. The rates of child maltreatment have persisted to an alarming degree despite state, national, and international efforts to address this insidious issue. There are individual, cultural, and systemic factors associated with child maltreatment that need to be understood to protect children effectively, to address the impact of maltreatment on families, and to remedy the challenges faced as children traverse the child welfare system. As these issues are explored, the three children whose cases were presented are further discussed throughout the chapters of this book to illuminate considerations for reducing maltreatment. The next chapter delves into the relevant cultural considerations that provide a context for understanding Black families.

1

Understanding Black Families

> No man can know where he is going unless he knows exactly where he has been and exactly how he arrived at his present place.
> —Maya Angelou, author, poet, civil rights activist

Overview

Context is integral to authentic understanding. In this chapter, we discuss the cultural considerations that provide a contextual framework for understanding Black families. We specify how the term Black is used as a collective racial descriptor. We delineate the historical journey of Black families, their cultural practices surrounding child-rearing, and the concepts of extended kinship and adaptable family roles. Additionally, we highlight the strengths and positive attributes of the Black community and the challenges they faced as a community.

Torn from Their Land and Culture

It is impossible to separate individuals from the context in which they have lived. For many racial and ethnic minorities, and for those of African descent specifically, that context is rooted within a tense and harmful history. During the slave trade of the sixteenth through nineteenth centuries, Blacks from the continent of Africa were held captive and then displaced to the Americas, the Caribbean, and other parts of the world. Black people were enslaved, oppressed, and dehumanized for hundreds of years (Miller, 2018). Organized efforts were made to strip them of their culture and disparage any amount of pride in their identity. In his book, *A People's History of the United States*, Zinn describes how "the blacks had been torn from their land and culture, forced into a situation where the heritage of language, dress, custom, family relations, was bit by bit obliterated except for the remnants that blacks could hold on to by sheer, extraordinary persistence" (1980, p. 26). For this reason, sheer, extraordinary persistence, and strength are imperative components of many Black families today.

The enslavement of Black people's bodies and the attempted enslavement of their minds has left lasting impacts on them individually, generationally within their families, and on society as a whole (Miller, 2018). One could argue that the past is never over, but instead, it manifests in the present in expected and unexpected ways. This notion appears true for many Black families who contend with the negative effects of the past in very present ways, including but not limited to ongoing prejudice, racism, and discrimination (Clark et al., 1999; Comas-Díaz, 2016; Gaylord-Harden & Cunningham, 2009; Pager & Shephard 2008).

Notably, such experiences are often tied to societal perceptions and stereotypes of the Black people, which are not always aligned with how Black people understand themselves and their culture. Culture is a distinct pattern of behaviors and traditions that groups use to regulate their daily lives (U.S. Department of Health & Human Services, 2001). It both shapes and is shaped by the beliefs of the people living within it and, through socialization, upholds the mores and core values that can make one culture distinct from another. Culture is therefore the lens through which people understand their experiences and express themselves. Through centuries of pain and suffering, Black families have developed a culture of strength, resilience, and identified ways of coping to ensure their survival. In this way, history and culture are interwoven into the fabric of their identity, family structure, and family functioning.

History of Black Families in the United States

It is important to note that Black families in the United States are a heterogeneous group who, as a result of forced and choice migration, constitute diverse subgroups of people from various places around the world. Notably, Black is intentionally used as a collective racial category to identify various ethnic groups that share a common identity as people of African descent. Such racial categorizations are heavily defined by the U.S. Census Bureau, which categorizes Black families as both people who identify specifically as Black or who identify as African American. In this way, Black families in the U.S. may include Black people who were born within the U.S. (sometimes referred to as Black, Black American, or African American), as well as Black people who were born outside of the U.S. (sometimes referred to as Black, Black foreign-born, or Black Immigrants). The majority of Black people who are living in the U.S., but who were born outside of the U.S. are from countries in the Caribbean (e.g., Jamaica, Haiti, and Trinidad and Tobago), Africa (e.g., Nigeria, Ethiopia, and Ghana), and South and Central America. However, there are also a small percentage of Black individuals who live in the U.S. but were born in Europe, Asia, Northern America, and Oceania. July 2017 population estimates reported that of the total U.S. population, 13.4 percent (approximately, 43.6 million people) identify as Black or African American (U.S. Department of Commerce, 2017). Further, reports from the Pew Research Center indicate that roughly one in ten Black people living in the U.S. are foreign-born/Black immigrants (Anderson & López, 2018). Thus, as the term Black is used throughout this book, it is referring to this collective of people of African descent in the U.S., which includes but is not necessarily limited to, African Americans. The research literature discussed throughout the book will sometimes refer to Black people as a collective, and sometimes refer specifically to African Americans. However, our use of the term is collective unless otherwise specified.

The history of these Black families residing in the U.S. is as diverse as the families themselves. First, African Americans are a diverse group of individuals whose ethnic background is of African descent, and whose ancestors were brought to the U.S. through the slave trade. They endured over a century of slavery, watched their loved ones lynched and beaten for nothing more than being Black in a White society, were denied education and rights that their White counterparts were freely given, and learned that they had to fight for everything they needed including freedom and equal treatment. This fight continued through the segregation of Jim Crow, the Civil Rights Movement, and even current movements such as Black Lives Matter. Throughout all of these movements, African Americans have fought for the betterment of themselves and their families. They have fought to obtain good education, own property and businesses, gain equal opportunity to work, and more, so that they could have better economic opportunities to advance themselves, their families, and the Black community as a whole. Throughout all of these movements, African Americans were viewed as less than others and not even a whole person. They have had to fight to remind society that they matter, that they are not inherently flawed or dangerous, and that they are deserving of the human rights to which all humans should be entitled. African Americans had to fight for freedom, fairness, and safety within their living environments, not only for adults but also for their children and the generations to come.

Black immigrants are also a diverse group of people, of multiple ethnic groups, who arrived in the U.S. through various migration patterns and motivation. Some immigrants migrated to the U.S. to seek asylum or refuge. Some migrated for economic reasons and needs. Others migrated for educational opportunities. Just as varied as the migration reasons for coming to the U.S. are the lived experiences of these families once residing in the U.S.

Acculturation and Enculturation are two important factors to consider when thinking about the lived experiences of any ethnic minority group in the U.S., including Black families. *Acculturation*, which typically occurs during migrant movement, is a process whereby one group of people experience change in their original cultural patterns and expressions as they come into continuous contact with the culture of a different group (Berry, 1997; Berry, 2015; Redfield et al.,1936; Schwartz et al., 2010). Black immigrants in the U.S. are tasked with developing an identity and operating within the U.S. through U.S. expectations versus their own. They may experience the tension of trying to hold on to cultural values from their heritage culture, and develop an identity and operate within the culture of the U.S. This conflict is also true for American- born, Black families who experienced acculturation over many generations as their ancestors were brought to the U.S. That type of acculturation may be better defined as *enculturation*, which is the process by which an individual is socialized into their own cultural group (Kim, 2007; Kizgin, Jamal, & Dey, 2018). From the time children are young, they learn the rules and customs of their family and larger cultural group. Their behaviors and understanding of the world grow through that cultural lens, and they continue the traditions they have learned. In this regard, enculturation is a part of what maintains cultural traditions, norms, behaviors, and expectations between generations of people.

There are expectations within acculturation and enculturation, whereby people are expected to abandon their ethnic culture, ways of being, and assimilate into U.S. culture in accordance with the "norms" set by the dominant group in society (Berry, 2003). There is also an underlying assumption that people should immediately understand and adopt the norms and expectations of the dominant group, and if they have recently immigrated, adjust to the new society they are in without hesitation or questioning of the new norms. Comments such as "they should speak English if they want to be here," or "they should learn how we do things if they want to live here" highlight the belief that people outside of the dominant group are expected to adapt fully to the dominant group's version of American society, if they want to survive in it. The challenge with this belief is that it ignores the culture of the person and assumes that people should replace their ethnic traditions with European White American culture and norms. This remains a prevailing theme within society despite research (Schwartz et al., 2010; Ward & Geeraert, 2016) showing that acculturation is a process that does not happen overnight.

In the time that Black families are learning the societal rules (in the case of acculturation), or attempting to balance societal rules within their own cultural understandings (in the case of enculturation), they are simultaneously being held accountable for dominant society's rules within many systems, including the child welfare system. Take for example, a Black Caribbean family living in the U.S. where some members of the family migrated to the U.S. and others were born in the U.S. There may be norms and traditions within this family that may be at odds with those of dominant society, such as the use of alcohol to provide relief from sickness. In the earlier case of Daniel (from the Introduction), his grandmother told his younger brother to give his sister a child's over-the-counter medicine for her nausea. What if, instead of nausea, the child was feeling feverish? In that case, a family with Caribbean background may choose to rub alcohol (e.g., rum) on the child's chest when they have a bad cough or on the entire body to break a fever. They may also rub a small amount of alcohol on a child's gum when they are teething or have other gum irritation. At times, these methods may be preferable to using over-the-counter medication, or a frozen teething ring, respectively. Notably, the latter methods are normative treatment according to European White American culture. Instead of viewing the Caribbean method of rubbing alcohol on a child as an alternative treatment that is culturally appropriate and normative for that family, dominant societal norms might lead those in power (for example, teachers; child welfare workers; mental health clinicians; other mandated reporters) to pathologize the behavior and view it as abusive. Here, and in other examples, it is important to acknowledge cultural differences of those who are outside of European White American culture, and to be mindful of the ways in which those differences manifest in systems of power. In discussing the overrepresentation of Black families within the child welfare system, and the connection to institutional racism, Hill (2004) urged child welfare professionals to show more of an "appreciation of diverse cultural beliefs and practices" and "disavow the belief that 'different' cultural values or practices are inherently 'inferior' to theirs" (p. 72).

Unfortunately, within U.S. society, Black people have been devalued and viewed as inferior for having their own cultural practices for centuries now; the negative implications are pervasive and widespread. From the beginning of the eugenics movement in the twentieth century, Blacks were deemed within society to be of lesser intelligence, weaker in strength and value, and of lesser worth than their White counterparts. They have been stereotyped individually and as a family, portrayed through a deficit-oriented lens, pathologized, painted as disorganized, and labeled as unfit parents (Frazier, 1939; Hill, 1998; Taylor et al., 1995; U.S. Department of Labor, 1965). Although based around portrayals within the United Kingdom, King (2004) highlights the way in which even sports broadcasting uses positive images of Black people excelling at sports, to discuss Black families in a negative light and claim that any success an individual has, is actually as a response toward a negative and disadvantaged home life. For example, when a Black person excels at sports to an extent they are able to make a career out of it, the media will often highlight stories of those who excelled in the face of deep poverty or within a violence driven neighborhood. The media rarely shares the stories of Black people who excel and come from middle class, suburban families without dysfunction or violence in the upbringing. Hill (1998) noted, "moreover, this 'deficit' perspective usually attributes the dysfunctioning of Black families to their internal structure or to the 'underclass' values of family members, and de-emphasizes the impact of external factors, such as racism, sexism, economic factors, or social policies" (p. 15). In more recent years, there have been scholarly attempts to shift the negative narrative about Black families by highlighting the truth of their strengths and framing their culture in the context to which it developed (Littlejohn-Blake & Darling, 1993; Mosley-Howard & Evans, 2000; Pollock et al., 2015). It is with this strengths-based framework in mind that the authors of this text will discuss the Black community and the maltreatment of Black children.

Culture of Black Families in the United States

Not all Black families are the same. There are similarities in experiences related to historical enslavement, displacement, and colonization. There are also differences in experiences related to historical political climates, economic opportunities, and their home country's race relations. All of these experiences shape and influence the structure and functioning of Black families. Collectively, Black families are a heterogeneous group where each family has a uniqueness that makes them different from the next. Although there is not one type of Black family that represents all the rest, research has shown that there are many shared experiences related to cultural identity, as well as commonalities in their expressed values (Boyd-Franklin, 2013; Hines & Boyd-Franklin, 2005; Kane, 2000). Commonalities within Black families can be seen through Afrocentric values of extended and adaptable family roles, family togetherness, family responses and adaptation (coping and resilience through education, work ethic, and spiritual grounding, as well as parenting and discipline practices.

To some extent, these values may be present in many types of families across the U.S., but to a greater extent the manifestation of these values in Black families can be in conflict with those of majority culture in the U.S. Again, take the case of Daniel that was discussed in the Introduction. Daniel's father chooses to parent him by teaching him the responsibility to care for others in his family. In addition to caring for his siblings, Daniel babysitting his siblings and potentially other relatives highlights the adaptable family roles and sense of family togetherness. Daniel's father likely saw this role as important and culturally congruent with his expectation of his son within a Black family. However, his expectation for his son is in conflict with societal expectations that might posit Daniel to be too young to help care for his siblings. If Daniel's father believes that Daniel has learned the lesson not to leave his siblings home alone, and is ready to resume the responsibility of watching them, should he be able to grant such responsibility to his son again? If he did, what might be the outcome for him and his family? To this end, Black families and their behaviors may be judged within systems of power (e.g., the child welfare system) as being right or wrong, and respectable or not respectable. Consequently, the repercussions of their behavior, even when culturally appropriate, can be detrimental to the family. Therefore, it is important to understand the individual in the context of their culture and not solely based on the context of majority culture.

Extended Kinship and Adaptable Family Roles

An important piece of understanding Black families involves understanding the structure of the family, which includes extended family kinship, adaptable and flexible family roles, and within family caregiving. First, extended family kinship is an important structure for many Black families (Kane, 2000; Moseley-Howard & Evans, 2000; Robinson, 2012; Taylor, Chatters, & Cross, 2021; Wilson, 1986). In a study comparing African American, Black Caribbean, and non-Hispanic White individuals, Taylor et al. (2013) found that African Americans and Black Caribbean Americans reported higher amounts of extended family, specifically "fictive kin." Fictive kin include family-friends, long-time neighbors, and other trusted individuals who become a true part of the family, not just in title such as cousin, aunt, or uncle, but also in terms of the family togetherness and bonding (Taylor et. al, 2021). Although these individuals may not be related by blood, they are accepted into the family and can be a part of child-rearing practices and/or family decision-making processes. For example, McCallum (2016) interviewed African American students to better understand the ways in which their families influenced their decision to enroll in doctoral education. Students noted that their decision to pursue doctoral studies, and their previous decisions to pursue any level of education, was influenced by family members over the course of their lifetime. Importantly, they defined family not only in terms of immediate family but also extended and fictive family.

Similarly, another part of adaptability and flexibility within family roles involves the structure around parenting roles and responsibilities. For example, older generations of aunts, uncles, and especially grandparents may participate in child rearing through supporting the parents or through parenting the child themselves. Additionally, friends and loved ones outside of the family may participate in parenting responsibilities, sometimes to the extent of informal adoption. Taylor et al. (2003) noted that informal adoption may be a temporary measure that is used when parents need assistance in raising children for a myriad of reasons. They note that during the great migration, younger mothers in the South had to leave their children with family or friends so they could establish life in the North. This is similar to Black immigrant families who migrated from other countries to the U.S. in pursuit of a "better" life. At times, these families may rely on loved ones in their home area to care for their children until they can reunite as one family. In fact, for Black immigrants, extended kinship can be an important source of support during and after the migration process, even when the family is geographically dispersed (Taylor et al., 2014). Take for example, the case of Oni, who was discussed in the Introduction. Oni and her family lived with other family in the U.S. during their migration process, and the family continued to care for Oni after her parents unexpectedly died. Even before Oni's parents died, her aunt and family were shared caregivers to her and her siblings because her parents needed the additional support, and because that can be a common experience for many Black families.

The historical pattern of shared caregiving continues in present day families in different ways, and may, at times, still be connected to socioeconomic status and specifically, economic difficulties (Armstrong, 2012; Kamo, 2000). Utilizing family support may be critical not only in terms of cultural family structure and tradition but also in terms of practicality of sharing resources and affording daily expenses. Take for example, single- or partnered-parents that need to work multiple jobs and long hours to provide for their family. In addition to needing extended family to help care for the children because of evening work hours, the family may struggle to pay escalating costs of daycare during their daytime work hours. As mentioned early, parents may need to share their parenting roles and responsibilities with trusted others such as grandparents, aunts, uncles, and so forth.

Older siblings may also assume responsibility within the parenting role. Hines and Boyd-Franklin (2005) note that children have the potential to become "parentified" (p. 91) when their parent works and there are younger children to care for, when parents abdicate their responsibilities, or more positively, when parents attempt to teach their child greater responsibility. There are obvious advantages and disadvantages to this, which we saw in the case of Daniel. Fifteen-year-old Daniel had the responsibility of watching his siblings while his parents were working. Here, Daniel was given an opportunity to learn responsibility, as the younger siblings were too young to be alone. Notably, this was not a daily responsibility for Daniel, but rather he was given this task a few times per week. Unfortunately, during one night of his watch, he decided to go out with friends and left his two younger siblings at home; the youngest of the siblings ingested their mother's prescription pills and was rushed to the emergency room. While this is a serious negative outcome of sibling caregiving, this is not always the case. One might debate that, in some cultures, Daniel may be perceived as old enough to watch his siblings and obtain this level of responsibility. Although leaving his siblings in order to spend time with his friends was certainly poor and flawed judgment, one might question if this is truly maltreatment on the part of his parents or worthy of the children being removed from the home. One might also ask if maltreatment would be questioned if the child ingested the pills when Daniel was home, or if an older family member (e.g., a grandparent) was present watching the children instead of Daniel. If his grandmother had left her pillbox out during her time watching the children, would it be maltreatment or a mistake? Notably, a global nonprofit organization, Safe Kids Worldwide, reported that there has been a significant rise in prescription and over-the-counter medications in the home, and that unfortunately, around 59,000 children are brought to emergency rooms each year because they found their way into medications in the home when no-one was looking (MacKay et al., 2016). These are instances where parents' attention may have been diverted, even if they were present in the home at the time. Safe Kids Worldwide recommend various strategies to prevent medicine poisoning, none of which are immediately removing the children from the home. Instead, they provide suggestions for keeping children safe within their homes. In the case of Daniel, another focus might include suggestions for supporting the family so that the parents can work and protect their children when they cannot afford daycare. Overall, considerations of the context in which the event occurred, and how it could be prevented in the future, are important aspects for those in the child welfare system to consider as they intervene to ensure children are safe.

A benefit to adaptable and flexible caregiving is that it can be an important buffer against family instability. Incarceration and economic hardship, both of which are disproportionately prevalent within Black families, are factors that contribute to family instability. Regarding incarceration, the U.S. Department of Justice's 2016 Prisoners and Jail Inmates reports showed that Black males continue to be disproportionately imprisoned compared to other racial/ethnic groups (Carson, 2018; Zeng, 2018). In fact, reports show Black males, age eighteen to twenty-four, were imprisoned at two times the rate of White males in the same age group (Carson, 2018), and Black males were incarcerated in jail at rates higher than any other group (Zeng, 2018). Sadly, 2.5 percent of all Black male U.S. residents were in state or federal prison by the end of 2016. As Browning et al. (2001) noted, "due to the disproportionate numbers of black men involved in the criminal justice system, issues of fathering behind bars have direct implications for the black parent-child relationship" (p. 88). Incarceration, single-parent households, unemployment, and low-paying jobs, to name a few, create economic hardship in Black families who have historically used the extended family for needed support. As already mentioned, many Black families depend on extended family to help care for the children of the family when they are faced with such dilemmas and hardships. This can be misconstrued as parents evading their responsibilities instead of seeing the strength in the family coming together to share in such responsibilities.

Family Togetherness

A strength and source of pride of many Black families is rooted in the spirit of family togetherness where families bond, stick together, support each other, and overcome the difficulties of life as a unified whole.

The family embodies a collective rather than an individualistic stance toward life that can be seen in the African proverb "I am because we are, and because we are, therefore I am," versus the European viewpoint "I think therefore I am." In this way, Black families view collectivism and a sense of family togetherness as an integral part of their familiar values and group identity (Boyd-Franklin, 2013; Hines & Boyd-Franklin, 2005; Kane, 2000), which can be seen through the principles of *Umoja* or *Ujima*. These principles occur within the African American holiday of Kwanzaa (Karenga, 1988), and are Swahili phrases meaning *unity* and *collective work and responsibility*, respectively. *Umoja* is about striving for and intentionally creating unity within the family and communities in which the family resides. Relatedly, *Ujima* is about maintaining a sense of togetherness in the family and surrounding community. In similar ways to the African proverb, "I am because we are . . . ," *Ujima* is about allowing others' problems to be your problems within a shared sense of problem solving and caring for each other. This shared sense of problem solving and caring for each other is also evident in the aforementioned extended and adaptable roles.

When child maltreatment cases are being investigated, or have become substantiated, and children are removed from their home, it is important that the child's cultural need for family togetherness is recognized within the child welfare system. *Kinship care* (placing children with relatives) is one example of continued family togetherness and family preservation. According to the Adoption Assistance and Child Welfare Act of 1980, the child welfare system is responsible for placing children in homes with the least restrictive environment, which often involves placement with other family members. This system of care is especially important for Black children as it allows family members to provide short-term care. In some ways, it can be seen as a culturally responsive plan to the challenging situation; however, it is also limited in that it does not allow or encourage family members to adopt their kin (Boyd, 2014), which might be needed when parental rights have been terminated. Perhaps the child welfare system will continue to evolve in valuing family togetherness so that kinship care can include kinship adoption. Perhaps it can also include extended kin care where close family friends, who are considered family, might also be considered appropriate caretakers.

Family Responses and Adaptation

For centuries, Black families have learned to function, cope, and thrive in the face of threat and danger. The aforementioned structure of the extended family and flexibility within caretaking are some examples of adaptive methods of coping. Indeed, the historical context around safety for Black children obliged families to take care of their own in order to keep them safe. Given that racism often leads to harm and death for Black people, extended family support and caregiving became a survival strategy. Black families have used role flexibility, extended bonds, and the "village" of their families and communities to survive societal stressors (Mosley-Howard & Evans, 2000).

Messages of Education and Work-Ethic. Additional coping responses and adaptations can be seen in the messages that are shared within Black families, such as the importance of education and a strong work-ethic (Hines & Boyd-Franklin, 2005; Kane, 2000; McCallum, 2016; Pearson & Bieschke, 2001), as well as the vitality of spiritual grounding (Boyd-Franklin, 2013; Hines & Boyd-Franklin, 2005; Kane, 2000). Many Black families teach their children the importance of getting an education and having a strong work ethic in order to literally and figuratively survive in this world. Parents value and promote these principles as they teach their children that they have to be twice as smart and work three times as hard as their White counterparts, not to get ahead, but to be equal in the pursuit of success. As Hines and Boyd-Franklin (2005) eloquently noted,

> Yet many Americans believe that most African Americans survive only because of welfare, despite the fact that the overwhelming majority work, often having more than one job. Unfortunately, they often secure less desirable jobs, receive less pay for the same work, are the last hired, and are more likely to be underemployed and/or stuck under "glass or cement ceilings" than their White counterparts. Most African Americans no longer believe that the American dream is intended to include them. (p. 94)

Unfortunately, Black immigrants may also hold this stereotype of African Americans by perceiving that African Americans have not worked as hard as Black immigrants have, in coming to the U.S. and building a life with fewer resources. Such stereotypes are not true of African Americans or other Black individuals. McCallum (2016) conducted semi-structured interviews with African American graduate students who noted that their parents instilled values of hard work and strong academics. Participants reported that their parents ensured that they completed chores, contributed (e.g., financially or emotionally) to the well-being of other family members and of the household, and engaged in academics with the expectation of going to college and even graduate school. In this way, some of the parentification of children might be viewed through parents' attempt to build a strong work ethic in their children. Some of McCallum's participants also noted the important role their extended family members played. No matter who the messages came from, obtaining education was seen as a means of coping, changing one's social status, and improving quality of life. For Black families that have immigrated to the U.S., messages of hard work and education are just as present.

Child welfare workers, mental health providers, educators, physicians, and others who are invested in and involved in keeping children safe should consider any racial biases or stereotypes that they may have as they interact with and respond to Black families. Given these individuals' positions of power and authority over others' lives, their biases can lead to harmful consequences for Black families. Consider the aforementioned notions around work ethic and the perceived necessity to teach children responsibility at an early age. These are strengths of the Black family but can be misconstrued as something else, such as parents not engaging in their own responsibilities as caretakers. Racial bias and over identification of Black children as being maltreated are seen as influential factors in the Black children being placed in foster care (Lash, 2013).

Use of Spirituality. As noted earlier, many Black families also use spiritual grounding through religious affiliation and spiritual identification as another way of coping and improving their quality of life. In fact, Black families have been identified as having higher identification with and belonging to religious affiliations.

Taylor et al. (2007) used data from the National Survey of American Life (NSAL) to examine religious and spiritual involvement among African American, Caribbean Black, and non-Hispanic White older adults and found that African Americans and Caribbean Blacks reported higher levels of religious participation, religious coping, and spirituality than their older White counterparts. The Pew Forum U.S. Religious Landscape Study conducted in 2007 highlighted African Americans as the most likely group to report some degree of formal religious affiliation, with 87 percent of African Americans reporting that they belonged to a religious group (Sahgal & Smith, 2009). They elaborate that 79 percent of African Americans reported that religion was very important in their lives, compared to 56 percent of all U.S. adults who reported the same. Religious importance was also self-reported in the 2006 Gallup U.S. Poll, which showed that 85 percent of non-Hispanic Blacks reported that religion was very important to them; this was the highest percentage of identification with religion of any of the racial/ethnic demographic group polled (Gallup & Newport, 2006). Similarly, the Religious Landscape Study noted that

> several measures illustrate the distinctiveness of the black community when it comes to religious practices and beliefs. More than half of African-Americans (53%) report attending religious services at least once a week, more than three-in-four (76%) say they pray on at least a daily basis and nearly nine-in-ten (88%) indicate they are absolutely certain that God exists. On each of these measures, African-Americans stand out as the most religiously committed racial or ethnic group in the nation. Even those African-Americans who are unaffiliated with any religious group pray nearly as often as the overall population of mainline Protestants (48% of unaffiliated African-Americans pray daily vs. 53% of all mainline Protestants). And unaffiliated African-Americans are about as likely to believe in God with absolute certainty (70%) as are mainline Protestants (73%) and Catholics (72%) overall. (para. 3)

To further elaborate religious diversity within African American families, the Religious Landscape Study results show that African Americans identify as Protestant (78 percent), Catholic (5 percent), Jehovah's Witnesses (1 percent), Muslim (1 percent), Buddhist (< 0.5 percent), Hindu (< 0.5 percent), and Mormon (< 0.5 percent) to name a few. While 12 percent identified as unaffiliated with any specific religion, only 1 percent described themselves as agnostic or atheist.

Regardless of affiliation, there is a common foundation of spirituality that has historically given Black families an outlet to cope with enslavement, continued oppression, and racism, and also to express their feelings (e.g., pain and joy), faith in a higher power who provides protection, comfort, and hope in times of trouble. In this regard, the role of spirituality and religion is another pillar of many Black families and spiritual communities and can be a great source of support and a buffer from their various stressors (Krause, 2006).

In fact, for some families, certain church members (e.g., ministers and other close members of the congregation) also become a part of the extended family who participate in childrearing and family decision making, especially for single mothers (Boyd-Franklin, 2010). Within their various religious affiliations, the role of the faith leaders or brothers and sisters of their faith community may be extremely influential in their overall family functioning (Carolan et al., 2000; Mattis & Jagers, 2001; Taylor et al., 2013). Here, one can see the connection between spirituality and extended family within the Black community. This is another important consideration for various providers to have when attending to the care of Black children and their families.

Parenting and Discipline in Black Families

There are many different culturally specific parenting practices that exist within families. In each cultural group, cultural beliefs, behaviors, and expectations influence how parents care for their children (Bornstein, 2012). While there are some similarities between parenting across cultures, there are also notable differences. For example, parents across cultures desire to keep their children safe, support their growth and development, and encourage a future that reflects a better life than their own. However, the ways in which parents engage with their children around these domains can be different.

The most influential work on parenting styles has stemmed from Baumrind (1966), where he described three parenting styles as authoritarian, authoritative, and permissive. An authoritarian parenting style involves high levels of demandingness from the parent to the child, with low levels of responsiveness. The authoritarian parent is seen as shaping and controlling the child's behavior toward a standard of conduct that is set by the parent, who is seen as the ultimate authority. Children are taught to respect their parents and there is little "give-and-take" in terms of negotiating within the relationship.

An authoritative parenting style involves high levels of demandingness and high levels of responsiveness. Authoritative parents also shape children's behaviors, but in more of a guiding manner that uses reason and power with an issue-oriented focus. There is also more give-and-take with negotiating where authoritative parents are firm but not overly restrictive.

A permissive parenting style involves low levels of demandingness and high levels of responsiveness. Permissive parents allow children to regulate their own behavior, without parental control, and without needing to conform to external standards of behavior. Permissive parents have little demands on their children and consult with the children about family business (Baumrind, 1966).

The literature around differences in parenting styles is not consistent. It is difficult to generalize the parenting style of any ethnic group given the influential nature of socioeconomic status, age, generational differences, support system, acculturation process, and psychological functioning of both the parent and the child, to name a few. Black parents may be strict and harsh in their punishments at times, and also lenient and forgiving of children's mistakes at other times. No matter the parenting style, Black parents typically demand respect within the adult-child relationships (even outside of interactions with the specific parent), and conflict may occur more often when such respect is not shown (Dixon et al., 2008).

Black parents and families have been compared to European parents whose parenting styles are considered the "norm;" subsequently, Black parents may be viewed in a negative light as their parenting practices may be different (Wilson et al., 2004). Take for example, the common practice in the Black community of a parent spanking a young child by smacking the buttocks with an open palm a couple times if the child misbehaves in an endangering manner (e.g., attempting to run into a neighborhood street). Or consider a parent spanking a child who has thrown a tantrum in the middle of the grocery store. Are these decisions appropriate parenting choices? Whose standards define what is appropriate in that case? Does the earlier historical and continued context about a Black family's need to protect their child from misbehaving in front of White individuals matter in this situation? What if such misbehavior has historically been life threatening? Like any other dimension of one's culture, it is important to explore parenting practices through the historical context in which they developed, and the social context in which they continue.

Appropriate behavior, conduct, and decorum are important facets of Black families. From an early age, young children are taught to sit still, behave, mind their business, don't stare, don't touch anything while in their local grocery store, and don't embarrass their parent (or themselves) in front of any White person. Children receive messages about how they will be perceived in the world, how they will be compared to the European "norm," and how they will be treated based on these perceptions. Whereas some White children are privileged to run free in spaces such as restaurants and stores, Black children rarely have such liberties without the judgments that their parents cannot control them or they do not have the proper amount of home training. As a result, many Black parents have long talks with their children before entering stores to review the rules and expectations. In spite of this, mainstream America continues to hold and perpetuate many negative stereotypes of the conduct and behavior of Black children. Like many stereotypes, these views can be linked to the historical racial context of the U.S.

Black parents and caregivers (of the immediate and extended family) have long known that their children's behavior, and perceived or reported behavior, could be life-threatening for them. This is similar to the survival points made earlier. Since the time of slavery, Jim Crow, and the Civil Rights Movement, Black children in the U.S. have been told not to draw attention to themselves, not to doing anything that could be perceived as threatening to any White person, and to be as polite as possible even when others are dehumanizing and harming them. Parents understood that these messages of safety were life and death matters. Take the example of Emmett Till, a young fourteen-year-old Black boy who, in 1955, was beaten and killed by White men because a woman, Carolyn Bryant, reported that he whistled at her. It has since been known that she recanted that story on her deathbed; however, the damage to Emmett Till's life and to that of his family cannot be undone. Unfortunately, these types of tragedies are not simply in the past. In the present, many Black families continue to prepare their children for surviving a routine traffic stop or any interaction with others who have more privilege and power than they do. In this way, the past is very much alive and in the present for these families, and interacting with authority figures, especially those who may threaten to take away their children, and/or those who are White, can be very difficult. Patton (2017) makes an important point in stating the spanking or "whupping" children has the potential to lead to negative outcomes, perpetuated family violence, and involvement from Child Protective Services (CPS) that can result in separation and additional negative outcomes that the parents initially hoped to avoid. Concurrently, Patton also acknowledges that such spankings and "whuppings" are connected to the fact that "Black parents have legitimate fears about the safety of their children, and the overwhelming majority believe physical discipline is necessary to keep black children out of the streets, out of prison or out of police officers' sight" (Introduction, para. 1).

People's racial and ethnic identities are intertwined in their interactions with others and within the world in general. Because of this, it will be useful to those working with Black families (e.g., child welfare workers, mental health providers, educators, physicians) to be aware of the interactive nature of each party's diversity identities. Specifically, those in power should approach the situation with awareness of their own culture, some knowledge of the family's culture, including historical context and implications, and skills to proceed respectfully throughout the interactions. Collectively, this is known as *cultural competence* (see Campinha-Bacote, 2002 for a review of cultural competence in health-care services, which is also applicable to other types of services). Consider the example of Madison from the Introduction. Are the parents' concerns about perceptions warranted? How might perceptions of them impact their experiences with daycares in the future?

Notably, Black parents incorporate racial and ethnic socialization into their conversations and teachings with their children. They discuss prejudice, discrimination, and racism as important factors to their child's interactions with others and success in the world, and they do so more than their White counterparts or other ethnic minority groups (Hughes et al., 2006; Lozada et al., 2017; McLoyd et al., 2000). Hurd et al. (1995) interviewed African American parents about aspects of their parenting that they perceived as going well. In this study, parents identified many of the themes that have been described in this chapter, such as connection with family, the importance of education, achievement and effort, and cultivation of spirituality. They also identified a theme of fostering self-reliance within their children and teaching children "survival skills." To the latter point, they noted life skills beyond the basics; however, many parents recognized the need to prepare their children to survive in a racist society. Children were taught to cope with discrimination, sometimes through assertiveness and sometimes through superior effort. One mother of two school-age daughters told her children, "Being a black child, you have to work extra hard" (p. 440). Similarly, Roopnarine et al. (2006) found that Black Caribbean parents also noted the significance of teaching their children the importance of education and appropriate behavior as a means of success.

It has already been noted throughout this chapter that there is a survival instinct within Black families; but it should also be noted that teaching survival is an important part of Black parents' responsibilities. Black parents need to teach their children to survive in a world that can kill them. Sometimes the lessons that parents give are verbal and come in the form of long conversations about what it means to be Black in a White world. Other times, the lessons that parents give come in the form of spanking and physical discipline. Historically, physical discipline has been employed as a technique to teach children how to behave so that they were not killed by others who were also eager to "teach that boy a lesson," which, at times, included lynching. In this regard, discipline within Black families should be understood in the context of generational trauma, continued institutional racism, and survival instincts.

It is important to note the difference between such physical discipline (also referred to in the literature as corporal punishment) and child maltreatment. Through the Child Welfare Information Gateway, the U.S. Department of Health & Human Services (2018a) provides a listing of resources that illustrate the differences among these areas. The list highlights resources specific to understanding cultural context and ethnic differences regarding physical discipline as a part of parenting styles versus abuse. They highlight an article from a health and wellness site, written by a social worker, Amy Morin, Licensed Clinical Social Worker (LCSW), who describes the federal and state laws that define abuse versus discipline. In the article, Morin (2018) states:

> In federal terms, physical abuse is generally defined as "any non-accidental physical injury." That may include burning, kicking, biting, or striking a child. Some states include threatening a child with harm or creating a situation where harm to a child is likely as part of their definitions of physical abuse. Local laws differ on the specifics. For example, California's law states, "Serious physical harm does not include reasonable and age-appropriate spanking to the buttocks where there is no evidence of serious physical injury." Meanwhile, Oklahoma's law states, "Parents/teachers/other persons can use ordinary force as a means of discipline, including but not limited to spanking, switching and paddling." (p.1)

When the current book authors discuss physical discipline in relation to parenting, they are not referring to any of the abusive methods of discipline mentioned above. Abusive methods of discipline are not acceptable means of parenting.

Like many parents, the child welfare system shares an investment in keeping children safe and is designed specifically to protect children when safety becomes a concern. Those who work in the child welfare system aim to promote and maintain children's best interests; however, the notion of "best interest" is subjective and interpretation is based on experience, which is ladened by cultural perspective.

Closing Summary

Overall, Black families are diverse groups of people who have overcome great obstacles so that their children can have better lives than they had. While every Black family is not the same, there are cultural similarities that tie them together; specifically, extended and adaptable family roles, a sense of family togetherness, family responses and adaptations, including education, work ethic, spirituality, and parenting styles. These cultural themes are important in the lives of many Black families and developed as coping and resilience in the face of great pain. Understanding these families within a historical, social, and cultural context is of most importance, as you cannot separate the individual from the context in which they have lived. Besides understanding the families and the cultural context of their lives, those who work with the families should attend to their own cultural backgrounds and be mindful of how different cultures have historically and presently interacted. Those who work with families should also be mindful of power dynamics, potential biases, and ways to be respectful to the cultural values and needs of the family. The next chapter delves into definitions of child maltreatment and provides relevant prevalence data related to the general U.S. population of children and Black children.

2

The Epidemiology of Maltreatment of Black Children

> The single story creates stereotypes, and the problem with stereotypes is not that they are untrue, but that they are incomplete. They make one story become the only story.
> —Chimamanda Ngozi Adichie, writer, feminist

Overview

Every social issue our society faces is embedded in a historical context that both created and shaped the issue. Child maltreatment has existed throughout humanity and the manner in which it is addressed has evolved as more has been understood about its scope and nature. It has become clearer over time that the ethnic, cultural, and socioeconomic contexts in which maltreatment occurs for each affected child and family is important to understand in order to prevent, intervene, and reduce the proliferation and insidious impact of maltreatment. It is from this standpoint that the issue of maltreatment of Black children will be discussed. This chapter provides definitions of child maltreatment, discusses types of maltreatment that occur, and delineates prevalence data that is general to the U.S. and specific to Black children and their families.

Demographics of Black Children in the United States

Black children are the offspring of the Black racial subgroup of the U.S. population. There are ten million Black children in the U.S., making up 15 percent of the national child population (Child Trends, 2018; U.S. Census Bureau, 2018). Black children in the U.S. include mostly African American children, followed by Black immigrant children from the Caribbean and African countries, then Black children immigrating from various other countries (Hernandez, 2012). The health and well-being of Black children looks different from that of children from other racial groups. As of 2017, Black children have the highest risk for infant mortality, with a rate of 11.4 per 1000 live births compared to 4.9 of White births and 5 per 1000 of Latino births (National Center for Chronic Disease Prevention and Health Promotion, 2019). Further, the highest frequency of pregnancy-related deaths occurs for Black mothers at a rate of 40 per 100,000 births, compared to 12.4 of White mothers and 17.8 of other races (Division of Reproductive Health, 2018). The impact of a child's mother dying during childbirth is immense in their growth and well-being. Thus, the disadvantages that Black children face more frequently than other children begin at infancy. Additionally, about 65 percent of Black children are being raised in single-parent households, typically by the child's mother (Fluke et al., 2011; National Kids Count, 2019). This figure is more than double the 24 percent of their White counterparts and more than the 41 percent of Latino children. Approximately 38 percent of Black children live in poverty, which is higher than the national average of 22 percent of American children living in poverty (Black Demographics, 2019). Additionally, Black children are approximately seven times more likely than their White counterparts to have a parent in prison (Martin, 2017). Overall, Black children experience multiple layers of disadvantages to a greater degree than other children that negatively impact their health and well-being. These adversities are interwoven into the lives of Black families and are likely influencing factors of child maltreatment.

The high rates of Black children being raised by single mothers means exposure to the effects of not only the child's direct experiences but also the difficulties that the mothers face. The 40 percent co-occurrence between intimate partner violence against women and violence against children indicates the volatility of the environment in which many children are raised (Nami et al., 2017). With that context in mind, it is not surprising, given the abuse women face in the home, that mothers are the most common perpetrators of child maltreatment. From that viewpoint, prevention and reduction of child maltreatment must be closely connected to supporting the mothers who primarily raise them.

In addition to these adversities, Black children experience child maltreatment at higher rates than most other racial groups (Child Welfare Information Gateway, 2017a; Statista Research Department, 2019a). However, it is notable that there may be many reasons for these higher rates. It is reported that approximately 13.9 of every 1000 Black children experience abuse, compared to 8.1 of White children (Statista Research Department, 2019a). Importantly, systemic efforts have been made to address child maltreatment by enacting laws and reporting policies, providing public education, funding, and creating reporting guidelines and standards, such as the Child Abuse Prevention and Treatment Act (CAPTA) of 1974 (Child and Family Services Reviews, 2018). There have also been efforts made to help mandated reporters better understand the ethnic, cultural, and socioeconomic contexts around potential child maltreatment situations, so that such maltreatment is not improperly identified or over-reported. There have been challenges with identifying occurrences of maltreatment, in part due to differing definitions of maltreatment, differences in what is defined as culturally appropriate treatment, as well as inconsistent implementation of monitoring methods (Collin-Vézina et al., 2013). Nonetheless, the existing demographic and prevalence data does provide some indication of the scope of this public health issue.

Relevant Laws

Most of the laws related to child maltreatment are focused on prevention and providing funding for intervention. The Child and Family Services Reviews (2018) outlined relevant child welfare legislation that provides legal protection and recourse for upholding the safety and well-being of children. The related legislation falls into two general categories of (1) providing funding for child welfare, and (2) focusing on the protection of children's rights.

The Social Security Act

The Social Security Act (SSA) of 1935 laid the groundwork for the welfare system now in place in the U.S. and has a primary focus on providing for the elderly, the unemployed, and minors. The SSA has two titles that have major provisions for child welfare. SSA Title IV-B funds services and programs that protect child welfare, prevent child abuse and neglect, support children remaining or returning to their families where appropriate, provides training and education to professionals, and supports research projects. Given that Black children are in the child welfare system at disproportionate rates, such legislation provides funding for their care while in foster care out of the home and provides funding for training of staff and foster care providers. SSA Title IV-E provides funding for monthly maintenance payments for care of eligible children and covers costs to maintain programs such as recruitment and training staff and foster care providers. Thus, the SSA is a main source of funding that allows for implementation of child welfare services. Providing further funding, CAPTA provides federal funds to U.S. states toward prevention and intervention activities regarding child welfare. Given that Black children tend to have longer stays in foster care (Fluke et al., 2011), laws that provide funding to keep foster care resources in place benefit Black children.

Family First Preservation and Services Act of 2018

The Family First Preservation and Services Act (FFPSA) of 2018 is legislation that focuses funding and resources on supporting child placements with their family (National Conference of State Legislatures [NCSL], 2020). Whereas SSA uses Title IV-E funds to help with child placement in foster care outside of the home, the FFPSA gives the option for Title IV-E funds to be used for placement with parents or other family who can be caregivers. This legislation provides support for keeping children in their family's care instead of mostly moving toward out-of-family foster care. In fact, the FFPSA limits funding for children staying in group care placements for more than two weeks. Of course, there are programs that can qualify for an exemption (e.g., residential treatment programs) but even within the exempt settings, children must be evaluated within thirty days to see if the family has the ability to meet their needs. This focus on family, kinship placement, is essential for Black families.

FFPSA allows for support for family placement and reunification (NCSL, 2020). Title IV-E funds can be used toward supportive preventative measures (e.g., mental health and substance use treatment) as well as in-home parent skill-based programs. Title IV-B of the FFPSA also supports family placement by eliminating the fifteen-month time limit for reunification funds, and by also allotting funds toward efforts to improve interstate family placement. Collectively, the FFPSA has the potential to lower the rates of Black children who are in the child welfare system.

Protection of Children's Rights

The remaining legislation covered provides, in some regard, for the protection of the rights of children. The Individuals with Disabilities Education Act (IDEA) offered provisions for CPS agencies to screen young children in substantiated maltreatment cases for IDEA eligibility evaluation (Child and Family Services Reviews, 2018). Given that Black children are the second highest racial group served under IDEA, providing screening for IDEA services while in the child welfare system is important for the educational outcomes of Black children (U.S. Department of Education, 2016). Some of the child welfare legislation has a particular focus on keeping families unified when possible, which is beneficial for Black children who tend to remain in foster care for longer periods of time than children of other racial groups.

The Adoption Assistance and Child Welfare Act of 1980 sought to ensure that reasonable efforts are made by CPS agencies to avoid removal of children from their families when possible. This act promoted providing families with resources to enable protecting the well-being of the child.

The Adoption and Safe Families Act (ASFA) of 1997 allowed for concurrent planning of reunification and other permanent placement options, which provided assistance for children who remain in foster care for extended periods. This act also gave preference to adult relatives over non-relative caregivers for child placement.

Further assistance for foster care children was provided by the Foster Care Independence Act of 1999, which assisted with children in foster care receiving skills training to prepare for leaving the system. The Act provided education, employment services, counseling, financial and housing assistance, and also increased funding for adoption incentive payments. Additionally, in the interest of foster care children, the Fostering Connections to Success and Increasing Adoptions Act of 2008 provided for more incentives for adoption.

In recent times, there has been specific legislation to protect against child sex trafficking. The Preventing Sex Trafficking and Strengthening Families Act of 2014 requires states to provide appropriate services for children in foster care who are victims or at risk of being sexually trafficked.

Negative Impact of Laws on Black Children

Black children and families have benefited from many of the laws that have been enacted to address child maltreatment. However, some laws have potentially added to the displacement of Black children and contributed to their disproportionality in the child welfare system (Committee on Child Maltreatment Research, Policy, and Practice for the Next Decade: Phase II, 2014; Fluke et al., 2011). While much of the legislation holds the promise of being beneficial to Black children who are in the child welfare system at higher rates, there has been some concern that the enactment of laws meant to protect all children from abuse may actually negatively impact Black children (Dixon, 2008). For example, Dixon made the point that the quicker time frames for reunification promoted by the ASFA could make it more difficult for parents who are struggling with substance abuse, which tends to take time to resolve adequately. Although overall substance abuse rates are not significantly different across racial lines (Thomas, 2019), access to substance abuse treatment tends to be more difficult for Black individuals (U.S. Department of Health & Human Services, 2016). In that regard, Black children may be more negatively affected by such legislation given the potential lack of access of their parents to substance abuse treatment if needed as it relates to reunification. Notably, the FFPSA allows for the use of funds toward mental health and substance use treatment, but one could argue that these efforts are preventative for foster care but not the abuse itself. Of course, the treatment has the potential to reduce future (e.g., additional) abuse from occurring and, in that case, could be considered a means of prevention and intervention.

Given the challenges caused by removal and separation of children from their home and parents, a focus on utilizing other methods to address abuse, such as providing in-home support services can be helpful. In the case of Oni, which was discussed in the Introduction, it may have been beneficial for CPS to provide in-home support for the family to avoid her removal from the home. Such efforts are provided in FFPSA, but the issue remains that there may not be enough programs that provide the in-home parent skills training that can be approved and receive the funding.

Mandated Reporting Statutes

One prominent area of legislation regarding child maltreatment requires certain professional individuals, such as health care practitioners and educators, to report suspected child abuse or neglect (Lau et al., 2009). As of 2016, all U.S. states have statutes that require particular professionals to report suspected child abuse to an appropriate authority (Child Welfare Information Gateway, 2016a). The standards for reporting are that a report must be made if the reporter, while working in an official capacity, has reason to believe that abuse or neglect has occurred (Child Welfare Information Gateway, 2016a). Thus, privileged communication—the legal requirement that communication between professionals and their clients remain confidential—is restricted and superseded by the requirement to report child maltreatment. Most of these statutes impose fines and/or imprisonment for willful failure to report maltreatment; that is, not reporting or impeding the reporting of known or reasonably suspected child abuse or neglect. Notably, most states have provisions for the identity of the reporter to be kept confidential, which can reduce barriers to reporting. Mandated reporters are not required to prove that abuse or neglect occurred; rather, they are required to report suspected abuse. In the case of Madison, that was discussed in the Introduction, the daycare owner, after learning that Madison had a bruise, reported suspected abuse to CPS. In Daniel's case, the emergency room staff also made a report of suspected abuse when it was determined that his younger sister ingested pills.

Defining Child Maltreatment

The Centers for Disease Control and Prevention (CDC) has made efforts to create consistency in the definition of child maltreatment. In 2008, the CDC defined child maltreatment as, "any act or series of acts of commission or omission by a parent or other caregiver that results in harm, potential for harm, or threat of harm to a child" (Leeb et al., 2008). Acts of commission are identified as physical, sexual, and/or psychological abuse. Acts of omission are identified as failure to provide for a child's basic physical, emotional, or educational needs, or to protect a child from harm or potential harm. Thus, acts of omission include physical, emotional, medical/dental, and educational neglect, as well as inadequate supervision and exposure to violent environments.

Types of Maltreatment

The types of abuse that are commonly specified are neglect, physical abuse, sexual abuse, and psychological maltreatment (Child and Family Services Reviews, 2018). Regarding sexual abuse, the widely accepted definition includes sexual contact such as penetration, and non-contact abuse such as exposure, voyeurism, and pornography (National Association of School Nurses [NASN], 2018). The CDC has focused on surveillance as an important method to identify and reduce child maltreatment (Leeb et al., 2008). Surveillance includes collection, analysis, and interpretation of data gathered from various sources, including hospital records, police reports, child death records, and CPS data. By casting a wide net regarding potential maltreatment cases, surveillance methods are used to identify those children that are currently experiencing maltreatment, as well as those who have previously experienced or have died due to maltreatment.

The number of reported cases of child maltreatment can vary greatly from agency to agency. Challenges with identifying the number of children experiencing maltreatment are problematic for monitoring any changes in prevalence and with providing appropriate and timely intervention to these children. Further, part of the difficulty is having consistent definitions of what child maltreatment is across professions and agencies (Collin-Vézina et al., 2013). It is particularly concerning that the issue of Black children being overrepresented in the child welfare system may point, at least in part, to an issue of accurate identification of cases of maltreatment of Black children, which will be explored later in this chapter.

Subtypes of Child Maltreatment

Under the categories of physical, sexual, psychological abuse, and neglect, there are also particular subtypes of abuse that can occur, such as Shaken Baby Syndrome (SBS), Factitious Disorder Imposed on Another, and substance abuse during pregnancy. There is limited demographic data on the prevalence of these subtypes; thus, the prevalence in the Black community is unclear. Nonetheless, it is important to know that these abuses are occurring and to be aware of the signs of each abuse. SBS refers to the injuries that result when an infant's body is violently shaken and is also referred to as abusive head trauma (Al-Saadoon et al., 2011). This type of abuse occurred March 2017 when a Black father turned himself in to police pursuant to a warrant for his arrest. The warrant was issued following a hospital evaluation of his son, revealing that the infant was violently shaken (Taylor, 2017). Another specific type of child abuse is Factitious Disorder Imposed on Another, more commonly known as Munchausen syndrome by proxy (MSBP). With this condition, sickness is intentionally induced in a child and/or efforts are made to convince others that a child is sick. One such case occurred in the Black community when an eight-year-old boy living with his mother and siblings in Texas was found to have over 300 hospital visits and eight surgeries during his lifetime (Eiserer, 2017). His mother reported that he had several medical conditions, including cancer and seizures, and at one point he was on a feeding tube. His mother was eventually arrested for child abuse, and the boy and his siblings were placed in foster care. CPS and doctors later determined that the boy did not in fact have the medical conditions the mother purported. Since leaving his mother's care, he has shown no signs of medical problems. Lastly, another subtype of child maltreatment is substance abuse during pregnancy. Babies born addicted to substances, such as opioids and alcohol, experience severe withdrawal symptoms and potentially lifetime ill-effects. This was the case for a Black infant boy born to a mother who was on methadone as treatment for her heroin addiction (Chatterjee & Davis, 2018). The infant spent his first few weeks of life in a hospital neonatal intensive care unit suffering through withdrawal symptoms, including stiffening and shaking.

Signs of Child Maltreatment

There are several warning signs associated with maltreatment (Child Welfare Information Gateway, 2019a). Signs of physical abuse can include bruises, sprains, soreness, and broken bones. Particularly in infants, poor alertness, shaking, irritability, and bruising and can be signs of abuse. Other signs of abuse can include depression, anxiousness, aggression, and emotional reactivity. Notably, visual signs of abuse such as bruises can be obscured by skin complexion, particularly on individuals with darker complexions, as is the case for some Black children. In Madison's case, from the Introduction, what led her daycare worker to suspect abuse was a bruise. Bruising on a child could sometimes be easily dismissed without further inquiry given that children can be prone to clumsiness, particularly a child as young as two who is still developing coordinated use of her limbs. In this case, it was not dismissed.

For specific types of abuse, such as Munchausen syndrome by proxy, signs of abuse can be frequent symptoms of sickness such as vomiting, diarrhea, fever, rash, allergies, and infections (Bhandari, 2012). Psychological abuse may be signaled by low self-esteem, mood dysregulation, irritability and anger, withdrawal, social discomfort, as well as abusive behavior such as bullying and fighting. Signs of sexual abuse can be genital infections, sexualized behaviors, difficulty sitting or toileting, and discomfort changing in front of others or joining in group or gym activities. Signs of neglect can be ongoing medical issues such as malnourishment, rashes, body odor, school absences, and being left home alone. Notably, visible signs of neglect such as rashes can be obscured by skin complexion. Auditory signs of abuse and neglect might entail the child reporting so. It is important to attend to the above cues that are seen, as well as those that the children report.

Prevalence Rates of Maltreatment

The primary approach to identifying prevalence has been to gather data from several sources to ensure as many points of identification are included. However, by virtue of having data from varying sources, there are difficulties that surface, including the financial burden of these efforts and then having a singular system to log all the data gathered (Leeb & Fluke, 2015; Leeb et al., 2008). Notably, since maltreatment definitions vary across agencies, identified cases of abuse may not include a particular aspect of abuse that another agency includes. Thus, if the definition of harm differs across agencies, then one agency may not deem a child as harmed by one definition, whereas another agency with a differing definition would identify that child as having suffered maltreatment. Additionally, cultural lenses through which these policies are developed and later understood are also important. There may be differences in the ways in which policies are developed that do not match cultural norms and traditions of groups who are not represented in the development process. Take for example, people of color who have not historically been given access to positions where such policies are created. How do those policies encapsulate the understanding of their cultural norms and traditions? Would a lack of reflected cultural norms influence the prevalence of reported maltreatment? We will continue to explore such questions throughout this book.

Despite these challenges, there is reported data on the occurrences of child maltreatment. As noted in the Introduction, CPS agencies received approximately 4.4 million referrals of alleged child maltreatment in 2019, of which 656,000 children were determined to be victims of abuse and/or neglect (U.S. Department of Health & Human Services, 2021). The highest rates of victimization are among infants under age one, and neglect is the most common form of maltreatment. Fluke et al. (2011) noted that "African American infants are more likely to be maltreated (including severe and fatal maltreatment), to have a case investigated and/or substantiated, to enter foster care, to have a longer duration of care and to be placed in adoptive homes than any other demographic group" (p. 25). This draws attention to the level of risk Black children, particularly infants, face.

The impact of specific types of child abuse is worth examining, given the particular outcomes and potential prevention methods that would be warranted to address each. SBS mostly occurs to infants under six months of age. There are about 1,300 cases in the U.S. per year and approximately 80 percent of victims suffer lifelong disabilities, generating billions in healthcare costs (National Center on

Shaken Baby Syndrome, 2019). Another type of child abuse that occurs is when a child is exposed to drugs during pregnancy. In 2014, 6.5 infants of every 1,000 births were born addicted to opioids (National Institute on Drug Addiction, 2019). Furthermore, 5.9 percent of pregnant women use illicit drugs and 8.5 percent drink alcohol according to a national survey (Forray, 2016). The rates of occurrence for MSBP are unclear in the research literature, but given that it occurs in all communities, understanding how to recognize the signs of the condition is important for prevention and protecting Black children.

Research on child maltreatment has been most extensive on child sexual abuse. The rate of sexual abuse among Black children is 2.6 per 1,000 compared to 1.4 per 1,000 of White children (Sedlak et al., 2010). There is a question within the literature whether difference in rates of prevalence is due to actual prevalence differences or other factors such as rates of disclosing abuse, which can differ for various reasons, including subcultural norms. Rates of incest, a specific type of child sexual abuse in which the child is assaulted by a family member, are difficult to determine as well due to stigma and the consequences the victim may suffer from disclosing.

Hussey et al. (2006) found that there are particular factors that are associated with child maltreatment. As we explore these factors, consideration of the impact of each in the Black community is notable. Children in low-income families are more likely to experience maltreatment (Hussey et al., 2006). This factor places Black children at higher risk, since Black children are three times more likely to live in poverty (Dixon, 2008). In Oni's case, she remained in the child welfare system for an extended period of time as her primary caregiver could not meet the financial standard necessary for reunification. Related to this, Black families tend to have less access to services, yet another factor that compounds the risk of maltreatment (Dixon, 2008). Lack of legal representation was found to effect high rates of entry into foster care, which places Black children at higher risk of entry to foster care given the high rates of poverty in Black families.

Disparity in Reporting Maltreatment of Black Children

There have been several indicators showing that the maltreatment of Black children is reported more than other racial groups, but questions have been raised about whether these children are abused at significantly higher rates than other racial groups (Committee on Child Maltreatment Research, Policy, and Practice for the Next Decade: Phase II, 2014; Dixon, 2008; Elliott & Urquiza, 2006). This question can be explored by examining the possible contributing factors to this disparity. Dixon (2008) found that hospitals over-report abuse and neglect among Blacks but under-reported maltreatment among Whites, even when controlling for insurance status and likelihood of abuse. Additionally, Fluke et al. (2011) have pointed to substance use during pregnancy as a contributing factor to child welfare involvement for Black children. Notably, Fluke et al. (2011) found that there is a higher prevalence of substance use among Black mothers; however, the rates of drug testing of pregnant women of color also tends to be higher than other racial groups. Thus, it is questionable whether the reported higher rates of substance use among Black women is accurate. Furthermore, Elliott and Urquiza (2006) found that abuse reports of Black children are more likely to be investigated. This factor yet again fuels the question of whether Black children actually experience higher rates of maltreatment or simply appear as such because the cases of other racial groups are not as likely to be investigated. And then there is the finding that Black children are more likely to be placed in foster care than White children (Dixon, 2008). In fact, Black children represent 37 percent of the children in the child welfare system, twice their number in the general population (Dixon, 2008). Children in single-parent homes are more at risk for maltreatment, and this is of particular concern for Black children, as there is a higher rate of prevalence of single-parent homes in the Black community (Fluke et al., 2011). In fact, twice as many Black homes are led by single mothers than the homes of White families, and about 10 percent more than Hispanic families (Livingston, 2018). Single parenthood has also been found to negatively influence reunification rates for Black children (Fluke et al., 2011) given the Child Welfare System's preference for two-parent households. Thus, while reported maltreatment rates of Black children may be higher, it would be dangerous to conclude that this reflects actual higher rates of abuse given the number of intervening variables that point to the race of the child and the parent as key factors associated with the higher reported rates. The uncertainty underlining the prevalence data on maltreatment of Black children warrants further understanding for accurate assessment of the problem and identification of appropriate prevention and intervention.

The disproportionality of Black children in foster care has become a problem unto itself. Lash (2013) found that racial bias was a main factor influencing the proportion of Black children in foster care. The over-identification of Black children for maltreatment is associated with an over-representation of Black children in the child welfare system (Lash, 2013). Additionally, race was found to impact decision-making at most stages in the process when children enter the child welfare system (Dixon, 2008). Furthermore, it has also been found that there has been a particular focus on Black single mothers (Lash, 2013). Specifically, a mother's race was found to be one of the strongest predictors of foster care placement of children, along with prior welfare history (Dixon, 2008). Moreover, there are slower rates of exit from foster care, lower likelihood of reunification with parents, and lower probability of adoption for Black children (Dixon, 2008). The disproportionate number of Black children in the child welfare system warrants unpacking to explore the contributing factors and to help with appropriately addressing this issue (Anyon, 2011; Boyd, 2014; Dixon, 2008; Knott & Donovan, 2010). Differences in foster care placement may be attributable to higher rates of poverty, lack of availability of resources, and discriminatory practices by caseworkers (Child Welfare Information Gateway, 2016b). Fluke et al. (2011) found that the length of stay of children of color in foster care is associated with issues related to caseworker-related factors, such as having multiple caseworkers and caseworkers' level of education and training.

Child sex trafficking has emerged as a particular type of sexual abuse in which a child is used for the purposes of a sex act in exchange for anything of value (Greenbaum, 2017). Sex trafficking includes using a minor for producing sexual exploitation materials, sex-oriented business, and online solicitation. As would be expected given the hidden nature of sex trafficking, it is difficult to obtain statistics that capture the prevalence of this form of abuse. Banks and Kyckelhahn (2011) pointed to statistics from the U.S. Bureau of Justice Statistics, showing that between 2008 and 2011, there were more than 1,000 incidents of child sex exploitation. It was also reported that 40 percent of sex trafficking victims in the U.S. were Black individuals. Additionally, statistics from the U.S. Federal Bureau of Investigation show that

52 percent of underage prostitution arrests are Black minors (Federal Bureau of Investigation [FBI], 2014). Given that most sex trafficking victims are female, and most trafficking suspects are male, Black girls are particularly at risk of being taken advantage of and engaging in prostitution, and Black young males of becoming trafficking suspects. There has been speculation that many of the missing Black girls in the U.S. may be victims of sex trafficking (Brown, 2019). These statistics draw attention to the importance of understanding the risk factors within the Black community and the need to develop preventative measures for Black children becoming sex trafficking victims or perpetrators.

Child Maltreatment Fatalities

One of the tragic and irreversible outcomes of child maltreatment is fatality. Child maltreatment fatality describes the death of a child where abuse or neglect was a contributing factor. Approximately 2.4 of every 100,000 children die as a result of maltreatment (Children's Bureau, 2019). Infants and toddlers are most vulnerable to maltreatment fatality, with infants accounting for 44 percent of fatalities, and children ages one to three accounting for 33 percent of fatalities. Most maltreatment fatalities result from neglect, followed by physical abuse (Children's Bureau, 2019). Certain types of child abuse are highly associated with fatality. SBS is the most common cause of death among infants who experience child abuse (American Association of Neurological Surgeons, 2019). Specifically, 25 percent of infant victims of SBS die (National Center on Shaken Baby Syndrome, 2019). Fatality was the result in a tragic case where a Black mother slapped her two-year-old son when frustrated with him, which pushed his head into a wall. As a result, he began to have seizures and later died (Beltran & St. Germain, 2018). In the same year, a fatality by neglect occurred when a five-month-old Black infant boy was found unresponsive in the bathtub (Shapiro, 2018). The infant's father claimed that after putting his son in the tub and running bath water, he exited the bathroom to play a video game and forgot his son was in the tub. These cases are tragic and raise questions as to how these fatalities could have been prevented.

Black children disproportionately experience fatal child abuse. Farrell et al. (2017) found that while Black children represented

16 percent of study subjects that were newborn to age four, they accounted for 37 percent of the fatalities discussed in that study. That study reveals that Black children are dying from abuse at a rate of 8 per 100,000 children compared to the rate of White children occurring at 2.7 per 100,000. One of the strongest predictors of child maltreatment resulting in fatality is the presence of a biologically unrelated caregiver (Santhosh, 2016; Yampolskaya et al., 2009). This may be a contributing factor to high rates of maltreatment fatality among Black children given the cultural normality of close bonds and integration of biologically unrelated individuals into the family context (Taylor et al., 2013). Related to this, the rates of Black children being raised by single mothers opens the door for the mothers' dating practices to be a factor, (i.e., dating brings biologically unrelated individuals into the family environment). Notably, Yampolskaya et al. (2009) found that biological mothers with behavioral health problems such as substance abuse, mental health conditions, and/or physical health problems, as well as male perpetrators with a history of domestic violence had significant probabilities of engaging in fatal child maltreatment.

Perpetrators of Maltreatment

Through a feminist theoretical lens, child maltreatment can be understood to occur in the context of a power differential in which an adult exerts control over a child (Herman-Davis, 2012). The unequal power dynamic that exists between adults and children leaves the child vulnerable to abuse and neglect—given that the adults in the child's life have the power to exert such control in acceptable and unacceptable ways. It is with this framework in mind that the data on perpetrators of child maltreatment can be understood. The perpetrators of child maltreatment are most commonly biological mothers (Santhosh, 2016). Given that mothers are typically the primary caregiver of children, this draws attention to the underlying factors related to this association. Notably, the presence of mental illness—which inherently introduces access to mental health care—and poverty increases the risk of child abuse (Kohl et al., 2011). These are both factors that particularly impact Black mothers. Additionally, and as previously mentioned, given that women are often the primary caregiver, children are impacted by the issues affecting women directly and indirectly. The high rates of co-occurrence between intimate partner violence against women and violence against children (Nami et al., 2017) points to the ways that oppressed groups such as women and children are subjected to maltreatment in a culture built on male dominance.

The second most common category of perpetrators are male partners of mothers who are not the biological father of the child. When examining specific types of abuse, the most common perpetrator can differ. Male partners of mothers show a high tendency to engage in child sexual abuse (Kohl et al., 2011). The most common perpetrators for shaken baby syndrome are males, and most commonly biological fathers (Al-Saadoon et al., 2011). It is again important to recognize that in a society that has male dominance interwoven and propagated at every systemic level, the abuse of children by males illustrates the implicit permission given to men to dominate those with less power.

There are factors that are correlated with becoming a perpetrator of child maltreatment. It has been found that perpetrators of abuse tended to be victims of child abuse themselves, and this is particularly evident for male perpetrators who have experienced child sexual abuse (Craissati et al., 2002). There are also socioeconomic factors associated with perpetrators. For females, having the experience of abuse in childhood or adulthood, lower socioeconomic status, and underpaid employment were associated with being a perpetrator of abuse (Santhosh, 2016). In the case of Daniel, presented in the Introduction, it is worth considering the socioeconomic circumstances. His mother asked him to babysit his younger siblings, and it is not unusual for parents to ask an older sibling to help in caring for and providing supervision of younger siblings. But now that a problem has occurred, do his parents have the resources to secure alternative childcare? Consideration of the support that Daniel's mother needs as the primary caregiver is important in reducing or removing the factors that led to the maltreatment. To that end, there could be medical follow-up services needed for Daniel's sister, and access to this will be impacted by the quality of health insurance that the family has. Access to healthcare is a known barrier in the Black community. Also, it is notable that the circumstances under which Oni (see Introduction) was removed from her aunt's home were related to poverty. The socioeconomic disadvantage of poverty created living conditions that were not adequate for children, which is a common circumstance for Black families.

Thus, the socioeconomic disadvantages that Black people face both directly and indirectly increase the risk of them becoming perpetrators and perpetuating the cycle of maltreatment.

There is a significant association between mental illness and child abuse. Children of mothers with mental illness have an increased likelihood of maltreatment (Kohl et al., 2011; Reupert et al., 2013). Furthermore, children of mothers with mental illness are more likely to be subject to recurrent maltreatment and to be placed in foster care. Mental illness in the Black community is a more significant risk factor, mainly due to treatment disparities when compared to Whites (McGuire & Miranda, 2008). Blacks have less access to health care, including mental health services, and often the healthcare is of lower quality. Thus, with less access to quality treatment, the effects of mental illness are likely more prevalent in the Black community. The oppression of those with less power is again evident in the lack of resources to which Black individuals have access, and this subjugation impacts Black children as a result.

Maltreatment in the Child Welfare System and Government Agencies

There has been a growing awareness of child maltreatment that occurs while a child is in the child welfare system. When reports of abuse occurring in foster care began to surface prominentlyin the 1990s, investigations led to increased awareness about the prevalence of abuse of children occurring in the larger child welfare system. The National Coalition for Child Protection Reform (2015) found that in studies across various states in the U.S., abuse in foster care was occurring at rates ranging from 28 percent to 34 percent. Wexler (2017) reported that surveys over the past few decades show rates of abuse in foster care as high as 40 percent. Such abuse can be re-traumatizing to a child who has been removed from their family because of maltreatment. In Oni's case, discussed in the Introduction, she was removed from her home and placed in the child welfare system, during which time she experienced sexual abuse on more than one occasion. Thus, she was placed at further risk of maltreatment when she was placed in the foster care system.

Taking a closer look at the child welfare system, there is a pattern of Black children remaining in the foster care system for longer periods than their White counterparts (Fluke et al., 2011). Given this extended placement pattern, there is a higher likelihood of Black children experiencing abuse in foster care than for other racial groups. This was the case for a Black six-year-old boy who was eventually discovered to be sexually abused by his foster father in San Diego, California (Cook, 2018). Despite several instances of the child reporting to adults that his foster father was hurting him, it took several months for the abuse to be confirmed and for the child to be removed from the home. This willful failure to protect the child based on the unacceptable amount of time it took for this child to be removed raises many questions. How much of a factor was his race before his cries for help were taken seriously? Were the individuals to whom he reported "being hurt" following mandated reporting guidelines? Who is to be held accountable for the length of time it took to address this child's needs?

There has also been growing attention on the treatment of immigrants who migrate to the U.S., which in turn has brought attention to immigrant children who suffer abuse during the immigration process once on U.S. soil. In 2018, the American Civil Liberties Union (ACLU) released a report detailing alleged abuse and neglect of unaccompanied immigrant children, many of whom were Black (American Civil Liberties Union [ACLU], 2018). Many of these children, when detained by U.S. Customs and Border Protection, were allegedly subjected to maltreatment such as being detained for longer than the seventy-two hours permitted by law, physical abuse including being punched and kicked, inappropriate sexual touching of female minors during body searches, denial of medical care of a pregnant minor which preceded a still birth, verbal abuse via derogatory name calling, and confinement in cold, small spaces (ACLU, 2018). In some cases, the ACLU has filed suit on behalf of immigrants because of children and parents being separated without clear or just cause once on U.S. soil during migration. This was the case for a mother and her daughter who were separated within days of arriving in the U.S. from the Democratic Republic of Congo (Samuels, 2018). They had been held separately in detention centers several states apart. There have also been cases of alleged abuse of children, including Black children, occurring in immigration detention centers (Associated Press, 2018). These incidents raise concerns about the safety of children and about whether the oversight of detention centers is adequate.

Reporters of Maltreatment

As noted previously, all the states in the U.S. have statutes that specify which professionals are required to report suspected child maltreatment to a central reporting authority. Mandated reporters include medical and mental health practitioners, educators, childcare providers, clergy, coroners and medical examiners, and law enforcement officers (Lau et al., 2009). In most cases, these professionals are the most frequent reporters of child maltreatment (Child Welfare Information Gate, 2017). Of professionals, educators are the most common reporters, followed by law enforcement, then social services staff.

Although reporting of child maltreatment is mandated by law, for the aforementioned professionals, there have been concerns about whether all suspected cases are reported. Barriers to mandated reporting have been found to include fear that reporting may cause more harm than good, believing there is insufficient evidence for a report to be made, and experiencing ethical conflict (Lau et al. 2009). These barriers leading to under-reporting can leave children vulnerable to abuse from which they need to be protected, and examples of this are not uncommon. This was the case when school staff did not report suspected abuse to CPS after being told by a parent that her nine-year-old daughter's classmate reported having sex with an adult (Saunders, 2007). In Madison's case, that was presented in the Introduction, there was at least a one-day delay in reporting to CPS. Daycare workers are considered mandated reporters and are therefore required to report suspected abuse. Thus, it is questionable whether waiting a day to report suspected abuse could fall under the umbrella of willful failure. In this case, the suspected abuse of Madison was not substantiated by CPS. Therefore, waiting a day did not ostensibly change the outcome, but the potential was there for further harm to occur. Notably, both the daycare worker and daycare owner are mandated reporters and are required to report this suspected abuse. Thus, the potential assessment of willful failure applies to them both. Madison's parents reported the daycare center based on their concerns that the bruise could have occurred at the daycare center. Parents are not considered mandated reporters, but they are well within their rights to report their concerns about potential abuse occurring at the daycare.

As previously noted, child maltreatment of Black children is reported at higher rates than any other racial group (Committee on

Child Maltreatment Research, Policy, and Practice for the Next Decade: Phase II, 2014). This disparity raises questions about the training of mandated reporters regarding the signs of abuse and ethical reporting practices, as well as the potential impact of racial bias on mandated reporters. Explicit training about the impact of race on the determination of suspected abuse could increase accuracy of identifying maltreatment.

Overreaching and False Positives

There has been some concern that the reporting systems in place for identification of child maltreatment have resulted in overstepping the boundaries of what is necessary to maintain the safety of children (Wallace, 2014). A case that occurred in 2014 in South Carolina raised questions about the overreach of child welfare efforts. When a Black, nine-year-old girl was found playing in a park by herself, her mother was arrested and charged with unlawful conduct toward a child (Wallace, 2014). Her daughter then spent fourteen days in foster care. This case garnered national attention, with dual outrage at this being just and unjust. The details of the case shed light on why such opposing viewpoints surfaced. This mother and daughter lived a six-minute walk from the park. The mother worked less than a ten-minute drive away from the park at a fast-food restaurant. The daughter had a cell phone, a key, and could walk home at any point. In this case, there was public debate as to whether there was legitimate abuse, at what age a child can play in the park without a parent, and to what extent the race of the mother and child was a factor in the outcome. It is also questionable whether the child's gender played a role. Would a boy the same age have been reported? Most states do not have a legal age at which a child can be left unsupervised. In this case, it is also questionable whether the child was harmed by the actions of her mother. Thus, the potential for overreaching and causing harm to a child and a family is worth further consideration when establishing safeguards to protect children.

Co-occurrence of Violence against Women and Children

Violence against children often occurs in a context where violence is occurring against women. As previously noted, as much as a 40 percent co-occurrence rate has been found between intimate partner violence against women and child maltreatment (Nami et al., 2017). Notably, Black women experience higher rates of intimate partner violence than women overall and, in particular, higher rates of psychological aggression (DuMonthier et al., 2017). This points to Black children being at higher risk of maltreatment in homes where intimate partner violence against women occurs. These children are not only facing maltreatment but also potentially witnessing the intimate partner violence. Also, one must consider the psychological impact of such violence on the functioning and responsibilities of women as primary caregivers to children, which they often are (DuMonthier et al., 2017). Examining these factors through a feminist lens raises many questions. How does the treatment of women, in turn, impact how they treat their children? To what extent does the prevention and reduction of child maltreatment need to have a dual focus on women's issues? These intersecting issues seem best addressed in tandem, such that both the needs of children and women are accounted for.

Outcomes of Child Maltreatment

As the longitudinal studies conducted on child maltreatment increase, so does the data on associated negative outcomes. There is a strong association between experiencing child maltreatment and negative health outcomes (Norman et al., 2012). For both Madison and Daniel's families, CPS involvement occurred, which can have a psychological impact given the potential for disruptive consequences when CPS is involved. Factors such as CPS staff visiting the home, interviewing family members, and having ongoing interventions and involvement with the family can be intrusive, impede family relationships, and have a negative psychological impact on each family member. The Adverse Childhood Experiences (ACEs) Study was conducted between 1995 to 1997 and yielded data on the effects of child abuse in adulthood (Feletti et al., 1998). Results indicated a strong association between child abuse and high-risk health behaviors in adulthood. Behaviors such as alcohol and drug abuse, smoking, and obesity were common. There was also a correlation to child maltreatment and risky sexual behavior, having multiple sex partners, and contracting sexually transmitted infections (Norman et al., 2012). Additionally, there was a correlation between child abuse and ill-health including heart and respiratory disease, and cancer. Associations between child maltreatment and juvenile justice involvement have been established, including social risk factors such as race predicting transition from child welfare involvement to juvenile justice involvement (Committee on Child Maltreatment Research, Policy, and Practice for the Next Decade: Phase II, 2014; Vidal et al., 2017). Additionally, rates of healthcare utilization are also higher for child maltreatment victims than the general population, thus having implications for U.S. overall healthcare costs (Collin-Vézina et al., 2013). Regarding mental health, there is a strong association between child maltreatment and developing depressive disorders, anxiety disorders, and conduct disorders (Norman et al., 2012).

There are also specific types of outcomes that result from particular forms of abuse. For example, SBS is known to cause numerous neurobehavioral impairments that permanently impacts the victim (Al-Saadoon et al., 2011). Retinal hemorrhaging is a common sustained injury as well as rib fractures. Other impairments can occur, including blindness, epilepsy, cerebral palsy, intellectual disabilities, behavioral disturbances, and in some instances, death (Al-Saadoon et al., 2011). Negative outcomes from abuse by prenatal exposure to alcohol and/or drugs are immense. Prenatal exposure to alcohol can lead to problems such as Fetal Alcohol Syndrome, low birth weight, premature birth, conduct problems, mental health conditions such as anxiety and depression, and attention problems (Sood et al., 2001). Exposure during pregnancy to illegal drugs can lead to issues such as poor growth, poor language development, lowered academic achievement, and attention problems (Behnke & Smith, 2013). Outcomes from child abuse stemming from MSBP can include unnecessary and potential life-threatening surgeries, as well as exorbitant healthcare costs (Eiserer, 2017).

Child sexual abuse is particularly associated with negative outcomes. There is an association between child sexual abuse and mental disorders (Turner et al., 2017). Child sexual abuse outcome research has shown that there is a substantial risk of developing particular mental health symptoms such as disassociation and post-traumatic stress, as well as delusions, hallucinations, depressive symptoms, and substance abuse problems (Collin-Vézina et al., 2013). There is also a propensity of child sexual abuse victims to exhibit inappropriate sexual behaviors, which can become a contributing factor to the perpetuation of child sexual abuse (Collin-Vézina et al., 2013). Collin-Vézina et al. (2013) also found that child sexual abuse victims are more at risk of experiencing domestic violence as well as adult sexual abuse. Moreover, there is an association between child sexual abuse and suicide attempts, with a stronger association in males than females (Turner et al., 2017).

Notably, chronic or repeated maltreatment tends to have worse outcomes (Jonson-Reid et al., 2012). Vidal et al. (2017) found that chronic maltreatment was a predictor for juvenile justice involvement. Furthermore, associations between child maltreatment and criminality have been found to continue into adulthood (M. Dargis, & M. Koenigs, 2018; Mersky et al., 2012). In Oni's case, she experienced negative social and emotional consequences from the sexual abuse she suffered, the full extent of which remains to be seen as she ages.

The healthcare costs of maltreatment are astounding though not unexpected given the impact of maltreatment on all aspects of health and well-being, including medical and mental health, education, employment, and criminality. As of 2010, the long-term health care costs were over six billion dollars (Statista Research Department, 2019b). When considering the cost in terms of productivity, the figure rises to over eight-five billion dollars (Statista Research Department, 2019b). Overall, child maltreatment has a far-reaching impact on the functioning of children into adulthood. This reality punctuates the importance of preventing maltreatment of children, thus preventing a host of associated issues across the lifespan.

Closing Summary

The insidious and far-reaching impact of child maltreatment warrants our continued efforts to prevent, identify, and treat the occurrence and consequences of abuse and neglect. Moreover, occurring at higher rates than any other race, Black children need specific attention to understand the cultural factors associated with the maltreatment they suffer in order to address the problem in the Black community. The study cases each provide a context for which suspected maltreatment can occur and allow for exploration of how each aspect of the case matters when seeking to prevent and/or reduce maltreatment. The lens through which maltreatment is explored has to consider factors at the individual, familial, and systemic levels in order to have an adequate impact. Using a feminist lens focuses on the power and oppression inherent in maltreatment and provides a more complete understanding of how to address child maltreatment adequately. As we delve into the scope of this problem, we will identify what is needed to promote prevention, treatment, and wellness in the Black community in order to successfully address the public health challenge that child maltreatment presents. But first, in the next chapter, we will consider the child welfare system as it relates to Black families in the United States.

3

Exploring the Child Welfare System

> There can be no keener revelation of a society's soul than the way in which it treats its children.
> —Nelson Mandela, former president of South Africa

Overview

The child welfare system is a comprehensive web of public and private agencies that serve a key role in the care of children who have experienced child maltreatment. This chapter explores the child welfare system, from inception through the evolution to its current standing. Specifically, the key legislative mandates that shaped and expanded the welfare system are discussed, as well as the impact of legislation on the provision of child protective services. The demographics of children in the welfare system are explored, focusing particularly on the overrepresentation of Black children in the system and the tendency for these children to have longer stays. As explained in chapter 1, Black will continue to be defined as the collective racial group that includes but is not necessarily limited to African American. The impact of child welfare involvement on Black children and families is reviewed. Lastly, improvements for the problematic aspects of the welfare system are outlined and a call for reform is made.

The Inception of the Child Welfare System

The inception of the child welfare system has been associated with different origin points that helped shaped the system, as it exists today. The current child welfare system is comprised of several agencies that intersect their efforts to provide wraparound support for children and their families (Children's Bureau, 2020). Public agencies partner with private agencies and community organizations to expand the reach and capacity of the services provided. However, the system was not always composed in this manner.

Orphanages

There have been several important developments across the chronology of the ever-evolving child welfare system that have shaped it into what it is today. One of the early and significant developments in building the child welfare system was establishing orphanages in the 1700s (Family and Children's Services Division, 1995). The development of these institutions has been thought to coincide with national socioeconomic problems and health epidemics. Orphanages were key in caring for children orphaned by war casualties, but also for children born to parents in poverty and unable to care adequately for their offspring(s). However, these institutions tended to focus on basic shelter needs, and did not address the complex and multilayered issues that caused children to need care outside their home. By the 1900s, concern about the deleterious impact of orphanages on the cognitive and social development of children sparked a movement toward more permanent care options for children, and various collaborations between government and community agencies were forged (Hostinar et al., 2012; St. Petersburg-USA Orphanage Research Team, 2008). As child welfare agencies and funding increased, the reliance and adequacy of orphanages decreased (Family and Children's Services Division, 1995).

Child Protective Agencies

The development of child protection agencies marked a key turning point in the evolution of the child welfare system. New York state was the first in the U.S. to establish an agency whose mission was the protection of children (New York Society for the Prevention of Cruelty to Children, n.d.). The inception of this agency is largely thought to have been in response to a notable case of child abuse. In 1873, the neighbors of an eight-year-old girl named Mary Ellen expressed to community leaders their concern and suspicion that the child was being abused (U.S. Department of Health & Human Services, 2020). Upon investigation, she was found to be physically and emotionally abused by her guardians. Criminal prosecution of her guardians resulted in sentencing to jail time. Notably, there had been several criminal cases of child maltreatment prior to this case, as early as the 1600s, however the criminal prosecution of parents did not subsequently lead to improved conditions for the maltreated child given the limited available resources for child welfare (Watkins, 1990). Subsequent to the prosecution of Mary Ellen's guardians, the New York Society for the Prevention of Cruelty to Children (NYSPCC) was created in 1874, the first of its kind (New York Society for the Prevention of Cruelty to Children, n.d.; U.S. Department of Health & Human Services, Administration for Children and Families, Administration on Children, Youth and Families, Children's Bureau, 2020). As such, Mary Ellen's case is often touted as the catalyst for the organized protection of children. Following the development of the NYSPCC, approximately 300 child welfare agencies developed across the U.S. over the next few years (Wildeman & Waldfogel, 2014).

Relevant Laws

In addition to child protection agencies, laws developed for child welfare helped to both shape and expand the boundaries of the welfare system. The Adoption of Children Act of 1851 provided legal parameters for the adoption process, which allowed for clearer guidelines for the process and expanded the permanent care options available for children in need (Herman, 2011; Kahan, 2006). This act helped shift the focus from facilities and institutions to families who could provide children with care. Prior to this point, adoption was informal and not regulated, and often occurred privately without assurances that the child was being given to an appropriate caregiver. The Social Security Act (SSA) of 1935 was another key legislative act for child welfare (Child Welfare Information Gateway, 2019c; Fluke et al., 2011; Wildeman & Waldfogel, 2014). Along with providing for the needs of the elderly and unemployed, SSA also focused on minors. The SSA is currently composed of two titles that fund services and programs to protect child welfare, prevent child abuse and neglect, support children remaining or returning to their families where appropriate, provide training and education to professionals, and support research projects. The SSA also provides funding for monthly maintenance payments for the care of eligible children, which covers costs to programs that recruit and train foster care staff and providers (Child Welfare Information Gateway, 2019c; Fluke et al., 2011; Wildeman & Waldfogel, 2014). The SSA is one of the most expansive legislative influencers of the child welfare system. Having federal funding for child protective services expanded the reach and scope of the services that could be provided not only to maltreated children, but to their families who were integral to the child's well-being.

The Family First Prevention Services Act (FFPSA) of 2018 seems to have taken the SSA a step further by specifically focusing on family placement as a means of supporting children in the child welfare system. In fact, FFPSA has a large preventative component targeted toward supporting children and family before they enter the system. Funds under FFPSA can be used toward supportive preventative measures for parents, including mental health and substance use treatment, as well as in-home parent skill-based training (NCSL, 2020). This is a welcomed change in support for families—whereas previous programs have focused training on staff within facilities, which is important and needed, FFPSA supports parent training programs. It also allows for reunification funds to be used for longer durations of time, and it requires that group placement programs evaluate children intending to assess their needs in relations to the family's abilities to meet them.

The Child Abuse Prevention and Treatment Act of 1974 (CAPTA) marked a significant shift in the involvement and role of the federal government in the protection of children, which is another pivotal component that shaped the child welfare system (Center for Advanced Studies in Child Welfare, 2016; Child Welfare Information Gateway, 2019b; Petersen et al., 2014). The enactment of CAPTA, which has been amended multiple times, required all states to have child abuse reporting laws, and allowed for the federal government to have a specific role in the prevention of maltreatment of children. CAPTA expanded what was deemed to be maltreatment and provided more specific immunity for good faith reporters of suspected child maltreatment from civil and criminal penalization (U.S. Department of Health & Human Services, Administration for Children and

Families, Administration on Children, Youth and Families, Children's Bureau, 2020).

It is important to note that the inception of the child welfare system, the related legislative acts, and the turning points for the provision of better services were not always intended for the betterment of Black children and families. Given the sociopolitical climate of the past few centuries, it is hard to imagine that these efforts reflected intentionality outside of providing services for the majority population at that time. For example, orphanages were not initially populated (or overpopulated as they are today) with Black children. In fact, Black children were excluded from orphanages until the 1900s and were in segregated orphanages until the 1950s and 1960s when churches and other religious groups stepped in to provide shelter and care for them. Although government and community agencies eventually collaborated to find more permanent options for children, Black children were originally being cared for by members of their community. This dichotomy of government versus community support remains a difficult balance for Black families to contend with today, especially because government involvement has historically been negligent, if not obstructive, toward responding to the needs and well-being of Black people.

Gateway to the Child Welfare System

The entry point to the child welfare system for most children is when there is referral of suspected abuse or neglect made to a child protective agency (U.S. Department of Health & Human Services, 2020; Wildeman & Waldfogel, 2014). This referral may come from any concerned individual who has come into contact with the child. Appropriate child welfare staff review the referral to determine whether there is sufficient reason to investigate if maltreatment has occurred. During the review process, referrals are either screened in, leading to further efforts being made, or screened out. The referral is screened in if there is adequate information and reason for investigation to occur. Conversely, the referral is screened out for reasons such as inadequate information for an agency response, the referral not being related to abuse or neglect, the referral being deemed more appropriate for another agency or jurisdiction, or the children concerned are older than age eighteen (U.S. Department of Health & Human Services,

2020). If it is determined that there is no basis for investigation, no further determination is needed. Child protection agencies have specific guidelines that are followed for screening, but there is also latitude for the individual judgment and discretion of the staff worker in making the determination. During the investigation process, most states use a two-tier or three-tier model with varying standards of evidence to substantiate maltreatment (Petersen et al., 2014). Most often, the conclusion of the substantiation process is that the referral is founded, unfounded, or inconclusive.

It is notable that a screened-out referral does not necessarily mean that child abuse or neglect has not occurred. Being screened out may mean that there is not sufficient data available to make such a determination (Petersen et al., 2014). For example, the referral may be received for a child who was seen being hit by an accompanying adult in a neighborhood store, but there may be no information that could lead to determining the identity of the child or the adult. Screening out might also occur when the behavior reported in the referral is not considered an indicator of maltreatment (e.g., a mother talking sternly to her child).

If the decision is made that the referral requires investigation, then efforts are made to substantiate whether or not maltreatment has occurred and/or whether the child is at significant risk for maltreatment. Investigations can include but are not limited to a child protective worker interviewing the child and caregivers, looking for physical indicators of maltreatment, (e.g., bruises), determining if there has been a prior report of maltreatment, inquiring about school attendance, and examining the living conditions of the child's home (Petersen et al., 2014). If it is determined that the child is either at significant risk for or has experienced maltreatment, then appropriate interventions are determined to remedy the maltreatment. Interventions may include providing referrals for community-based support services to the family, providing in-home interventions, and in some cases, removal of the child from the care of their caregiver(s). When removed, the child may go to a kinship placement, which involves placing the child in the care of a blood relative, or the child may be placed in a foster care agency or foster care home. Overall, most referrals do not result in children being placed in foster care (Petersen et al., 2014). But the number of foster care placements is significant enough to warrant the continued utility of oversight and repeatedly reviewing the efficacy of the child welfare system in managing the needs of those children.

Racial Demographics of Children in the Child Welfare System

The foster care system has been a significant resource for children to be cared for when they are removed from their caregivers. U.S. child protection agencies receive approximately three million annual referrals for approximately six million children (Wildeman & Waldfogel, 2014). The U.S. Children's Bureau established that there were 676,000 reported child maltreatment victims during the 2016 fiscal year (DePanfilis, 2018). Many of these child victims were placed in the foster care system for various lengths of stay. In 2018, approximately 437,000 children were in foster care (Child Welfare Information Gateway, 2020). Although children are being increasingly placed in alternative placements, such as kinship care, the numbers of children in foster care have not decreased over time (Child Trends, 2019). A review of the racial demographics of the children in the child welfare system reveals that Black children are disproportionately placed in foster care (Child Welfare Information Gateway, 2020). Specifically, Black children are placed in foster care at higher rates than White and Hispanic children (Child Welfare Information Gateway, 2020). Moreover, not only do Black children have a higher likelihood of entering foster care, but they also stay in care for longer periods of time (Adopt .org, 2020). Thus, more Black children are being removed from their homes and also kept away from their homes and caregivers for longer periods of time than children of other racial groups.

The case study of Oni, which was presented in the Introduction, provided an example of a Black child being removed from her home and caregiver. Her removal was predicated on there being too many occupants in her aunt's home, which raised questions about the living arrangements being adequate and suitable. How would her case have been different if community resources or in-home interventions were able to be provided in lieu of her being removed? In other words, what would be necessary in order for Oni to have stayed in the care of her aunt? If her aunt were provided resources to allow the home to be more amenable to the number of individuals staying in the home (i.e., adequate beds per person), could Oni have remained in the home? You might remember that there were no noted concerns about her being in danger, only that the number of people residing in the home was not appropriate. Is the number of people in the home enough to determine endangerment of a child? The answers to these questions are dependent on a number of factors including the available resources in Oni's aunt's community, whether they could access those services, whether in-home interventions were available, whether such interventions were provided efficiently, and whether Oni's aunt was agreeable and capable of engaging with those services and interventions. On the caseworker's part, there are also factors to be considered such as the size of the caseworker's caseload, which impacts the time and attention the worker can spend addressing each case, and whether the caseworker used culturally informed criteria in decision-making.

It is the multilayered considerations in each case of founded child maltreatment that can make it difficult to determine the best course of action. Presumably, the overarching goal would be to keep children in the care of their family, and to provide the resources needed to ensure that the home environment is safe and adequate for the child's needs. In Oni's case, the goal of family preservation would have prioritized any efforts to keep her in the home and have the first tier of action focused on interventions that allow for this to happen. But there are clearly a number of factors that lead to that tiered approach not being employed in every case.

Racial Disproportionality throughout the Child Welfare Process

According to statistics from the 2014 U.S. Census Bureau report, as well as the U.S. Department of Health & Human Services, Black children are disproportionately identified by child protective services as victims, entered into the foster care system, and wait longer for permanent adoptive placement than children of other racial groups (Child Welfare Information Gateway, 2016b). Additionally, when involved in the child welfare system, Black children were more likely than their White counterparts to receive out-of-home instead of in-home services (Foster et al., 2011; Watt & Kim, 2019). The disproportionality of Black children in the child welfare system has been a longstanding pattern (Anyon, 2011; Boyd, 2014; Dixon, 2008; Knott & Donovan, 2010; Watt & Kim, 2019). Thus, the existence of this disparity is not a new phenomenon, but it has become a more glaring issue as racial disparities have come into national focus in recent years.

There are a number of influencing factors that have been raised to explain the disproportionate number of Black children in the child welfare system, including race-related biases, poverty, parental challenges, and other institutional factors. Additionally, influencing factors may vary by state and locality, particularly given the difference in state allocation of funding, available resources, and differences in racial demographics across states.

The Association between Race and Disproportionality

Race has been found to impact decision making at most stages in the process when children enter the child welfare system (Dixon, 2008; Watt & Kim, 2019). For example, at the first stage of entry, which is child welfare referrals, research has indicated that there is an over-identification of Black children for maltreatment referrals (Lash, 2013; National Conference of State Legislatures, 2021). Moreover, in general, not all reports of maltreatment lead to investigations; however, when reports of maltreatment involve Black children, scholars have found that the reports are more likely to be investigated (Bernstein et al., 2020; Elliott & Urquiza, 2006). And as noted above, Black children are disproportionately identified by child protective services as victims of maltreatment. To this end, there are now indicators that a Black child's injuries are much more likely to be interpreted as being caused by abuse than for a White child, in some cases leading to wrongful convictions of Black parents (Bernstein et al., 2020).

The role of race in child welfare system involvement extends beyond the stages of referral and identification of maltreatment. Research has shown that race is a prominent factor in foster care placement. Specifically, a mother's race was found to be one of the strongest predictors of foster care placement of children, along with prior welfare history (Dixon, 2008). Rising female imprisonment rates could also be a contributing factor to Black children being disproportionately involved in the child welfare system (Kajstura, 2018; Wildeman & Waldfogel, 2014). Specifically, female incarceration has increased from 26,000 to more than 200,000 in the past thirty years, with Black women being incarcerated at twice the rate of their White counterparts (Maxwell & Solomon, 2018). Women are most often the primary caregiver of children, and this is particularly the case in the Black community. For example, single mothers lead Black homes at five times the rates of White homes (Prince, 2016). Thus, as the rates of incarcerated Black mothers increase, the rates of Black children in the child welfare system may rise in tandem.

Poverty and Disproportionality

In addition to the disparities that are thought to be associated with decision making regarding child welfare, there are also influential population-based factors. Not surprisingly, poverty has often been touted as an overall component of the racial disparity of Black children in the child welfare system. Some scholars have noted that there are disproportionate rates of Black children in the child welfare system because there are disproportionate and disparate needs of the children and their families, mainly related to high rates of poverty (Child Welfare Information Gateway, 2016b). However, this has not proven to be a sufficient explanation for the racial disproportionality in the child welfare system. Research has shown that poverty is not as strong of a factor as race, and even when socioeconomic factors are controlled for, the disparity is not fully explained by poverty (Child Welfare Information Gateway, 2016b).

Other Associated Factors in Disproportionality

There are other noteworthy factors that are potentially associated with racial disproportionality in the child welfare system, including issues relating to caregivers, child welfare staff, and other external factors. Parental substance use and mental health problems are also associated with increased risk of child maltreatment. Although substance use and mental health problems plague all racial groups, it is the lack of adequate access to treatment resources for such conditions that can create additional disadvantages for Black parents and therefore become a risk factor for more Black children entering the child welfare system. In looking at these data, the intersection between inadequate resources for the needs of parents and the increased risk of children for maltreatment and for entering the child welfare system becomes clearer. In considering these factors within the Black community, it would stand to reason that addressing the disproportional numbers of Black children in the child welfare system must include providing resources for the needs of the families of Black children.

There are also institutional factors (e.g., policies and procedures) related to child welfare staffing that could contribute to the racial disparity of children in the system. Fluke et al. (2011) found that the length of stay of children of color in foster care is associated with caseworker-related factors, such as having multiple caseworkers and caseworkers' level of education and training. Additionally, research has shown differences in the risk thresholds caseworkers used to decide whether maltreatment has occurred related to race (Lash, 2013). Moreover, it makes sense that higher caseloads can compromise a caseworker's judgment and ability to focus on particular variables in individual cases. Additionally, Harris and Hackett (2008) found that attitudinal factors contributed to this disproportionality. Specifically, they asserted that the less caseworkers were aware of institutionalized racism, the more likely they were to engage in inept decision-making. The authors recommended an intervention that addressed this compromised cultural consciousness, so that caseworkers can use their own informed sphere of influence to develop and utilize more effective strategies, practices, and policies. In chapter 4, we offer suggestions for raising cultural consciousness, developing cultural competence, and maintaining cultural humility.

Other institutional factors that have been noted in the literature include the impact of government funding on the services that are provided at the state and agency level. In particular, varying funding from state to state may reflect reduced funding in Black communities, which in turn reduces the resources that are available to support Black children remaining in the home or returning home more expediently (Child Welfare Information Gateway, 2016b). Thus, having adequate community resources can affect whether a child has to be removed from the home to address maltreatment. If community resources can be developed in Black communities, this could positively impact the racial disparity within the child welfare system.

The Three Risk Factor Framework

Many of the aforementioned areas can be viewed through the three risk factors that Hill (2006) highlighted related to the disproportionate rate of children of color in the child welfare system: parent and family risk factors, community risk factors, and organizational and systemic risk factors.

Parent and family risk factors are related to children who come from families with increased risk for child maltreatment. Factors that influence parent and family risk include, but not limited to, unemployment, mental health issues, substance abuse, domestic violence, and teen parenthood.

Community risk factors are similar to parent and family risk factors, but are focused within the community. For example, community risk factors include attention toward the unemployment rate within the community instead of the specific family that is unemployed. Additional risk factors include poverty, homelessness, welfare assistance, and crime rates within the community.

Organizational and systemic risk factors focus on policies, institutional structures, organizational culture and climate, and more. For example, biased beliefs, prejudicial attitudes, and discriminatory practices that undergird government employees' behaviors, policies that are developed, and agency practices that are implemented.

It is hard to discuss any of these factors without discussing all of them, as they are all interrelated. Risk factors for parents, families, and the overall community cannot be understood outside of the context of organizational and systemic factors, such as racism and discrimination. Take for example incarceration, which can be a parental risk factor; incarceration rates, which can be community specific; and the prison system, which maintains a structure that systemically disadvantaged certain people and communities. As we discussed in chapter 1, Black males (i.e., parent and non-parents in the Black community) are disproportionately imprisoned compared to other racial/ethnic groups (Carson, 2018; Zeng, 2018). And as discussed earlier in this chapter, there is also the impact of Black women/mother's incarceration on the child welfare process. These incarceration numbers not only make the parenting relationship challenging, but they also impede on the parent's ability to assume responsibility for their child or participate in their child's permanency planning. In thinking about Black men specifically, biased and prejudiced beliefs about Black fathers and Black men in general may also lead to discriminatory practices that prohibit their involvement in permanency planning. This notion can be even more challenging when fathers have served jail or prison time. Further, when fathers are included in the case planning processes, it is important for them to feel respected and for them to be seen in their desire and right to care for their child. Coakley (2013) interviewed twelve fathers, the majority of whom were Black, and noted that even when they attempted to be involved in the case planning process, they experienced personnel and policy issues that became barriers to successful participation. For example, the fathers experienced racism, discrimination, and blatant disrespect by social workers assigned to their child's case. Conversely, when fathers were included in the case planning process, and were adequately involved with their children while they were in foster care, the children had an increased chance of being placed with their fathers and had shorter stays in the foster care system (Coakley, 2008). It is important for child welfare agencies to have policies and procedures that better engage fathers, and to have training in cultural competence to engage Black fathers specifically. Perhaps focusing efforts on improving organization systemic factors, overall, will better support the Black children and families and reduce their lengthier involvement with foster care.

Why Do Black Children Stay Longer?

Taking a closer look at the child welfare system, beyond the racial disparity of child welfare involvement, there is a pattern of Black children remaining in out-of-home care for longer periods than their White counterparts (Fluke et al., 2011). There are a number of factors that may contribute to these longer stays, including higher rates of kinship care, lower rates of reunification, and greater placement instability (Boyd, 2014), all of which can contribute to a longer process of finalizing adoption.

We discussed kinship care in chapter 1 and noted that placing children with their relatives was one example of continued family togetherness and family preservation. Kinship care can be a significant part of Black children's experience in the child welfare system. While there are many benefits to kinship care, there are also ways that kinship care can unintentionally influence longer out-of-home care. As we noted in chapter 1, family members are not always encouraged or supported in their desires to adopt their kin (Boyd, 2014). In fact, Boyd (2014) reviewed the notions that there is less support for family/kinship caregivers as opposed to non-kinship caregivers. In some ways, this is related to the first points about family members not being encouraged or supported to adopt their kin, but is more specific to support in terms of resources such as financial assistance and case planning. Family caregivers receive unequal assistance than non-family caregivers (Berrick & Boyd, 2016; Berrick & Hernandez, 2016) and some even debate if family should receive assistance at all. Also, family members may be less likely to proceed through the adoption process because it means terminating the parental rights of their family member, which, as one might imagine, may come with mixed and complicated emotions. Taken together, the frequency of Black children receiving kinship care can be beneficial, but it can also unintentionally delay the process of children being placed in permanent foster care, whether that be within or outside of the family.

Similar to the delay of being placed outside of the family, there can be a delay in Black children being reunited with their parent(s). One of the major provisions of the Adoption and Safe Families Act established in 1997 mandated that states initiate termination of parental rights for children who have been in foster care for fifteen out of twenty-two months (Congressional Research Service, 2004). Although some families are able to meet this deadline, some are not. This is an example of how laws meant to protect children can also create barriers to reuniting families. Another factor that has been noted to negatively influence reunification rates for Black children with their family is single parenthood (Fluke et al., 2011), largely thought to be a reflection of an inherent preference in the child welfare system for two-parent households.

Lastly, Black children face greater placement instability in being sent to more out-of-home placements than their White counterparts (Fluke et al., 2011; Foster et al., 2011). It is well known that aging children may be harder to place in foster care and may move from one home to another. However, this may be more of a factor for Black children than White children (Foster et al., 2011). Further, Black children are also at higher risk of placement mismatch, receiving substandard care (Sattler et al., 2018), and running away from out-of-home, but not kinship, care (Courtney & Zinn, 2009). Each of these factors can contribute to greater placement instability and contribute to a longer process of finalizing adoption.

How Children and Families Are Impacted by Child Welfare Involvement

Many of the risk factors affecting parents of children who end up in the child welfare system are also negative outcomes that children face. One particularly concerning reality is that some children who are placed in the child welfare system experience maltreatment within the system (Szilagyi et al., 2015). This was the case for Oni, who experienced abuse while in the care of a foster family, which caused her to experience mental health concerns. Her placement in foster care exposed her to further maltreatment and a potentially worse outcome than if she had remained with her family and the family were provided resources. When reports of abuse occurring in foster care surfaced prominently in the 1990s, investigations led to increased awareness of the prevalence of abuse of children occurring in the larger child welfare system. The National Coalition for Child Protection Reform (2015) found that in studies across various states in the U.S., abuse in foster care was occurring at rates ranging from 28 percent to 34 percent. Surveys over the past few decades show rates of abuse in foster care as high as 40 percent (Wexler, 2017).

There is expansive data indicating the negative impact of child welfare involvement on children, ranging from educational achievement and employment to potential criminality (U.S. Department of Health & Human Services, 2020). Those children in foster care have been shown to score lower on achievement tests, have higher rates of repeating a grade, and have lower high school graduation rates than youth who are not in foster care (Burley & Halpern, 2001). Factors found to maximize the educational success of children in the child welfare system include permanency placement in order to have greater stability of school placements, mentoring relationships, and overall educational support (Pecora, 2012). Employment support may also be a needed intervention to counteract the negative impact of child welfare involvement. A study exploring employment rates for youth in foster care found that youth who were approaching their eighteenth birthday and aging out of foster care had lower earnings and a slower progression into the job market compared to youth who were not in foster care (George et al., 2002). Moreover, Black youth who have been in foster care have worse rates of employment than their White counterparts (Watt & Kim, 2019). Scholars have also found significant results connecting child welfare involvement to adult criminality and noted that the age children are placed can influence their future criminal record (Lindquist & Santavirta, 2014; U.S. Department of Health & Human Services, 2020). A systematic review of literature from 2004 to 2015 showed that children engaged with the child welfare system continue to struggle in all the above areas once they leave the system (Gypen et al., 2017). It is notable that placement instability has been connected to many of the issues regarding educational achievement, employment, and criminality. This connection further supports the notion that permanency placement may be a helpful intervention for supporting youth in the child welfare system.

From the family perspective, the disruptive nature of child welfare involvement also takes a toll on family bonds, and the sense of empowerment family members have as a familial unit. The intrusion of an outside party on the structure of how a family functions and the external control that can be exerted can disempower caregivers, create a lack of stability for the children, and can add to the uncertainty the family members feel about future involvement of the child welfare system. Thus, although the system is designed to protect and ensure the safety of children, it is an intervention that is inherently unnatural and disruptive in nature. In Oni's case, the end result of being in the child welfare system was not only being removed from her home for an extended period of time and separated from her siblings, but also facing abuse that occurred in the system.

Child Welfare Reform

The problems within the child welfare system have led to many reform efforts. The primary routes to reform have been legislative mandates, often resulting in amendments to child welfare laws that expand the scope of policies and the responsibility of the federal and state government as well as child protection agencies in managing the safety and welfare of children (Center for Advanced Studies in Child Welfare, 2016). As the factors that contribute to the disproportionality of Black children in the child welfare system are explored, of particular interest are solutions that address the root of the issues rather than those that provide temporary, superficial means to address the problem. A key starting point would be to provide greater access to resources for Black families. Using parent mentors (i.e., parents who have previous involvement in the child welfare system) to provide support, guidance, and resources to parents within the child welfare system has proven to be one helpful means of supporting families (Cohen & Canan, 2006). Additionally, parent training and support programs can be useful as in-home interventions to assist parents while their children remain in their care, or as interventions to assist parents in the reunification process of getting their child back (Barth et al., 2005).

Program Development and Monitoring

The manner in which states implement child protection laws is important in improving the effectiveness of child welfare efforts. Monitoring of state government and agency compliance with child welfare laws and ongoing assessment of the efficacy of child welfare programming is as important as the existence of the pertinent laws. Monitoring efforts range from formalized reviews to performance improvement planning. Specifically, in an effort to ensure state compliance, the Children's Bureau, which is under the umbrella of the U.S. Department of Health & Human Services, conducts Child and Family Services Reviews (CFSRs), examines state level child welfare programs and requires a review of child welfare data (U.S. Department of Health & Human Services, 2020). If the state is not in compliance with child protection laws, a performance improvement plan (PIP) is required to outline how compliance will be achieved. Additionally, the manner in which child protection services are provided differ greatly from state to state, which can create difficulty with having uniform criteria and data to measure outcomes (U.S. Department of Health & Human Services, Administration for Children and Families, Administration on Children, Youth and Families, Children's Bureau, 2020). This variability can present challenges with the monitoring of compliance with child protective laws, but this challenge is minimized by having standard evaluation criteria for CRSRs and PIPs.

Cultural Competence and Humility

Another area of focus needs to be the training and protocols followed by the child welfare staff who receive the referrals for suspected maltreatment. As mentioned earlier in this chapter, child welfare workers are not immune to the negative stereotypes, biases, and beliefs that society has traditionally held about Black parents, children, and families. Training in cultural competence, as well as cultural humility, is needed to address cultural nuances and individual and family differences. Cultural competency is defined as attitudes, actions, and policies that respect cultural differences and similarities and promote effective functioning during diverse cultural interactions and settings (Greene-Moton & Minkler, 2019). This concept is related to but separate from cultural humility, which reflects commitment to self-evaluation and critique, to redress power imbalances and develop beneficial partnerships (Greene-Moton & Minkler, 2019). These concepts are differentiated by their scope and nuances of their focus, but they both speak to continued effort to treat others from any background with respect. Training reflecting these concepts is important to ensuring that Black children receive competent assessment and care by child welfare staff. Thus, cultural competency and humility training can serve a key role in improving service provision in the child welfare system. To this end, training is needed in the areas of understanding the privilege and power that child welfare workers hold over the families they work with, as well as trainings that illuminate and challenge the structural ways that the child welfare system may perpetuate biased and discriminatory practices against Black families. This can be accomplished by states requiring ongoing cultural competency training of child welfare workers. Such training is available, for example, through the U.S. Department of Health & Human Services, which offers information, presentations, articles, and training materials that promote appropriate cultural and linguistic training for individuals providing healthcare services (U.S. Department of Health & Human Services, 2020).

Child Welfare in Real Time

Currently, across the globe, there is heightened awareness of an increased risk of harm and a greater need to protect those that are vulnerable in society. The Coronavirus-19 (COVID-19) pandemic that is currently plaguing the world at the time of publishing this book is having a negative impact on the health, mortality, and economic circumstances of individuals, families, communities, and socioeconomic systems. The pandemic has had an amplifying effect on existing social issues. There are several social factors that are associated with increased risk of violence, for example, increased overall stress, reduced social support, and increased financial stressors (Abramson, 2020). In particular, increased parental stress is associated with child abuse and neglect (Abramson, 2020). Given that these risk factors have been intensified during the pandemic, concerns have increased about the heightened potential of child maltreatment.

One example of the importance of being vigilant about the risk of child abuse and neglect in the current climate is the case of a seventeen-year-old girl named Marie (name changed to ensure confidentiality). Marie was a Black teenager who was entering her senior year of high school in the fall; the pandemic precipitated many sudden changes for her. She transitioned from in-person to distance learning, from daily in-person contact with friends to only texting and phone calls, and from spending most of her days outside of the home (e.g., in school or spending time with friends) to being in the home. Marie's family, which consist of her parents and two younger siblings, were now spending more time together. Marie's parents were both working from home since stay-at-home orders began with COVID-19, and tensions were more evident, sometimes erupting over simple issues. There is a history of emotional and physical abuse by Marie's father, and with the recent COVID stressors, she worried that her father's stress about potential job loss and financial strain might mean the return of him yelling and being highly critical, which in the past has been a precursor for abuse. Despite these initial worries, over the past few months, her family found a rhythm with giving each other space, spending time together, and spending socially distanced time with selected friends, which worked fairly well.

For Marie, her risk for potential abuse was managed effectively. But for many children, this may not be the case. For some children, the child welfare system may become a part of what helps to keep them safe. As noted, Marie's family stressors are associated with increased risk for child maltreatment. As discussed in chapter 1, Black families rely on the extended family network for additional support; for example, back-up caregiving when a parent has to spend more time at work. During a global health pandemic, where social distancing is recommended and socializing across households can result in increased risk of illness, many Black families may not have the additional support they would typically rely on. This lack of support can increase the risk of child maltreatment and also decrease potential solutions to family problems. If Black families and networks choose to support each other in-person, out of necessity for keeping their jobs or providing needed emotional support for each other, then they are also risking their health. This decision, like many decisions for Black families, is complex.

Closing Summary

The child welfare system has evolved from nonexistence to mostly providing basic shelter needs to the comprehensive system of agencies, foster care facilities and homes, and kinship care options that children have today. The development of a comprehensive, regulated child welfare system has allowed for a large expanse of care for children when parents/caregivers are not able to do so. A system of this magnitude is far-reaching, but not without its challenges. While the system has offered protection to the welfare of children, it is also associated with additional perils that need to be addressed alongside the dangers the children faced before entering the system. Black children are of particular concern as they, more than other racial groups, are overrepresented in the welfare system, more frequently receive out-of-home services, and remain for longer stays in out-of-home placements before returning to their families.

In a system that was not designed with the particular needs of Black children and families in mind, it is not surprising that there are race-related disparities in service provision. Ensuring that service provision is delivered with reduced blind spots and increased cultural competence when working with black fathers and black mothers—who each face unique challenges when they and their children become involved in the child welfare system—is important to develop, monitor, and maintain. Requiring ongoing cultural competency training to improve the awareness of child welfare staff regarding the biases that may influence their decision making and handling of welfare-involved children and families can be key to reducing negative outcomes. The racial disparities and the risk of experiencing maltreatment in the welfare system are strong indicators that reform is needed to reduce the chances of such maltreatment occurring. More stringent oversight of out-of-home placement is necessary to reduce maltreatment from occurring within the welfare system. And providing resources to families can be an effective way to help keep a child in the home and reduce the need for placement outside of the home. The training and protocols followed by the child welfare staff who receive the referrals for suspected maltreatment needs to include content that improves cultural competence. In the next chapter, prevention and intervention efforts are explored, including efforts that protect the victims of child maltreatment, and strategies to manage and rehabilitate perpetrators of abuse and neglect.

4

Child Maltreatment Prevention and Intervention

It is easier to build strong children
than repair broken men.
—Frederick Douglass, American
social reformer, abolitionist,
author, orator, and statesman

Overview

This chapter discusses current prevention methods and interventions utilized to address child maltreatment at the individual, family, and community levels. The role of public policy in prevention and intervention is discussed, with a particular exploration of the implications for Black children. As discussed in chapter 1, Black is used to describe the collective racial category. Notably, in some instances, we cite research that refers to a specific sub-group of Black children, e.g., African American children. In this chapter, primary, secondary, and tertiary levels of prevention programming are delineated. The common child abuse prevention methods of school-based educational programs and offender management efforts are reviewed. Methods such as registries and sex offender treatment programs are explained. Data on factors that are associated with treatment efficacy are discussed. Broader interventions, such as awareness campaigns, online technologies (e.g., social media and phone apps), and professional training on child maltreatment are explored. Examples are provided of various prevention and intervention approaches that have proven results in the U.S. Lastly, relevant prevention and intervention efforts are discussed in connection with the cases that were introduced in the Introduction.

Defining Prevention and Intervention

The terminology used to discuss child maltreatment services are sometimes used interchangeably, reflecting a variety of definitions for terms. Defining key terms, such as prevention and intervention, will allow for clearer understanding and better context for the services and programs discussed within this chapter. Prevention refers to efforts, services, or programs that focus on or include a component related to preventing child maltreatment from occurring or reoccurring (Child Welfare Information Gateway, 2017). In this regard, prevention services can be provided to children and families who have not experienced maltreatment, as well as those who have experienced maltreatment. In the latter case, the prevention services would have the purpose of preventing further abuse or neglect. Prevention services are therefore proactive in nature as such services seek to empower children and families with the knowledge and resources needed to avoid exposure to or re-exposure to maltreatment.

Interventions generally refer to services provided once maltreatment has occurred (van der Put et al., 2018). As such, interventions are in response to the need for support once abuse or neglect has occurred in order to mitigate the impact of maltreatment. Notably, prevention services that are geared toward preventing the re-occurrence of maltreatment can also be described as interventions, given that they are provided subsequent to the occurrence of maltreatment. For example, as is the case for chemical interventions for sex offenders, hormonal drugs that reduce one's sexual drive can be used to lower their ability to act on sexually inappropriate urges (e.g., before they abuse) and also after they abuse in an effort to prevent further abuse. Overall, both prevention and intervention services have the overarching goal of empowering children and families with knowledge, support and resources, and mitigating the impact that maltreatment can have on individuals, families, and communities.

The Role of Public Policy in Child Maltreatment Prevention

There have been great strides through the last century in the U.S. with developing awareness about child abuse and neglect. As the spotlight has grown on child maltreatment, more comprehensive efforts have been made at local, state, and national levels to protect children from being maltreated and to help those who have experienced maltreatment. These prevention and intervention efforts have been focused not only on children but also on their families, communities, and the U.S. healthcare system. This all-encompassing approach echoes an ecological perspective that acknowledges the interconnectedness of life such that changes of individuals, families, and systems have a ripple effect, and that changes need to occur beyond the individual level (Jason et al., 2019).

From a top-down perspective, examining public policy is an entry point to addressing child maltreatment. In line with an ecological perspective, public policy shapes prevention and intervention resources and service provision, which is key to organizations receiving funding. The development of public policy involves determining what prevention services are appropriate at the primary, secondary, and tertiary levels; accurately identifying individuals, families, and communities that are at greater risk of child abuse and neglect; ensuring that adequate finances are made available to fund programs; and promoting ongoing data-driven assessment of the efficacy of prevention programs.

The Child Abuse Prevention and Treatment Act of 1974 (CAPTA) has been a hallmark law providing funding for prevention and treatment services for child maltreatment (Chasnoff et al., 2018). CAPTA provides funding to be awarded at the state level for developing policies, procedures, or protocols for the development of community-based and prevention-focused programs for children and families (U.S. Department of Health & Human Services, 2018b). CAPTA was amended several times, allowing for a wider breath of covered services. This act has far-reaching mandates, ranging from services for infants who experience prenatal drug exposure to services for children in the child welfare system to child victims of sex trafficking (Child Welfare Information Gateway, 2019b). Prevention programs can include organizations providing crisis care, parent education, family support programs, and home visiting programs. CAPTA also provides funding for the training of health professionals and health system leaders related to state mandatory reporting laws, and for appropriate screening and assessment of child maltreatment. There are also provisions for partnerships between agencies, including health, mental health, court judges, substance use programs and early intervention programs with the aim of coordinating the implementation of child maltreatment prevention, assessment, and interventions for children and families.

Historically, there has been more focus on providing interventions once maltreatment has occurred; however, in more recent decades, there has been a greater focus on prevention efforts. The first efforts in this regard were geared toward in-home services (Child Welfare Information Gateway, 2017). Specifically, programs were focused on services for new mothers and at-risk mothers. Programming included teaching basic child-rearing skills and promoting bonding. The hope was that these interventions would nurture child development and aid in creating a positive home environment. By focusing on the mother's needs and parenting ability, this approach had the potential to reduce the impact of negative factors affecting mother, which could lead to maltreatment.

Organization and Implementation of Child Maltreatment Prevention Services

Prevention services are organized into three tiers—primary, secondary, and tertiary programs (Child Welfare Information Gateway, 2017). Each tier is designed for different target audiences and range from broad to specific efforts to prevent maltreatment. Each tier is discussed next with examples of programs and services that are available.

Primary Prevention

In an effort to prevent child abuse from occurring, primary prevention programs are provided to the general population. Sometimes referred to as universal programs, primary prevention programs and services offer information about child maltreatment, provide parenting support, and educate children about safety. Such efforts can range from television commercials and advertising campaigns to more comprehensive in-person programs providing information about child maltreatment. Primary child maltreatment prevention programs have the greatest reach, tend to be less costly, and are easiest to implement. For example, the American Psychological Association (APA) has developed and implemented the Adults and Children Together (ACT) Raising Safe Kids Program, which offers information, materials, and classes for parents and caregivers related to healthy parenting of children, particularly from infancy to age ten (American Psychological Association [APA], 2017a). This program has been shown to increase prosocial parenting practices and decrease harsh parenting and negative discipline.

The Keep Kids Safe program of the Pennsylvania Department of Human Services (2017) is another primary prevention program. This program offers information to the public about when and how to report child abuse and neglect through their website, informational videos, and other related resources. One of their published video advertisements includes several children speaking about abuse. Each sad and tearful child shared a different experience that, as they described it, ranged from being repeatedly hit to being told not to talk about the abuse. The video ended with a call to action to report suspected abuse and provided a phone number. This ad not only provided tangible examples of what can constitute abuse, but it also helped with understanding that the threshold for reporting abuse is suspecting, not necessarily knowing with certainty, that it is occurring.

Secondary Prevention

Secondary programs, sometimes referred to as selected prevention programs, are designed to focus on children and families that are identified as being at risk for child maltreatment to occur (Child Welfare Information Gateway, 2017). One such program is the Coordination, Advocacy, Resources, Education and Support (C.A.R.E.S.) program, a comprehensive, California-based prevention program that offers evidenced-based, family-focused prevention services, with measurable goals and outcomes that promote the preservation and stabilization of families (National Center for Innovation and Excellence, 2020). One of the programs C.A.R.E.S. offers is Child First, which provides home-based mental health services to children, prenatal to age five, living in environments with risk factors such as violence and neglect. This program also connects the families of these children to community-based supports and services in the hopes of increasing family stabilization and reducing parental stress (California Evidence-Based Clearinghouse for Child Welfare, 2019). The program also includes data-driven components, such as documenting measurable changes from inception of services to discharge in order to determine statistical significance of the changes that occur. Programs such as these are targeted to not only children but also their families. Such programs help reduce the risk of maltreatment occurring to these children and within their families.

Tertiary Prevention

For families and individuals who have experienced child maltreatment, tertiary prevention programs are provided in an effort to reduce and eliminate the recurrence of abuse (Child Welfare Information Gateway, 2017). Also referred to as Indicated Prevention programs, tertiary services include family preservation programs, parenting support and mentoring, and mental health services for children and families affected by child maltreatment. In the cases provided in the Introduction, each child and family received tertiary services, occurring after suspected or actual maltreatment had transpired. For example, once concerns about two-year-old Madison's bruising was reported to Child Protective Services (CPS), a caseworker was assigned and in-home services were provided, which included home visits with guidance on how to keep Madison physically safe in her crib. Both Daniel and Oni received individual therapy that was recommended by the CPS caseworkers in their respective cases. Daniel's parents also participated in some of his therapy sessions. It is unknown whether these children and their families had exposure to primary or secondary prevention services. Exposure to those levels of prevention services would have the potential to increase awareness about what constitutes child maltreatment, which could have shaped behavioral choices and the eventual outcomes in each case. For example, exposure to primary or secondary prevention services could have increased the awareness of Oni's aunt toward the potential issues posed by living in an overpopulated home and could have encouraged her to seek resources to address this issue. Of course, this also requires that resources to support families in overpopulated homes are available to the families and, given the cultural normativity of multiple generation homes, such resources are culturally appropriate.

Integrating Tiers and Types of Prevention Services

Efforts have been made to coordinate prevention strategies by integrating primary and secondary service systems (Herrenkohl et al., 2016). Such programs offer services to the general public and to those identified as being at higher risk for child maltreatment. These programs also offer multiple delivery methods, such as family support, parenting training, and child education about maltreatment. Programs and services might range from home-based to center-based, and from individualized to family and group formats (Mikton & Butchart, 2009; Waid & Choy, 2021).

Home-Based vs. Center-Based Services

Home-based services are one of the more heavily utilized delivery methods for preventing child maltreatment. For example, there were over 1,000,000 home visits carried out through the Health Resources & Services Administration's (HRSA) Maternal, Infant, and Early Childhood Home Visiting Program in 2019 (Health Resources & Services Administration [HRSA], 2020). Delivered by trained professionals, home visits provide information and support to families in their home environment. Home visits are intended to improve parent and child functioning in many areas, one of which includes reducing child injuries, abuse, and neglect. There is substantial evidence supporting the efficacy of home visits, although the extent to which they are truly preventative of maltreatment is unclear (U.S. Preventative Services Task Force [USPSTF], 2019). Specifically, the U.S. Preventative Services Task Force (2019) noted the difficulty in assessing benefits or harm of services that are aimed at preventing an abuse that has not occurred. Nonetheless, that does not negate other benefits that may come from in-home services, such as improving maternal and newborn health, reducing crime or domestic violence, improving coordination of community referrals and services, and other areas that may help to reduce child maltreatment.

There are also services outside of the home that may utilize a center-based format. For example, parent education programs occur in centers and tend to be delivered in group formats across families, versus in-home with one family at a time. One such program is the Family Connections Program housed at the Progressive Life Center (2016), a family support organization with locations in the Washington D.C. metropolitan area. This program has goals that include providing emotional support to families and empowering families to be independent. Regardless of whether it occurs in-home or within a center, family interventions can be a critical preventative method for intervening and keeping at-risk families out of the child welfare system.

Prevention Services Specific to Type of Abuse

There are also programs and campaigns that utilize education about child maltreatment as a means of prevention. Some prevention services are designed to address specific types of child maltreatment. For example, infant education programs have been created to help reduce the dangers of infant injury (e.g., abusive head trauma such as Shaken Baby Syndrome) and fatality. One such program is the Period of PURPLE Crying program, which provides education on typical infant behaviors, including patterns around crying and accepting soothing, being unpredictable, and having pained facial expressions (Joyce & Huecker, 2019). Such programs can help parents understand what to expect from their infants and to improve their ability to manage their own frustration with the infant's behaviors. Ultimately, the goal would be to reduce emotions and behaviors that might lead to child maltreatment. There are also mutual support groups, in which parents and families support each other and create a social network for resources, support, and education.

Prevention Services through Media

The use of media has also become an avenue to address child maltreatment. For example, the United Nations Children's Fund (UNICEF) has created the #ENDviolence advertising campaign, which promotes creating safe environments for children, provides education on what constitutes maltreatment, and makes reporting maltreatment easily accessible to the public (United Nations Children's Fund [UNICEF], 2020). Leveraging the societal reach of social media, there are prevention programs that use this forum to disseminate information. The Michigan Children's Trust Fund is an agency that provides social media links and messages related to child maltreatment prevention (Children's Trust Fund, 2020).

Effectiveness of Prevention Programs and Methods

There now exists an array of programs and services for prevention and intervention for child maltreatment. The successful delivery of child maltreatment prevention programs requires several dimensions of implementation factored into the development and dissemination of programming. The quality of programming and the reach of services are key (Berkel et al., 2011). Other specifics, such as the number of program sessions, and the particular content areas covered, are also important. It is also key to determine the effectiveness of services by gauging the responsiveness of the participants and monitoring the fidelity of the services that are provided.

The effectiveness of these services has been examined and evidenced a range of findings. Home visits, one of the most extensively used prevention methods, have been found to be an effective method in reducing incidence of child maltreatment and improving the health of young children (Peacock et al., 2013). In particular, home visits were more effective when initiated by the parents. Notably, it is not known what particular aspects of home visits make them effective. For example, is it the length of the visit(s), the structure of the information that is provided, the families' receptiveness to the services, or some combination of each of those? In another study, a systematic review, the effectiveness of seven child maltreatment prevention interventions was assessed (Mikton & Butchart, 2009). The interventions included home visits, parent education programs, child sexual abuse programs, abusive head trauma prevention, multi-component interventions, media-based interventions, as well as support and mutual aid groups. Results showed that four interventions of out the seven interventions evaluated were effective for preventing child maltreatment, which included parent education, home visits, abusive head trauma prevention, and multi-component programs. More data on the effectiveness of child maltreatment will be discussed in later sections as different types of maltreatment are discussed (i.e., child sexual abuse).

Prevention of Child Sexual Abuse

Child sexual abuse (CSA) has been of particular focus on the development of child maltreatment prevention efforts. Factors in establishing and providing prevention services are influenced by defining what is considered CSA, as this impacts what is addressed when providing prevention education. The definition of child sexual abuse has evolved, broadening over time to include sexual acts perpetrated by force, intimidation, or manipulation (Collin-Vézina et al., 2013; Mathews & Collin-Vézina, 2019). There are some aspects of defining child sexual abuse that remain varied, including the legal age that a child can consent to the sexual activity, and what constitutes child-to-child sexual abuse (Mathews & Collin-Vézina, 2019). In particular, the age of consent differs from state to state in the U.S., ranging from sixteen to eighteen (Glosser et al., 2004). At one point, a two-to-five-year age difference was thought necessary to consider sexual behavior between siblings to be abuse (Collin-Vézina et al., 2013; Mathews & Collin-Vézina, 2019). However, this range of age difference has since been challenged by substantiated cases of sexual abuse in which there were smaller age differences (Collin-Vézina et al., 2013; Mathews & Collin-Vézina, 2019). These aspects of CSA can create a challenge for targeted prevention education about what constitutes child sexual abuse.

CSA Prevention and Intervention Efforts Geared toward the Victims

Child sexual abuse (CSA) prevention programs have been channeled through two pathways, services for the victim or the perpetrator (Collin-Vézina et al., 2013). Primary prevention services for victims provide the public with general information about the nature of CSA, which have commonly been delivered as ad campaigns, and publicly available community-based programs (Bonnar-Kidd, 2010). Prevention efforts for victims of CSA have entailed education programs and have primarily been provided through schools (Collin-Vézina et al., 2013). School-based prevention programs focus on educating children on maltreatment, and interventions such as teaching skills to avoid its occurrence, and helping children build advocacy skills to report abuse and neglect if it occurs (Cowan et al., 2019). Thus, school-based programs are driven by specific efforts to increase student knowledge of child sexual abuse, and there is data to suggest that such programs are working (Walsh et al., 2015; Walsh et al., 2018).

Many CSA prevention programs offer education directly to children and families, about appropriate touch, recognizing abusive situations, assertiveness skills, and training with how to disclose abuse. The KIDS Center, an Oregon-based child abuse prevention center, is one such program that offers curriculum for children from kindergarten to fifth grade (KIDS Center, 2019). Designed to be provided to elementary schools, the five-day curriculum uses stories, discussion, and activities that teach children ownership over their body, identify what is an appropriate and inappropriate touch from others, learn how to respond to an unwanted touch, develop strategies to leave an uncomfortable situation, and know how to tell a trusted adult. Such programs empower children to trust their instincts. In another example, the Committee for Children offers an online activity aimed at helping caregivers teach children the names of their body parts, and explains types of touch, such as safe, unsafe, and unwanted touch (Committee for Children, 2017).

In addition to school-based prevention services for victims, there are also community-based organizations that provide prevention programming. Some organizations are focused on providing prevention services for adults and families. For example, Darkness to Light is an organization that uses a social-behavior-change approach that focuses on encouraging adults to prevent abuse within their sphere of social influence (Darkness to Light, 2021).

Keeping in mind that mothers are often the primary caregivers of children, particularly in Black families, programs geared toward helping mothers are important to addressing child maltreatment. The Mothers of Sexually Abused Children (MOSAC) website is geared toward supporting mothers of sexually abused children (Mothers of Sexually Abused Children [MOSAC], 2020). This site offers comprehensive information to mothers ranging from what to expect after a child discloses that abuse occurred, to various resources, including videos, book recommendations, website links, and legal advocacy information. By educating mothers, children are more likely to receive the tailored support they need from their primary caregiver.

CSA Prevention and Intervention Efforts Geared toward Offenders

Prevention services for offenders typically fall into the tertiary prevention tier as these services are interventions that are implemented with a focus on eliminating or reducing the recurrence of sexual abuse.

Offender management programs tend to monitor the known perpetrators of child sexual abuse through the use of identification tools, such as sex offender registries and background checks. This is a relatively new approach, given that there was no legally enforceable system for public awareness of sex offenders prior to twenty-five years ago (Office of Sex Offender Sentencing, Monitoring, Apprehending, Registering and Tracking [SMART], 2020). When the Violent Crime Control and Law Enforcement Act (Violent Crimes Act) of 1994 was passed, one stipulation was that all states were required to establish and maintain a registry of sexual offenders. The U.S. Department of Justice established the National Sex Offender Registry, providing a log of offender registries for each state and province in the U.S. (U.S. Department of Justice, 2020). Sex offenders were therefore required to register, verify their current name, and provide their current address to local police after release from serving jail time. Additionally, in 1996, Megan's Law was passed, which amended the Violent Crimes Act and made it easier to access detailed information about registered sex offenders. Subsequently, photographs, names, and addresses of sex offenders were publicly available via the internet. Many states have residency restrictions related to where sex offenders can live. There is also the option for individuals in local communities to receive notifications if a sex offender is living in their community (Bonnar-Kidd, 2010; Mancini, 2018). Notably, it is questionable whether community notification of sex offenders is effective in reducing sex crimes (Bonnar-Kidd, 2010; Mancini, 2018).

Some states have passed legislation with even more specific requirements in an effort to reduce repeat sex offense and protect the public, such as banning sex offenders from loitering in particular locations, and from wearing Halloween costuming, requiring them to be indoors with the lights outside of their home turned off on the day of Halloween (Bonnar-Kidd, 2010). Other legislative actions have mandated the use of hormonal drugs to reduce the sexual drive of sexual offenders (Iati, 2019), also known as "chemical castration." This form of treatment has been controversial in terms of its effectiveness (Sauter et al., 2020; Turner & Briken, 2018), and also because of questions of whether this intervention constitutionally violates the eight amendment which prohibits cruel and unusual punishment.

The existing data show a higher rate of recidivism among child molesters than offenders committing other sex crimes (Przybylski, 2017), and a significant aspect of increasing the safety of victims of childhood sexual abuse is deterring sex offenders from repeating the abuse. Thus, identifying repeat sex offenders has been an area of legislative, research, and public focus (Przybylski, 2017). However, it is difficult to know the precise extent to which recidivism occurs, in part because sexual abuse is not reported or discovered to the degree that it occurs, and thus many cases of repeated sexual abuse may go unreported (Przybylski, 2017). Therefore, the extent of the difference between occurrence and reporting is not clear.

One approach to determining the recidivism risk for sex offenders can include establishing protocols for determining the level of risk a sex offender poses to the community in which they reside (Bonnar-Kidd, 2010; Mancini, 2018). High-risk offenders are subject to stricter registration requirements, such as additional residency restrictions and global positioning system (GPS) monitoring. Risk level determination assessments are often utilized in this process. The most widely used offender risk level assessment is the STATIC-99R, a ten-item assessment that rates risk of re-offense from Level I, very low risk, to Level IV a or b, above-average risk (STATIC99 Clearinghouse, 2020). This assessment is given to male offenders at the time of their release into the community from serving jail time. Specialized supervision is also used to manage sex offenders, which entails having specially trained probation and parole officers assigned to work with sex offenders (Lobanov-Rostovsky, 2017). This type of supervision typically includes a supervising officer coordinating with treatment providers to enforce special release conditions, such as GPS monitoring and polygraph testing.

Sex Offender Treatment

Treatment is an important component of sexual abuse prevention. Sex offender treatment programs generally include psychoeducation and psychotherapy delivered in individual and group psychotherapy formats. Particular interventions, such as aversion therapy, i.e., pairing pleasant stimuli with unpleasant stimuli, are commonly used (Lee & Cho, 2013). Family therapy is also a treatment approach used, in which the needs of significant others of the offenders are a part of the treatment focus. Family therapy, can take place in the form of group therapy for parents of offenders, where the focus includes psychoeducation about the parents' patterns of behavior, guidance on providing parents support, directives around their supervision of their child to help improve recidivism (Bustnay, 2020), and improving overall parent-child communication and mutual support (Letourneau et al., 2009).

Surgical and chemical interventions remain controversial treatments for sex offenders (Lee & Cho, 2013). The permanency of surgical castration raises questions of its legitimacy as a humane punishment. Regarding chemical castration, although it evidences some effectiveness with reducing sex re-offending, there are limitations with this form of treatment including that it is not effective once it is discontinued, and it has significant potential side effects such as osteoporosis and heart disease (Lee & Cho, 2013).

Factors Influencing Sex Offender Treatment

Treatment for sex offenders is an avenue to address child sexual abuse by potentially reducing the likelihood of repeated sexual offenses, increasing children's safety from sexual abuse, and providing data about sex offenders to further develop treatment programming. However, there are inherent challenges to this type of intervention. Notably, sex offender treatment is typically court ordered (Hardeberg Bach & Demuth, 2018). The involuntary nature of this treatment can impact the degree of the offender's cooperativeness, openness and effort in treatment, and ultimately the likelihood of positive treatment gains. It also begs the question of whether treatment is therapeutic when it can be experienced by the offender as a form of punishment.

Sex Offender Treatment Providers

As the focus on child sexual abuse increases, it has become clearer that, in addition to the victim and the offender, the mental health treatment provider is also impacted in the course of providing treatment. Sex offender treatment services and interventions are delivered by trained professionals who coordinate and provide direct treatment services, and therefore, by virtue of service provision, have increased exposure to the offenses the sex offender committed. Research has shown that providing sex offender treatment was associated with the treatment provider experiencing a significant degree of work-related stress and negative emotions (Hardeberg Bach & Demuth, 2018). Some researchers speculated that this may be due to a number of factors, including vicarious exposure to the offenses committed by the offenders and the negative perception of conducting this work, which can diminish collegial support (Hardeberg Bach & Demuth, 2018). These ill-effects can negatively impact the retention of treatment providers. The difficulty of sustainment of this work can limit the treatment options available to sex offenders, a limitation to the scope of prevention options available for child sexual abuse.

Does Child Sexual Abuse Prevention and Intervention Work?

The effectiveness of child maltreatment prevention services has been examined regarding the association between exposure to service and reduced incidence of child sexual abuse. Research suggests that some programs are effective. For example, in a meta-analysis of twenty-six articles on school-based child sexual abuse prevention programs, findings indicated that such programs were effective (Fryda & Hulme, 2014). There are mixed results regarding the effectiveness of sexual abuse interventions in reducing recidivism among sex offenders. In particular, sex offenders subject to supervision that included polygraph testing were found to reduce recidivism rates, while no change in rate was evident in other studies (Przybylski, 2017). Studies on the use of electronic monitoring, such as a GPS, are also mixed, with some studies showing reduced rates of recidivism but not to a statistically significant degree (Przybylski, 2017).

Cultural Adaptations for Prevention and Intervention

An imperative process for understanding responsiveness to services, as well as determining the true effectiveness of them, involves ensuring that such services are culturally appropriate for the communities they intended to benefit. Such cultural adaptations are necessary because, as was discussed in chapter 3, the origins of services within the child welfare system were not developed with Black families, e.g., Black, Black American, African American, in mind. Instead, many prevention efforts and intervention services have been developed, tested, and normed with groups that reflect the dominant cultural group of the time.

Child maltreatment prevention services should reflect an understanding and true consideration of the values of people who they are meant to benefit. For example, in chapter 2, we spoke about the values of extended kinship, adapting family roles, family togetherness, etc. It is ideal to have services and interventions that reflect these values from the beginning stages of development through the completion of testing and putting an evidence-based or empirically supported stamp of approval on it. Such a process would reflect culturally grounded interventions. Okamoto et al. (2014) noted that,

> Culturally grounded interventions have been designed from the "ground up" (that is, starting from the values, behaviors, norms, and worldviews of the populations they are intended to serve), and therefore are most closely connected to the lived experiences and core cultural constructs of the targeted populations and communities. (p. 2)

One example of a culturally grounded intervention is the Strong African American Families (SAAF) Program. SAAF is a family-centered prevention intervention that was designed specifically for African American families (Brody et al., 2004). It is a seven-session program targeted toward rural, African American youth, ages 10-14 and their parents/caregivers (Center for Family Research, 2010). The intervention has been shown to help with adolescent risky behaviors, parenting skills, and parent's mental health (Beach et al., 2008; Brody et al., 2010).

The Progressive Life Center (PLC) is another organization that provides culturally grounded services to children and families, many of whom have experienced child maltreatment (Progressive Life Center, 2016). PLC has several locations throughout the Washington, D.C., Maryland, and Delaware areas providing center-based and home-based prevention services and interventions to children and families. PLC operates from a culturally grounded framework named NTU, pronounced "in-to" (Progressive Life Center, 2016). The concept of NTU is rooted in Afrocentric and humanistic principles that are spiritually, culturally, and holistically oriented.

Interestingly, there are many more culturally adapted interventions than there are culturally grounded ones, for reasons that include the ease and low cost of adapting versus developing culturally grounded services (Okamoto et al., 2014). Culturally adapted interventions are ones where the original intervention was not developed with salient cultural factors of a particular ethnic group in mind, but later, the intervention is adapted to take those cultural factors into consideration (Okamoto et al., 2014). This may, at times, be an appropriate course of action when there is good reason to suggest that a prevention or intervention strategy that is not culturally grounded might still benefit a family. In that regard, thoughtful considerations for approaches to culturally adapted interventions should occur. Furthermore, it is important when working with Black children and families to provide services with a framework that shows awareness and sensitivity to the racism and racial trauma they have faced, and to provide services that promote empowerment and autonomy (French et al., 2019).

There are different methods of adapting an intervention as well as different levels of depth to which the adaptations might occur. Lau (2006) describes the need for adaptations that improve engagement as well as adaptations toward contextualizing content that help with the 'fit' of the intervention. Contextualizing content includes "the addition of novel treatment components to target these group-specific risk processes, or the addition of components to mobilize group-specific protective factors. Alternately, treatment content may be altered to target symptom presentation patterns that require distinctive intervention elements" (p. 300). There are additional differences in adaptations between surface level or deep structural changes. Surface level changes are minor modifications to elements, such as images or terminology used in the intervention curriculum or program. Whereas deep structural level changes involve more systematic methods of infusing complex cultural elements (Okamoto et al., 2014).

Culturally grounded and adapted interventions are not without their challenges and mixed findings on the necessity and effectiveness of them (Castro et al., 2010; Shehadeh et al., 2016). There must be a thoughtful balance between adapting interventions and changing core components of the program/service so that the latter does not occur at the expense of the positive outcomes that one would have typically seen with the program (Kumpfer et al., 2020). Still, scholars have noted the importance of culturally adaptive interventions for supporting parent management training that reduces child conduct problems and abusive parenting (Lau, 2006; Van Mourik et al., 2017).

Closing Summary

The efforts to reduce and eliminate child maltreatment are steadily expanding and becoming a priority for lawmakers, healthcare providers, school officials, and our overall society as more is learned about the far-reaching deleterious impact of this insidious public health issue. With CAPTA as a major legislative starting point for prevention programs to be adequately developed and funded, prevention programming has been created with a three-tier program dispersion system at the primary, secondary, and tertiary levels. These strides have allowed funding to be channeled toward educating the general public about child maltreatment through primary prevention services, but to also identify those at greater risk of maltreatment and those that have experienced maltreatment, to provide secondary and tertiary prevention services as well. Legislative support for child maltreatment prevention programming is key, but it is also important to have methods of ensuring that state mandates are executed in each state in the U.S.

One glaring issue is that there is not adequate data about the efficacy of these programs. Given this, it is difficult to determine whether the programming is working to reduce and eliminate child maltreatment, and to decide how to improve the reach of these programs in effective ways. More robust efficacy data would allow for more strategic building of programs and help with determining to which programs funding should be funneled.

Addressing the impact of treating sex offenders on the treatment providers is another area needing more focused attention. Without adequate support in treating this population, providers will experience vicarious trauma and burnout, which impacts the provider's ability to provide quality treatment, and can potentially reduce the number of providers open to doing this work. Additionally, the moral and constitutional questions that arise from forms of prevention and intervention such as chemical castration need further exploration to determine the appropriateness of potentially expanding the legislative reach of such treatment mandates. Furthermore, it could be valuable to understand propensity to re-offend as it relates to different type of child sexual abuse. Such specific data can help with protecting children from sexual abuse. Lastly, it is unclear whether there are treatment services that are specifically geared toward individuals who are experiencing urges to engage in a sex offense but have not yet done so. Focusing prevention services on this particular group of individuals could reduce the likelihood of them engaging in sex offenses, and, in turn, reduce child sexual abuse.

Notably, much of the research data on child maltreatment prevention and intervention services does not offer adequate information on whether Black children and families are sufficiently receiving these services. Given the disproportionate number of Black children in the child welfare system, it would be important to track with more specificity if they are receiving the services needed. Lastly, it is imperative that maltreatment identification systems continue to be a focus so that children experiencing maltreatment are more readily identified and interventions, support, resources and services are deployed efficiently. More culturally grounded programs such as SAAF and the services offered through Progressive Life Center are needed to address the needs of Black children and families who are at risk for and those who have experienced child maltreatment. In the next chapter, we explore strategies to promote health and wellness in Black children and families.

5

Promoting Health and Wellness

> We as parents are our children's first and best role models, and this is particularly true when it comes to their health.
> —Michelle Obama, 44th first lady of the United States

Overview

Preventing child maltreatment can be strengthened by promoting protective factors of positive health and wellness. In earlier chapters, we discussed how Black children experience multiple layers of disadvantages that influence child maltreatment and negatively impact their health and well-being. We also explored the generational impact of how the health and wellness of parents can influence factors for child maltreatment. We continue that exploration in this chapter. Just as we have noted that child maltreatment may be reported from interactions with healthcare professionals, we also use this chapter to address ways that healthcare professionals can support protective factors to further health and wellness and reduce the likelihood of child welfare involvement. We consider any barriers to children's health and wellness as oppressive factors that negatively influence them and their families. In that regard, using a womanist perspective around strengthening families, we focus on their health and wellness as a protective means of guarding against oppression factors (e.g., child maltreatment) toward them. Overall, we continue to focus on promoting wellness in the Black community, defined as the collective racial group, as a means of successfully addressing the public health challenge that child maltreatment presents.

Defining Health

The World Health Organization (WHO) defines health as "a state of complete physical, mental, and social well-being" and specifically states that it is more than the absence of disease or illness (McCartney et al., 2019). Notably, this definition emphasizes more of a holistic view of health in terms of overall wellness rather than emphasizing health as only the absence of sickness. In this regard, health can be viewed as a state of well-being; it can be seen from a proactive stance that is promoted and maintained, rather than from the reactive stance of responding to a decline in health. Understanding health in a complete or holistic manner can also be understood from both internal and external influencing factors, such as physical, mental, and spiritual wellness. This focus is aligned with the term "wellness," which is interchangeably used to describe health and reflects the proactive standpoint of maintaining well-being. Given the impact of access to health education, resources and living conditions on an individual's health and wellness, it is important to understand the status of health and health outcomes in the U.S.

Overview of Health and Health Outcomes in the United States

The healthcare system has historically and primarily focused on treating and intervening once issues have occurred. Thus, mitigating the impact of health problems has been a central part of the approach. This reactive approach to dealing with physical and mental symptoms of illness and the harm caused by abuse and neglect leans heavily on cures and remedies rather than prevention and wellness. Far too often, the reactive nature of healthcare services is limited in its scope and/or effectiveness and does not address the root of issues. As discussed in previous chapters, addressing child maltreatment has followed a similar path, with a historical focus on intervention rather than prevention. The shift toward prevention is a move in an important direction regarding the needs of children and families dealing with abuse and neglect. And while prevention measures tend to focus specifically on educating about maltreatment as a means of reducing the likelihood of its occurrence, there is value in promoting health and wellness as an all-encompassing approach to prevention. From this broader perspective on prevention, health and wellness can become a primary goal rather than preventing harm or sickness. In this chapter, prevention is discussed from the standpoint of promoting the health and wellness of children, families, and communities.

Healthcare expenditure in the U.S. continues to rise along with increasing rates of disease (National Center for Health Statistics, 2015), and the extent to which the Black community is impacted is concerning. From obesity to disease to mortality, U.S. health outcomes have begged the question of what can be done to keep Americans healthy. An estimated 40 percent of adults in the U.S. are considered obese (Fryar et al., 2018). Child rates of obesity are 21 percent for adolescents age twelve to nineteen, 18 percent for children ages six to eleven, and 9 percent for children under age five (National Center for Health Statistics, 2015). Obesity is a condition that is associated with many other health conditions, such as cardiovascular, pulmonary, and heart diseases, and is known to negatively influence health outcomes (Wong et al., 2014).

Health Outcomes in the Black Community

It has been well established that health disparities exist in the U.S. and that they fall along racial and ethnic lines (Collins & Rocco, 2014; Rowland & Isaac-Savage, 2014). Health disparities, or health inequities as they are also referred to, are differences in health status that are systemically connected and related to contextual factors around people's lives. These factors include education, employment, poverty, access to health care, and more. Disparities are connected to health and wellness as they influence physical, mental, and social well-being.

Throughout this book, we have discussed the importance of understanding the historical context of the issue at hand; the same is true for understanding overall health outcomes for Black families. Within the U.S., there is a history of deceptive medical practices that have led to the sickness and deaths of many Black people. For example, in the infamous and unethical Tuskegee research study, 600 Black men voluntarily participated in an experiment on the sexually transmitted infection Syphilis (Centers for Disease Control and Prevention [CDC], 2020a). Initially expected to last six months, this study was conducted over forty years, during which time the participants did not receive proper treatment. It was later determined that the men were not adequately informed of the risk involved in the experiment (informed consent) and the study was unethical. More egregiously, curative medication (i.e., penicillin) was withheld from the participants (Muvuka, 2020). Although reparations were provided to the surviving men, and to their wives and offspring, the damage had been done. The procedural practices in this study not only caused the participants unnecessary suffering but had also led to some of their deaths. And the ramifications of the study impacted the lives of the families of these men. Furthermore, the deliberate deception and resulting damage of this experiment aligned with, in the minds of many Black people, an American history of devaluing the life of Black people. The Tuskegee experiment remains an indelible mark on the continued American legacy of Black people being taken advantage of and not having their life and liberty valued. Thus, there is a legacy of distrust toward the medical profession that has lingered in the Black community (Rowland & Isaac-Savage, 2014). Such mistrust can impede Black people from seeking care and from accepting the recommendations of healthcare professionals. Additionally, there are other associated factors that influence the health disparities within the Black community, including poor accessibility of affordable healthcare services, implicit bias of healthcare professionals, and financial constraints prohibiting healthcare use and follow up (CDC, 2020b).

Medical Health Outcomes

The health disparities that Black people face are particularly concerning. Many factors that correlate with poor health outcomes tend to occur at higher rates in the Black community. For example, the rates of obesity are highest among Blacks compared to other racial groups (Wong et al., 2014), with U.S.-born Blacks evidencing greater rates of obesity than foreign-born Blacks (Mehta et al., 2015). Black children also evidence the highest rates of obesity among racial groups (Taveras et al., 2013). Black men and women have the highest prevalence of hypertension than other racial groups (National Center for Health Statistics, 2015). Black mothers, compared to other racial counterparts, experience the highest rates of preterm (premature) births (National Center for Health Statistics, 2015). Black mothers also experience physical inattentiveness to their pain during pregnancy as well as during labor and delivery. The rates of Black mothers dying during childbirth are three to four times more than the rates of White mothers (National Partnership for Women & Families, 2018), which devastates the family and also leaves children in a single parent or extended family care households. In chapters 3 and 4, we noted the pressures and challenges of single-parent households involving additional traumas and stressors, as they related to potential child maltreatment. In addition to concerns about Black maternal birth and pre-birth experiences, Black women are also in need of postpartum medical support.

Infectious disease rates in the Black community are also alarming. For example, the Black community has higher rates of newly diagnosed HIV cases annually than any other U.S. racial groups (CDC, 2018). Blacks and other people of color are affected by higher rates of diabetes and diabetes-related mortality than their White counterparts (American Diabetes Association, 2019; Clements et al., 2020). In fact, overall rates of mortality are higher in the Black community compared to their White counterparts (Cunningham, 2017). Another example is the novel Coronavirus-19 (COVID-19) disease, which has caused a global health pandemic and affected the lives of countless individuals in the U.S. To date (November 2020), there have been almost 11,000,000 people in U.S. who tested positive with COVID and close to 250,000 people who have died from it (CDC, 2020a). According to the CDC (2020b), Black Americans account for a disproportionate percentage of COVID-related deaths in many states throughout the country. Still, according to a Pew Research Survey, Black families may be less likely to trust medical doctors and accept the COVID vaccination when it is made available (Gramlich, & Funk, 2020). Some of this hesitance may be related to a history of negative medical experiences of Black, particularly, African American, families within the U.S. medical and healthcare system, such as the Tuskegee Experiment described earlier (Newkirk, 2016). Taken together, given the extent to which the Black community is burdened by poor health and health outcomes, it becomes clear that the health and wellness of Black people needs to be front and center as an issue to be addressed and improved.

Mental Health Outcomes

There are concerning mental health trends in the Black community. As discussed in chapter 2, there is an established connection between parental mental illness and increased likelihood of child maltreatment (Jonson-Reid et al., 2012; Reupert et al., 2013). This association highlights the importance of the state of mental health in the U.S. given the impact on other public health issues, such as child maltreatment. The prevalence of mental disorders such as major depression is increasing in the U.S. (Jorm et al., 2017). Notably, child maltreatment is known to be associated with mental health problems. For example, males who experience child sexual abuse have a higher likelihood of experiencing mental health issues, particularly suicide attempts (Turner et al., 2017). These associations between mental health and child maltreatment are indicators that addressing mental health needs is as important as physical health. Mental health is a core component of health and wellness that influences health outcomes. Focal points for improving health and wellness must therefore include attention to mental health.

Such attention to mental health should also include attention to families who are in their beginning stages of forming. Take again, for example, the topic of Black mothers' maternal health. In addition to their physical health, attention to their postpartum mental health is imperative. Postpartum depression, which describes depressive symptoms that can occur after giving birth (CDC, 2020a), effects many mothers and can be debilitating to their functioning in ways that they could not predict (O'Hara & McCabe, 2013). There can be serious consequences for the family, including the care of the child and the additional stress on the other parent or other extended caregivers. Despite the potential serious consequences of postpartum mental health conditions, such as depression and the lesser-known postpartum anxiety (Ali, 2018), Black mothers may be less likely to reach out for help because of the stigma associated with mental health concerns; the expectations and pressure of being a "good" mother; the lack of access and resources for help; and also the fear of child welfare involvement (Ali, 2018). Black families have seen and heard all too often the real-life stories of children being taken away when a Black parent appears to struggle. Black mothers and Black fathers may not be eager to turn to helping professionals for fear of what the help might look like. An article in the *Philadelphia Inquirer* (Feldman & Pattani, 2019) highlighted this topic by interviewing Black mothers who struggled with postpartum depression. One mother spoke about struggling to manage her emotions and connect with her newborn child, while also being in an abusive relationship. She reported that she did not reach out for help because of fear that she would be perceived as a bad mother and her child would be taken away from her. A community health worker also noted that Black mothers have minimized their depression and anxiety when the worker inquired about it during their home visits. She again noted the fear the women have as it relates to the possibility of losing their children. Being able to assist these women is beneficial to the women, and also to the children. It is imperative that we create a system where Black parents can be honest about their struggles, especially as they relate to mental health, and receive help without fear of losing their children. In fact, focusing on improving the health and wellness of these parents may help to prevent the very thing that they fear.

Health Outcomes for Child Welfare-Involved Youth

Delving further into the health outcomes of children involved in the child welfare system brings to the forefront some concerning realities. Children who have been in the foster care system have worse outcomes than the general population (Ahrens et al., 2014). More specifically, children in foster care have been shown to have a high prevalence of health problems, with a third of foster care children having a chronic health condition, and a larger percentage having a physical health problem (Szilagyi et al., 2015). Furthermore, young adults who have been in the foster care system have shown a greater degree of chronic health conditions (Ahrens et al., 2014). Studies have shown that there are higher rates of mental health conditions, such as Post-traumatic Stress Disorder and Depressive Disorders for children in the child welfare system compared to children in the general population (Haselgruber et al., 2021; Keller et al., 2011). Thus, child welfare involvement is a factor that is associated with poor health and highlights the need to address the wellness of youth involved in the child welfare system. Returning to the cases discussed in the Introduction, while not much is known about the overall health of each of the children, it is worth considering what their health status might have been, and considering how health might be associated with their involvement in the child welfare system. It is not clear if they received regular healthcare, and if they were healthy. In Oni's case, it is known that due to financial struggles, her aunt's health insurance had lapsed at particular points. This lapse in coverage could have negatively impacted Oni's access to healthcare for some period of time and therefore impacted her health and wellness. Paying attention to the health of children, particularly those who become involved in the child welfare system, is an important part of their care and well-being.

Health Disparities and Inequities

Health disparities and inequities are more than differences in health status among groups. They are differences that negatively impact marginalized people in systematic ways that people who have more social privilege do not have to contend with (Braveman, 2006; CDC, 2021). Health disparities and inequities impact the health and well-being of Black families across many areas. For example, we spoke about the disproportionate rate of Black families that experienced COVID-related deaths. The disproportionate rate has been connected to long-standing social and health inequities (CDC, 2020b). In general, there are a number of associated factors that influence health disparities within the Black community, including health literacy, social determinants, race and racism, and incarceration.

Health Literacy

Given the complexity of managing individual healthcare, and for parents, the healthcare of their children, how individual health consumers understand health-related information matters. Health literacy is the ability to understand health information and services, and to make decisions that influence health and health-seeking behavior (Mantwill et al., 2015). When researchers reviewed thirty-six studies on health literacy, findings supported an association between health literacy and health status (Mantwill et al., 2015). As such, it is becoming more evident that health literacy is a mediating factor in health disparities (Mantwill et al., 2015). Health can be impacted by an individual's understanding of specific factors such as knowledge of disease-prevention methods and disease-control strategies, knowing what constitutes concerning health symptoms, and having an adequate understanding of the importance of adhering to medical recommendations and of following up with recommended medical care. It is likely that variables such as exposure to health information, education level, and cultural attitudes about health differ across racial and ethnic groups, and therefore relate to the health disparities that occur. In other words, for socioeconomically disadvantaged families, health literacy could be a barrier to maintaining health and wellness, could contribute to lack of access to adequate healthcare, and could relate to not seeking healthcare as often or as early as needed, ultimately tying health literacy to poorer health outcomes. In the Black community, there is a disproportionate degree of low health literacy, which has been associated with poor health outcomes (Prins & Mooney, 2014).

Social Determinants of Health

Historically, medical care has been a significant focus for addressing health and illness. Over time, research trends have shifted toward examining other factors, besides medical care, that could be shaping health and health outcomes. The conditions in which people live and the circumstances of their birth are now understood to be significant influencers of health (Braveman & Gottlieb, 2014). To that end, living in a neighborhood that has easily accessible resources for nutrition, health, and exercise can result in different health outcomes as compared to living in a neighborhood with limited access or subpar resources. Take for example President Barack Obama's previous Task Force on Childhood Obesity along with First Lady Michelle Obama's 2010 "Let's Move" campaign. These initiatives sought to decrease childhood obesity by focusing on generational health issues within families, access to healthy food, increased movement, healthier choices, and overall more positive health outcomes (ObamaWhiteHouse, 2017). Other factors, such as an individual's income level, accumulation of wealth, and educational achievement can also shape an individual's health (Braveman & Gottlieb, 2014). These socioeconomic factors can impact the level of stress, access, and resources that are available for an individual. As such, poverty can significantly limit the health choices an individual can make, from dietary choices, access to exercise, access to healthcare and health information, to a host of other resources that contribute to health.

Race, Racism, and Health

The understanding of racism as a social determinant of life outcomes is growing. The racialized nature of life in America has created an environment that is fraught with race-based traumatic stress (French et al., 2019). Racism has been increasingly found to negatively impact health and is thought to be associated with health inequities (Heard-Garris et al., 2018). The nature and recurrences of race-based incidents can be experienced as distressing and can have a cumulative impact on the mental and physical health of individuals and communities, with a greater association to poorer mental health outcomes than physical health outcomes (Paradies et al., 2015). Experiences of racism can include indirect exposure or direct hatred that can be suffered at the hands of friends, associates, and strangers across familial, work, and communal settings. Thus, the paths of exposure to racism are just as varied as the adverse consequences that result. For Black people, both born in the U.S. and foreign born but residing in the U.S., the experience of being Black in America comes with stress that is both a product of life circumstance and choices, and from the sociocultural context and nature of being Black in a racist society. Specific to Black women, who tend to be the primary caregiver for children more often than not, the experience of racism has been associated with reproductive problems (Heard-Garris et al., 2018). There has been a link between experiences of racism and the parent-child relationship. More specifically, racism has been found to be associated with harsher parenting practices (Heard-Garris et al., 2018). Moreover, exposure to vicarious racism, which describes the indirect effects of the racism that another person has experienced, is associated with poor health outcomes for children (Heard-Garris et al., 2018). Healing from racial trauma is vital to health and important to having a sense of wellness.

Incarceration and Health

America has been a leader in the world community in many innovative and positive respects. However, there is an underside of significant adverse conditions that America leads the way with as well. With approximately one in every one hundred adults in jail or prison, the U.S. is leading the world in incarceration, despite the fact that incarceration rates have fallen in the U.S., within the past few years (Gramlich, 2021). The rate of Black imprisonment is also decreasing, still incarceration remains particularly high for Black men who are far outnumbering their White and Hispanic counterparts (Gramlich, 2020). In 2018, Black men were almost six times more likely than their White counterparts to be imprisoned (Carson, 2020). Moreover, the racial disparity in incarceration is most pronounced in men ages eighteen and nineteen (McDaniel et al., 2013). The incarceration disparity is not only impacting men, but women as well. Although less prevalent, rates of female incarceration of Black women are also declining, but still, in 2018, Black women were incarcerated at almost twice the rate of White women (Carson, 2020; Maxwell & Solomon, 2018).

The impact of incarceration is well documented, from the impact on the inmate to their significant others and offspring. For example, incarceration has a direct impact on the health of inmates, with higher rates of infectious and chronic disease, and lower rates of health follow-up (Brinkley-Rubenstein, 2013). Specifically, inmates have a higher rate of health conditions, including HIV, hypertension, hepatitis, tuberculosis, and asthma. Specific subgroups of inmates also experience poor health outcomes. For example, for women, there are higher rates of cervical cancer among inmates (Brinkley-Rubenstein, 2013) and infant mortality (Maxwell & Solomon, 2018). For adolescents, incarceration is associated with greater rates of depression and poorer physical and mental health in adulthood (Barnert et al., 2017).

Not only is physical health a concern for inmates, but their mental health suffers as well. Incarceration is associated with higher rates of depression, anxiety, and antisocial personality disorder (Brinkley-Rubenstein, 2013). Furthermore, the healthcare infrastructure within jails and prisons has challenges in terms of delays in receiving medical supplies and medication, facility hygiene, and errors in medication administration (Brinkley-Rubenstein, 2013). These issues with infrastructure likely exacerbate the poor health outcomes of inmates.

In addition to the direct impact of incarceration on the inmate, the impact on those that are related to the inmate is becoming clearer. It is estimated that 25 percent of Black children will experience parental incarceration, that is, at least one parent who will be imprisoned (Wildeman et al., 2018) and parental incarceration has been shown to have a direct impact on the health of Black children's lives. For example, parental incarceration is associated with increased infant mortality for Black children, greater levels of behavioral and mental health problems in children, and higher body mass indexes for young Black women (Wildeman et al., 2018).

Given the disproportionate number of incarcerated Black people, the Black community is inordinately impacted by the ill-effects of incarceration. Incarcerated Black parents are less available for child-rearing, have a higher degree of health problems, and their children have pressing physical and mental health issues. Taken together, the plethora of factors influencing health disparities drives home the significant extent to which Black families and children are placed at risk for poor health, and the dire importance of focusing on health and wellness in the Black community.

Wellness in the United States

Promoting wellness over curing disease can represent an important shift in how health and wellness is addressed in the U.S. The subject of wellness has several important facets, including factors associated with improved health, western versus holistic approaches, healing from racial trauma, and spirituality. Each of these facets holds promise in helping to improve health and wellness and reducing child maltreatment.

Factors Associated with Improved Health

Now that concerns about the health and health outcomes in the U.S. have been outlined, and the particular health issues plaguing the Black community have been laid bare, turning the focus to promoting wellness is needed. There are several factors that have been associated with improved health outcomes. One important factor is the format of intervention service provision. For example, for children, home visits are health promoting. Specifically, in a study of the effectiveness of home visits, there was a positive association with health outcomes, including the cognitive and social development of children, and reduced behavioral problems (Avellar & Supplee, 2013). Thus, it bodes well that home visits are one of the most commonly used interventions for child maltreatment (Casillas et al., 2016).

Western Medicine and Holistic Approaches

The distinct differences in how wellness is approached in Western countries versus Eastern countries have been established and have spawned often dichotomous thinking about which path may be best. Western countries lean heavily toward scientifically based treatment options for physical and mental health, while eastern methods focus on holistic, spiritually based approaches. In recent decades, more attention has been directed toward merging these approaches for added health benefits. Additionally, research has shown that the use of traditional or alternative medicine is substantial among Black people, with prevalent use of such practices as prayer for health reasons, deep breathing and relaxation techniques, and herbal supplements (Agu et al., 2019; Barner et al., 2010). Thus, merging these paths can create a more all-encompassing and comprehensive approach to wellness in the Black community. A true commitment to a culturally congruent, biopsychosocial model embraces an African-centered approach that recognizes the "interdependence and interrelatedness of spiritual, mental, physical, social and environmental well-being" (Myers & Speight, 2010, 76).

Healing from Racial Trauma

The clearer understanding of the impact of racial trauma on the health of those experiencing racism warrants attention being turned toward healing such trauma. Healing from racial trauma is becoming a greater clinical focus in mental health treatment practices. Recommendations for psychology practice include viewing healing from a continuous process standpoint, where the healing from racial trauma is ongoing because the exposure to racism is continual (Liu et al., 2019). Recommendations are geared toward both practitioners and clients with regard to approaching the healing process. Practitioners are advised to be mindful that general psychology practices originate from a White, heteronormative ideology, where traditional cultural values and standards are the default perspective. With this biased reality in mind, practitioners may become more aware of the oppressive nature that can come into play when treating clients who do not fit into such homogeneous thinking and approaches. It is recommended to use a treatment approach that empowers people of color. Regarding clients, researchers encourage "microprotections" through emulating parental warmth and acceptance of children's experiences, and also preparing children for racial bias (Liu et al., 2019). Researchers also promote the importance of clients understanding the purpose of racism, in that it is a deliberate act against people of color, to buffer themselves from internalization of racist views (Liu et al., 2019). Understanding the nature of racism can be discussed in the context of the experiences' clients bring up, and through non-specific examples of instances where racism occurs. The researchers also promote a collaborative approach for people of color to heal from racial trauma such as connecting with White allies, that is, White individuals who have a conscious awareness of how their race creates privilege, power, and oppression, can be a conduit for increasing the awareness of other White people regarding race relations, racial bias, and racism (Liu et al., 2019). Such collaboration can be encouraged by the practitioner by discussing the potential value of these collaborations and discussing how such collaborations can be forged in various life settings.

Spirituality and Wellness

It is clear that physical and mental health greatly factor into wellness, but the role that spirituality plays in health and wellness is not as evident and clear cut. Some research suggests that religious or spiritual practices can have a protective quality, promoting resilience and well-being (Brewer-Smyth & Koenig, 2014; Brooks et al., 2018). Specifically, spirituality and religion have had a robust role in the lives of the Black community (Rowland & Isaac-Savage, 2014). Churches with predominantly Black members have been a center-point in Black communities and are often where individuals first seek support and guidance, which can sometimes be seen as a replacement, or at least a supplement, for healthcare. In fact, church involvement has been associated with positive health care practices, which has been recognized by healthcare professionals and can become a means of collaboration for improving families' health (Felix Aaron et al., 2003). Over time, church leadership has sought to develop more community involvement and resources, which has also helped to bridge the health gap. For example, many churches create initiatives to increase physical wellness through food pantries, meal delivery, and community dinners; they promote mental wellness through providing additional needs such as clothes, spiritual guidance, and other family resources. Importantly, many churches provide these supports to the members of their congregations and also to members in the community the church resides in. Additionally, initiatives to form partnerships with houses of worship and other organizations in the community are gaining traction as a means of addressing the health disparities in the Black community (Bryant, 2014). Utilizing the strong ties of churches and community centers, health care centers forming collaborations and partnerships with these institutions has become a means of disseminating health education and offering some healthcare services. Collaborations can take various forms to connect Black children and families with needed services. For example, non-profit organizations in Los Angeles developed grant-funded partnerships with predominately Black and Latino church congregations to address the disparities impacting the congregants and their community (Derose et al., 2019). These partnerships resulted in increased resources and community engagement to achieve goals, such as providing health programming to reduce obesity through exercise and nutrition education. Collaborations and partnership can occur in other ways, such as healthcare and mental health practitioners including a religious and spiritual component in client assessments, as well as educating clients about the scope of resources offered by faith-based organizations (Hodge, 2020).

Wellness and Spirituality for Black Women

It is worth considering wellness and spirituality in terms of the role it can have for women. As discussed in previous chapters, Black women are often the primary caregiver of Black children. The wellness and healing of a Black mother is therefore critical to that of their children. Religion and spirituality have well-established roots in the Black community, with the church playing a particularly vital role in the lives of Black women (Bryant-Davis et al., 2014). Some researchers have highlighted that religion is a part of the coping mechanisms of Black women (Bryant-Davis et al., 2014). Black women prominently utilize their religious and spiritual beliefs to manage stressors and life changes. Thus, their spirituality can be a tool to bolster wellness and be a buffer for stress, which ultimately helps the children in their lives. It is worth considering how the spiritual base of Black women can be more robustly incorporated into the care and support of Black women, and the extent to which such a focus can positively impact children and reduce child maltreatment.

Culturally Grounded Health and Wellness Services for the Black Community

The disproportionate rates of health issues the Black community face warrant health care that is geared to their particular needs.

Identifying programs in Black communities that are geared toward promoting health, healing, and wellness can be crucial in improving the health outcomes in the Black community. In this section, we will discuss programs that are specifically geared toward Black women, children, and families.

Programs for Black Women

Given the primary role Black women have in raising Black children, their wellness directly impacts that of their children. To this end, Black women have specific needs that programs geared toward them must take into account. With few programs specifically developed for the health and wellness of Black women, the ones that exist are paving the way to culturally grounded care that is more suited for their particular needs. The Center for Black Women's Wellness (CBWW) is one such organization (Center for Black Women's Wellness [CBWW], 2022). Based in Georgia within a Black community, this center houses a wellness clinic that provides women's health care services such as physical exams, pap smears, sexually transmitted infection testing, and health screenings. This organization offers various programs geared toward maternal and infant health. The center also has an initiative that encourages fathers to develop healthy parenting techniques. Additionally, CBWW seeks to empower Black women through economic independence. Their Women's Economic Self Sufficiency Program (WESSP) provides workshops that focus on developing business, marketing, and advertising strategies as well as record keeping and tax preparation knowledge and skills. WESSP also offers one-on-one coaching, peer-to-peer support, and financial resources. Through their comprehensive palette of services, CBWW is a quintessential example of focusing on the health and wellness of Black women, which in turn improves health outcomes for their children. The Black Women for Wellness is another program that is geared specifically toward the wellness of Black women (Black Women for Wellness, 2022). With a primary goal of addressing the health disparities that Black mothers face, this California-based organization offers various programs geared toward improving health and promoting wellness in the Black community. This organization provides a community forum that focuses on educating about healthcare issues affecting Black women. They also offer a sex education program that is particularly geared toward youth and young adult Black individuals who are in the foster care system or at high risk for sexually transmitted infections. So, the organization not only helps Black women but also Black youth.

Programs for Black Families

Programs that are developed to address the unique needs of the Black community are integral to making a difference and equalizing health outcomes. One such program is the Center for African American Health, which focuses on providing culturally sensitive programming (Center for African American Health, 2020). This organization offers counseling, workforce readiness training, aging support for older adults, and a social movement forum where members can express their opinions regarding social issues. Some programs are tailoring their services within the Black community. Take for example the African American Health Program (AAHP), which has the mission of reducing health disparities for African American people (African American Health Program [AAHP], 2022). This Maryland-based organization offers services for medical care, including maternal, child, sexually transmitted infections, heart and dental services within the Black community, as well as men's health and senior resources. AAHP utilized a tailored approach to identify the communities with the most need for services. More specifically, this organization uses county research data to identify Black communities with health disparities as indicated by emergency room visits for conditions such as cardiovascular diseases, cancer, and diabetes (AAHP, 2020). Taken together, these organizations are examples of programs that serve the Black community in a culturally grounded manner that is geared to improving health and wellness of Black people.

Programs for Children

Programs for children generally focus on clinically based interventions that primarily provide interventions such as counseling, pharmaceutical intervention, and home visits. Examples of culturally grounded programs for Black children were discussed in chapter 4, which are geared toward meeting the specific needs of these children. There are also programs that use holistically focused interventions. Zensational Kids is an example of one such organization providing holistic services for children (Zensationalkids.com, 2017). A key part of this program's mission is to empower and support children in a natural setting, such as school, to thrive through the use of holistic strategies to support mental health. For example, their program helps school staff integrate breathing and movement practices to help children self-regulate emotions, increase attention, and cultivate a positive mindset. The program provides in-class support and professional development for educators and school staff to utilize in the classroom and school setting. Another example of a holistically based program is Leg Up Farm, a Pennsylvania-based organization, that offers services that are non-traditional (Leg Up Farm, 2020). Ranging from equine therapy to nutrition counseling, they provide various holistic intervention options for children.

Resilience as a Part of Wellness

There have been initiatives among researchers and practitioners to focus on and improve the resilience of children. In a review of studies, DeAngelis (2014) found that parents, religious leaders, coaches, and even barbers have the potential to have a positive impact on the resilience of Black boys. Further, the American Psychological Association (2014) developed a parent tool kit to promote resilience in children. Listed tools include establishing routines, e.g., meal, bed, and homework times, as well as routines for family traditions such as family game night. The tool kit also encourages parents to work on their children's life skills, such as having strong communication skills and problem-solving ability. Thus, fostering resilience can be a meaningful part of promoting wellness for Black children.

Prioritizing Wellness in Clinical Practice

Focusing on wellness in clinical practice can create a strengths-based approach to helping clients. Practitioners of mental health are in an influential position and can advocate for prioritizing wellness through educating clients about how to identify resources and access health needs. By focusing on prevention via wellness, practitioners can promote behaviors that reduce a need for a cure.

Addressing Wellness in Clinical Practice

Mental health approaches have been improperly developed and imposed on communities of color. For example, Myers and Speight (2010) argued that mainstream psychology has continued to oppress and ostracize individuals of African descent by ignoring African cultures, practices, and epistemologies. They observed that "by exploring and analyzing the interdependence of the various institutions within the society (e.g., educational, legal, religious, and political), we can see how the status quo is maintained, social realities are fostered, and the development of potential for human growth is negatively influenced" (p. 68). Informed by optimal psychology (Myers, 1992), these authors examined ways to promote psychological well-being in Black communities, despite the oppressive realities they face. They asserted that mainstream psychology approaches and assumptions leave Black communities psychologically fragmented, ignoring their African-centered histories and traditions. They called for an Africana/Black psychology that recognizes the interconnectedness of physical, mental, spiritual, social, and environmental well-being. Through this approach, a system that informs, research, teaching training and practice will evolve. This system will focus on illuminating and freeing the spirit, allowing for the resolution of physical and mental ailments while promoting optimal functioning.

Additionally, empowering women, given that they are frequently the primary caregivers for children, is key to improving the health of children. Incorporating holistic care in clinical practice has potential to improve client wellness. There are particular Western treatment approaches that have made efforts in this regard. For example, dialectical behavior therapy (DBT) is a well-researched, manualized form of cognitive behavioral treatment that is used to treat mental health disorders ranging from mood, anxiety and trauma disorders to personality disorders (Linehan, 2015). DBT stands out from other forms of clinical treatments in that this approach specifically includes a treatment module that is focused on incorporating mindfulness practice into the clinical treatment of mental disorders.

Above and beyond a particular treatment intervention, it is important to attend to the cultural identities of the client within clinical practice. For Black families, being aware and watchful of microaggressions toward them, avoiding misdiagnosing them, and promoting a strengths-based as well as culturally grounded approaches to their treatment are crucial elements to addressing wellness in clinical practice. Racial microaggressions, which are race-based slights and insults toward people of color, have the potential to minimize the families' experience and to make them feel unwelcomed in the treatment setting. Similarly, misdiagnosing families, either by underdiagnosing symptoms of depression and anxiety or by over-pathologizing symptoms of anger, also have the potential to minimize the experience of the person, prevent support, and ultimately hinder the promotion of wellness. We mentioned the ways in which Black families, mothers in particular, are ignored within the medical system. The mental health system is another place where Black families are not seen as vulnerable as they may actually be, and where their pain is often overlooked. Stereotypical perceptions of Black men and women as overly strong and stoic may lead clinicians to overlook, and even discourage, moments of vulnerability and attempts to ask for help. Attention to such moments is important for promoting wellness and also protecting against child maltreatment.

Given the susceptibility of treatment providers to the blind spots that stereotypes, implicit bias, and systemic norms create, ongoing self-evaluation is crucial to providing culturally sensitive treatment (French et al., 2020; Goodman et al., 2004). Self-evaluation that focuses on becoming aware of deeply held beliefs that may be negatively impacting treatment can help treatment providers consciously make efforts to counteract the potential negative effects. Lastly, not all evidenced-based treatments are appropriate for all clients. There are ways of culturally adapting treatments and also utilizing culturally grounded treatment (e.g., developed for the specific population) that are imperative to explore when working with Black families.

Closing Summary

The interconnectedness of families and communities necessitate improving health outcomes for children from a more comprehensive approach that includes not only the child but those who care for and surround the child. The well-documented health disparities that occur along racial lines not only put Black children at risk, but negatively impacts them into adulthood. Every opportunity needs to be taken to equalize the health and well-being of these children. Children involved in the child welfare system are at particular risk for poor health outcomes. But these children often enter the system with existing disparities. In this manner, disparities in one sphere tends to be associated with disparities in other life spheres. Prevention that provides targeted information about child maltreatment is helpful, but focusing on the health and wellness of Black children, mothers and families can address the social determinants that lead to maltreatment and promote optimal functioning in the Black community. By bolstering the health of the Black community, child maltreatment is potentially thwarted. From community resources, to the church, to clinical treatment, health and wellness needs to be a prominent aspect of care and support for the Black community. Ultimately, with health and wellness as a preventive focus, the health of the Black community, Black women, Black parents, and, therefore, the lives of Black children can be positively affected. In the next chapter, we discuss the role of advocacy in addressing child maltreatment, and in addressing the disparities Black families and children face.

6

Advocacy and Child Welfare Reform

My humanity is bound up in yours,
for we can only be human together.
—Desmond Tutu, archbishop,
human rights advocate,
Nobel peace prize winner

Overview

This chapter explores the importance of advocacy in addressing child maltreatment. Laws and policies that specifically address the needs of Black people and children living in the U.S. are discussed. Advocacy is explored in terms of how it occurs through the micro to macro levels of a social ecological model. Discussion includes a detailed exploration of the article, The African-American Child Welfare Act: A Legal Redress for African-American Disproportionality in Child Protection Cases. This article proposes a law, the African American Child Welfare Act, that would specifically address the needs of Black children regarding their disproportionate presence in the child welfare system by establishing new requirements and changes throughout the decision-making process for a Black child to be removed from the home. Lastly, the potential impact of such a proposal being enacted into law is discussed.

The Role of Advocacy

Advocacy is generally understood as an active process of supporting a particular area, or areas, for the benefit of specific groups or causes (Jason et al., 2019). Advocacy efforts are typically aimed toward key decision makers, who can influence policy and promote the interest of others. Key decision makers are commonly thought of as political and elected officials, such as lawmakers. However, social and health care professionals and administrators are also important decision makers. For families that are involved in the child welfare system, they can be essential to the outcomes of their case.

The historical role of advocacy has been a powerful amplifier that places a spotlight on societal issues. Issues that occur at the micro-level of society, in a household, a community, or in a subgroup of individuals, are not visible to larger society without a propellant to the public eye. To that end, the prevalence and severity of the issues occurring in households and communities becomes clearer when attention is brought to the issue at national and international levels. Thus, advocacy broadens the breadth of awareness for social problems, injustices, and areas of deficiency, and in doing so, creates a call to action for change to be discussed and implemented. Lating et al. (2009) noted that "advocacy initiatives may include helping those who are underserved access care, promoting social justice through the recognition of diversity and multiculturalism issues, securing funding for training and research, and understanding and becoming involved in public policy issues that affect the profession at local, state, and national levels" (p. 106).

Advocacy amplifies the voice of those who can speak for themselves and becomes the voice for those who cannot. The developmental stage and ability of children is often an inherent limitation to their ability to recognize their autonomy, set personal boundaries, and speak about when they have been violated (Lagaay & Courtney, 2013). Take for example a five-year-old child who is developmentally at an early stage of learning how to read, how to develop friends, and developing a clearer understanding of the difference between real life and make believe. One can imagine the complexities and difficulties involved in a child that age comprehending that she is being neglected if left alone at home and not fed regular meals, and what cognitive and emotional skills it would take for the child to have the wherewithal to say what is happening to someone who could help. The limitation a child faces in ability to recognize and say that maltreatment has happened often means that they do not have the capacity to report the abuse, or that there are varying lengths of delay in the child reporting the abuse, perhaps delayed to when they have aged and have a greater retrospective understanding of what they have experienced (Alaggia et al., 2017). Furthermore, a child's voice is often lost in the child welfare process where adults decide about the child's care and protection once maltreatment has occurred. Fortunately, there has been some efforts to shift the focus of advocacy to promote that a child's voice needs to be considered as a part of providing care and protection from maltreatment (Lagaay & Courtney, 2013).

Advocacy at Different Social Ecological Levels

Advocacy can occur at varying levels, ranging from advocating on behalf of an individual or small groups of individuals, to larger groups and more pervasive issues. In this way, advocacy can be understood across all levels of the social ecological framework, from the micro to macro levels. Bronfenbrenner's ecological framework consists of the microsystem, the mesosystem, the exosystem, and the macrosystem. Advocacy at each level will be discussed next. Additionally, the following case will be discussed in terms of how advocacy was used or would have been helpful.

This case involves a young Black mother, who will be referred to as Monica, whom one of our authors provided individual therapy to as a psychologist. As a single mother raising a daughter, Monica led a busy life working full time while attending online college classes. She received regular child rearing support from her family and had a close relationship with her parents and relatives. One of the presenting issues in therapy was Monica's desire to raise her seven-year-old daughter somewhat differently than had been traditional in her family history. Through the generations of Monica's family, children were expected to show deference to adults, from listening to their elders, doing what an adult tells them, using respectful titles, i.e., Sir, Ma'am, even down to hugging or kissing any adult on the cheek, who initiated such physical contact as a greeting, even if the child was showing signs of not wanting to greet in such a way. These social conventions of respect for elders are a common tradition in Black families (Dixon et al., 2008), and are seen as a part of how to raise respectful children into respectful adults. Monica, having experienced molestation as a child, had quietly wanted to teach her daughter "body autonomy" and how to disclose if maltreatment had happened.

Microsystem Advocacy

The microsystem involves environments that directly engage with the child, such as the home, school, neighborhoods, and community settings, like recreational centers and faith-based institutions (Campos-Gil et al., 2020). The direct person-environment interactions of the microsystem provide a fertile ground for direct advocacy that can address maltreatment. Advocacy at this level can take many forms. For example, advocacy can occur on behalf of the child, such as when a parent advocates for their child to receive school intervention when bullied by peers. Teachers can advocate for students, for example, when supporting a child in receiving tutoring or school-based accommodations. Advocacy can occur for the family on behalf of the child. For example, a faith-based clergy advocating for a family to receive financial support in order to afford tutoring for their child. Advocacy can also take the form of encouraging and teaching children how to advocate for themselves. For example, a mother can teach a child self-advocacy through role playing what to say when being teased or bullied.

In the case of Monica, microsystem advocacy with this mother took the form of validating her feelings and parenting preferences, and helping her identify assertive yet diplomatic language she could use when talking to her family members about her preference for her daughter to learn "body autonomy" early and to gain comfort with asserting herself appropriately with adults. Helping Monica identify what language and body language to teach her daughter to use when in such situations seemed to help her be more assertive with teaching her daughter. There was also a therapy session in which Monica invited her parents to attend, and the session focused on supporting Monica as she talked to her parents about her fears for her daughter given the molestation she suffered at a young age that she did not disclose until older. She felt supported by the information her psychologist shared in that session about how parenting norms have been evolving around teaching children to speak up and to have autonomy over their body. Monica was eventually able to assert more of what she wanted for her daughter when family members approached for a greeting, and she felt more assured that her daughter had tools to protect herself, even at a young age.

Mesosystem Advocacy

The mesosytem involves interactions between the microsystems, such as between home and school. Advocacy at this level illustrates the value of interconnectedness between microsystems. For example, mesosystem advocacy can be when a school offers a parenting program to their students' parents that broadens their knowledge on child development and promotes healthy disciplinary skills. Another example would pertain to the use of school-based websites designed to be information portals for parents to know about their child's education progress. Using the case discussed above, Monica could check whether her child's school has a parent portal and utilize it to help keep track of her daughter's academic performance. In the case of Oni, who was discussed in the Introduction, advocacy could have included her aunt, foster parents, or child protection services caseworker helping Oni receive in-school counseling to manage the impact of her mental health on her academic performance. Thus, advocacy between microsystems can create more integrative and interactive webs of support around children, and in so doing, can allow for a wider reach when advocacy efforts are made.

Exosystem Advocacy

The exosystem includes settings that do not contain the child, but can affect the child, such as the local school board or the parent's workplace. Advocacy in the exosystem demonstrates the degree of influence these environments have on children. For example, advocacy at a parent's workplace could include flexible work schedules that allow parents to perform their employment duties while tending to family obligations. Some may deem paid family leave as a form of advocacy, as it could promote optimal family functioning and prevent child maltreatment. Resources that support caretakers and parents such as an employee assistance programs, parenting services, domestic violence support, and trauma-based treatment can all provide benefits for children in that healthy parents can better raise healthy children.

In Monica's case, exosystem advocacy could have taken the form of her place of employment offering mental health care options, which could improve Monica's psychological health and allow her to be a healthier and more attentive parent. Using one of the cases from the Introduction, Daniel's caseworker could have encouraged his parents to take parenting classes in order to improve the quality of parenting in the home. Thus, even though indirectly influencing children, advocacy in the exosystem can provide meaningful support and can be a powerful agent of change.

Macrosystem Advocacy

The macrosystem includes societal or cultural influences that affect the child's development and well-being. This system has a broader breadth and scope regarding how advocacy efforts are made. One example of advocacy at this level includes national or state laws that allow or prohibit corporal punishment. In California, the Democratic committee passed a resolution to ban the physical or corporal punishment of children (Bennett, 2019). Additionally, other forms of advocacy at the macro level can include when prominent organizations, such as the American Academy of Pediatrics or the American Psychological Association (APA), issue a statement calling for a ban on physical punishment or highlight the impact of poverty on the developing child. These efforts have the potential to promote policies and practices that foster child wellness and well-being.

At the macro level, advocacy can also take the form of organized efforts, such as political action committees, organizations, and social movements, which can propel issues to the forefront of the national and international conversations and call for change. The phrase Black Lives Matter was sparked by outrage over the acquittal of the man who killed Trayvon Martin, the Black teenager who met his death while walking home with candy and a soda he bought from a convenience store. What was initially a phrase and hashtag added to social media posts became an organized movement that has endured. The Black Lives Matter (BLM) movement has gained momentum over the past seven years through the Black Lives Matter organization that includes local and national chapters throughout the U.S., Canada, and the UK that coordinate protests, petitions, and provide advocacy for social issues that need to be addressed (BlackLivesMatter.com, 2020). The BLM movement has brought not only national attention, but has extended to other countries of the world as a global message and platform. While the movement is largely focused on violence against Black people, particularly unarmed Black people at the hands of police officers, the movement speaks to a broader message of addressing the systemic racism that Black people face and the need for Black liberation (Clayton, 2018). From seeking legal policy changes, police reform, and new protections under the law specific to Black people, the BLM movement has provided advocacy that has amplified the voice of victims of violence that may not have been heard otherwise. The maltreatment of Black children and their disproportional representation in the child welfare system is a component of the inequities facing the Black community that can potentially gain more attention and redress through a movement such as BLM. Advocating for justice to be received for the killing of Black children such as Trayvon Martin and Tamir Rice is an example of how the BLM movement connects to advocating for Black children by bringing attention to the maltreatment Black children face.

As professionals, many of us belong to professional organizations that engage in extensive advocacy. For example, the APA maintains an impressive Advocacy office that engages in a range of advocacy efforts at the macro level, ranging from health promotion to social justice concerns (American Psychological Association [APA], 2017b). APA, like other organizations, facilitates the advocacy process by issuing action alerts, allowing us to communicate with our elected officials with just a few clicks. We urge child maltreatment professionals to seek out and engage in these critical efforts. For more on the APA Advocacy office, please see https://www.apa.org/advocacy.

Women's Rights and Child Welfare

As the often-primary caregiver of children, women and the rights and protections afforded to them can have a significant impact on the children they care for. Seeking equal rights for women has a positive ripple effect for the Black family and Black children. As women are empowered and afforded rights and protections that are legally enforceable, this has a positive impact on their ability as caregivers and is likely to reduce incidence of child maltreatment.

Safety is a right that all people hold. However, the safety of women is disproportionately jeopardized by abusive relationships, such as domestic violence (Office on Women's Health [OWH], 2019). Domestic violence is also understood to be a risk factor for child maltreatment and child welfare involvement (Coulter & Mercado-Crespo,

2015; Guedes et al., 2016). We spoke, in chapter 5, about the fear that Black families feel when they seek help related to caring for their children or dealing with family difficulties. Domestic violence is no exception. Women who experience domestic violence may fear losing their children because of perceived judgment from the child welfare worker, presumption that the child was exposed to the domestic violence, or concern that the children were physically abused themselves. It is widely known that a double standard exists within society, and within our social services systems, where a great deal of responsibility and accountability is expected of mothers while fathers are held to lower standards. In this regard, women can be seen as responsible for what occurs in the household, including domestic violence perpetrated against them.

This view highlights gender inequalities, which can be addressed through advocacy efforts. Womanist advocacy recognizes the impact of gendered inequality, with specific attention to the intersection of identities for Black women. Black women already contend with cultural pressures and expectations that they hold their families together as the strong caretaker who can rise above anything. Advocacy is needed to prevent heaping additional undue expectations on Black mothers who are being abused as opposed to the fathers who may be doing the abusing. Advocacy should focus on keeping the child safe and with the non-offending or victimized parent, rather than taking the child away from the victimized parent. The program "Safe and Together" is an example of such advocacy efforts. The Safe & Together Institute (2020) offers trainings, tools, interventions, and more for child welfare workers and related organizations who would benefit from better understanding the dynamics of domestic violence and the need to shift perspective toward the protection and safety of children and the victimized parents, typically the mother. Such efforts are well aligned with the philosophy we exposé throughout this book, that caring for mothers helps the children they care for.

The Role of Laws in Addressing Disparities

African American Laws

Over the past half century, there have been laws enacted that seek to address the racism, inequities, violence, and loss of life that Black people have historically experienced in the U.S. These race-specific laws are tailored to address issues that have negatively impacted Black people. For example, the Emmett Till Unsolved Civil Rights Crime Act was enacted in 2008, and was followed by the Emmett Till Unsolved Civil Rights Crimes Reauthorization Act of 2016 (Congress.gov, 2016). These laws expanded the responsibility of the Federal Bureau of Investigation and the U.S. Department of Justice to investigate civil rights crimes occurring prior to 1980 that resulted in death. These acts also urge these agencies to have regular meetings with civil rights organizations and other relevant institutions to communicate about what efforts have been made regarding investigating these crimes. The Illinois African-American Family Commission Act is another example of a race-specific law. The purpose of this act is to advise the Governor, General Assembly, and work directly with state agencies to improve existing policies, programs and services for African American families (Illinois African American Family Commission Act, Title 20 ILCS 3903, 2015). Thus, having laws in place that are specific to a group of people and/or particular injustices can allow for a more targeted approach to addressing the problems faced. To this end, having a specific law(s) designed to address the child maltreatment of Black children could be beneficial for reducing the disparities facing them.

Proposed Laws for African American Children

There have been bills proposed in various states to address specific needs of African American children. For example, the Minnesota African American Family Preservation Act was proposed, but not ratified (Cooney, 2019). This proposed bill would stipulate that social service agencies make reasonable and diligent efforts to provide appropriate services to families to prevent out-of-home placements of children. The bill would have also required diligent efforts to reunify families if out-of-home placements had occurred, increase the minimum requirements for visitation, and assess fines for social services agencies that were non-compliant with the act. Other requirements of the bill would have been to require the completion of in-home safety plans before removal could occur, cultural competency training for child protection case workers, increasing minimum visitation for parents and siblings when a child is removed from the home, and fines for social service agencies not in compliance with the bill's requirements. The bill was ultimately not approved, and dissension to the bill reflected that the scope of the bill was thought to be overly broad (Cooney, 2019). Although this bill was not approved, it delineated a framework of legal redress to reduce the unnecessary removal of Black children from their home and to improve the quality of out-of-home placement experiences. Additionally, proposing bills that seek to rectify inequities faced by disempowered social groups (i.e., children, women) hold promise that society is moving in a positive direction regarding addressing equality.

A Published Proposal: The African-American Child Welfare Act

There is historical precedence for laws enacted to address the needs of particular races of children and this is needed for Black children. For example, the Indian Child Welfare Act (ICWA) of 1978 was established to address Indian children being removed from their homes at rates that were greater than the general population (Association of American Indian Affairs, 2020). These high rates of out-of-home placements of Indian children were having a negative impact on the children and on the unity of the families these children were removed from. Providing guidelines at various levels of intervention, ICWA provided guidance for the decision-making during child custody proceedings in an effort to preserve Indian families, to maintain the best interest of Indian children, and to preserve Indian tribal authority. ICWA created a higher burden of proof to determine if Indian children should be removed from their family (National Indian Law Library, 2020). For example, ICWA stipulates that in order to determine termination of parental rights, it is necessary for there to be evidence beyond a reasonable doubt, such as testimony of qualified expert witnesses, to demonstrate that parental custody is likely to result in maltreatment of the child. By having a higher decision-making threshold, the removal of the Indian child is less likely to occur without clear efforts to preserve the family.

As noted earlier in this chapter, laws have been proposed and some enacted for African Americans to improve the life and outcomes of the Black community. But, no laws have been put in place to deal specifically with the needs of African American children and their disproportionate placement in the child welfare system. In 2008, law professor and researcher Jessica Dixon Weaver published a comprehensive proposal for a legal act that would specifically address the needs of Black children at each stage of the process in the child welfare system. The proposed act delineated detailed methods to reduce this disparity (Dixon, 2008). The proposed act focused appropriately on Black children, while also giving attention to the needs of the parents and the relative support network surrounding the children. The proposed act therefore promoted the approach that, in order to help children, assistance also needs to be provided to those who care for the children.

Framework for the Proposed African-American Child Welfare Act

As a framework to support the need for the proposed act, Dixon asserted that universal social policies are helpful and important, but do not address the specific factors that relate to identities, such as race. Without specificity, social policies are less likely to address the needs of subgroups of people. To this end, the unique challenges that individuals of a particular race face are not directly and likely not adequately addressed by policies that do not acknowledge race-specific circumstances in its provisions. This is particularly relevant to Black children, who are facing a number of factors that make them more likely to end up in the child welfare system and remain in said system for longer lengths of time (Child Welfare Information Gateway, 2021; Fluke et al., 2011). It is necessary to consider the unique factors that lead to such a disparity by addressing as many contributing factors. Furthermore, the differences in legal statutes across states regarding the burden of proof for removal of a child from a home and termination of parental rights warranted some degree of uniformity for how particular children are impacted by these differing regulations (Child Welfare Information Gateway, 2017).

Proposed Stipulations

Dixon's proposed act includes several stipulations concerning the removal of children from homes where maltreatment has occurred. The proposed act stipulates that, similar to the ICWA, there should be a higher burden of proof for the removal of a Black child from their family. Specifically, there should be clear evidence for why a child needs to be removed from the home. For example, a parent testing positive for drug use would not be an adequate reason for the removal of a child. There would need to be corroborating circumstances such as the parent being unwilling or unable to enter a substance use treatment program, or the parent being highly likely to flee with the maltreated child. These stipulations create a higher threshold for the removal of Black children, making the odds of removal less likely. Another stipulation of the proposed act is mandatory establishment of paternity with provisions for free legal services to identified fathers if needed. This requirement supports proactive efforts to involve the father of a child in their care, safety, and home placement. Furthermore, the proposed act stipulates that efforts be made to include incarcerated parents and immediate relatives, i.e., aunts, uncles, grandparents, when a child is removed from the home. Moreover, the proposed act specifies that an incarcerated parent is contacted within thirty days of a child being removed from the home.

The proposed act would require judges to use early intervention services for African American cases. By focusing on early intervention, this requirement has the potential to reduce the likelihood that maltreatment occurs or continues to occur, thereby decreasing the need to remove the child from the home. The proposed act would also mandate cultural competency training for judges and attorneys. Along these lines, the proposed act included having a racial bias risk assessment added to the out-of-home placement process. More specifically, caseworkers would be given a racial bias screening assessment when they are considering removing a Black child from their home.

In addition to the proposed stipulations that guide the placement process of children, the proposal specifies how funding should be used, for example, to provide support services when children are in kinship placements such as daycare, after school care, and affordable family therapy access. The act also requires that funding be provided for maintaining an advisory committee to study the dynamics of disparity.

Lastly, the act proposes that there be an amendment to one of the stipulations of the Adoption and Safe Families Act of 1997, which mandates a one-year deadline for permanent child placement. The amendment would allow judges to use their discretion to extend the deadline at least two times for six-month intervals, therefore allowing greater latitude for Black caregivers to address the issues that may preclude a child from safely remaining in the home.

Limitations of the Proposed African-American Child Welfare Act

This proposed act provides a comprehensive foundation for addressing racially based disparities that impact Black children who experience maltreatment. Although there are a great deal of potential benefits if such a proposal were enacted into law, we observe some foreseeable limitations. First, increasing the burden of proof for removal of a Black child from their home requires increased funding and staff or staff hours for the time that it takes to follow through with the data that needs to be presented and reviewed. Provisions would need to be made for required funding for child welfare agencies to provide this level of service. Second, it is meaningful that provisions are included to address racial bias. Using a racial bias screening tool for child welfare professionals, who are making a recommendation for a child to be removed, can help to identify the presence of racial bias. However, these professionals will likely have repeated exposure to the screening measure and can quickly gain an understanding of how to answer questions in a manner that could create favorable results. In other words, it would not be difficult to fake the test. Thus, while screening theoretically addresses racial bias, in practice, there would likely need to be a more robust way to identify and address racial bias, such as diversifying the workforce, promoting cultural competence, and broadening racial consciousness. In addition to screening, it could be helpful to have a case review process in which the caseworker needs to discuss with a supervisor or colleague, specifically someone who could help challenge their decision-making process in comparison to similar cases. This may help to highlight patterns with decision making that could reflect racial bias. Despite these limitations, the potential for this proposal to offer viable solution-focused efforts to address disparities plaguing Black children is worth pursuing.

A Promising Act

Developing a child welfare act that specifically protects Black children, their families and communities could be immensely advantageous. Keeping with the major themes of this book, we implore policy makers and child welfare advocates to be guided by the tenets of multiculturalism and womanism, should this idea come to fruition. French et al. (2020), developed a comprehensive model promoting "radical healing" with communities of color that can aptly guide these efforts.

Within this model, they adopt principles of liberation psychology, Black psychology, ethnopolitical psychology, and intersectionality theory to guide this major framework. They assert that through collectivism, critical consciousness, radical hope, strength and resistance, as well as cultural authenticity and self-knowledge, we can start to address the pernicious effects of oppression and promote optimal wellness with our Black children and their respective communities.

Closing Summary

Advocacy has served an important historical role in bringing attention to the presence and prevalence of issues that individuals and groups face and creating a call to action for decision makers to address the issues. For child victims of maltreatment, advocacy from the micro to the macro levels can be instrumental in reducing the prevalence of abuse and remediating specific issues such as the disproportionate number of Black children in the child welfare system. Addressing maltreatment and disparity will take implementing change at every stage of the child welfare process. The historical precedent has been set for laws to be enacted that address the needs of particular subgroups, and such laws can promote increasing the attention paid to the particular needs of Black children, and by extension, the Black families from which these children emerge.

In this chapter, there was detailed focus on a published proposal for an Act that would specifically address the disproportionate presence of Black children in the child welfare system. The African-American Child Welfare Act proposal published in 2008 offered feasible and reasonable steps to be taken by those directly involved in the care and placement of maltreated Black children. If efforts can be made by politicians to propose a law that would address the issues as outlined in this proposal, tangible changes and remediation of the placement disparity could occur, with more Black children able to be kept safe from abuse in a manner that is less disruptive to the Black family.

The pervasive extent that disparities exist in the Black community warrants specific efforts to address, reduce, and prevent such disparities from persisting. Advocacy and legislation are key components to addressing the needs of Black children. Reducing the disparity of Black children in the child welfare system requires a multi-prong approach and advocacy will play a pivotal role. If legislation were put forth that specifically addresses the needs of Black children, this could reduce out-of-home placement to only when necessary, and help preserve the Black family through less disruptive means of support and intervention. In chapter 7, we introduce a case study to explore the applications of prevention and intervention.

7

Application of Prevention and Intervention

A Case Study

> I never met a Black boy who wanted to fail.
>
> —Ta-Nehisi Coates, writer, journalist, educator

Overview

In an effort to provide a complete overview of the process involved when a child experiences maltreatment and enters the child welfare system, this chapter presents the case of James, a nine-year-old boy, who had a substantiated case of child maltreatment and entered the child welfare system. The case is presented with identifying information that has been redacted to protect the family's identity. This case is discussed in four parts that include: (1) developmental history and background; (2) the prevention methods he was exposed to and those that could have been implemented; (3) intervention methods that were used and that could have been used; and (4) additional relevant factors that may have impacted the outcomes in this case. This case is utilized as a means of considering all data and resources discussed throughout this book and further illustrates the importance of policy, prevention, intervention, wellness, and advocacy as elements to address and reduce child maltreatment. This chapter also includes discussion questions that can be used in a training setting to build awareness of the signs of child abuse, the preventative measures that can be implemented, the interventions that are appropriate, and the systemic issues and policies that require advocacy to produce change. Notably, the events of this case occurred before the COVID-19 pandemic, when students were being educated in the physical school setting.

The Case of James

Demographic Data

James was a nine-year-old African American boy who lived in a two-bedroom apartment in the Washington D.C.-Maryland-Virginia (DMV) area, with his mother and his ten-year-old sister. He was born in an urban city in Georgia. His family moved to the DMV area one year ago. James was a fourth grader in an urban public elementary school, which his sister also attended. James had a substantiated child sexual abuse case in the child welfare system. He was assigned a Child Protective Service (CPS) caseworker and received both in-home and center-based intervention services.

Developmental History

James's mother noted that her pregnancy with him was unplanned. She received prenatal care throughout her pregnancy, attending monthly appointments with an obstetrician through Medicaid health coverage. She experienced gestational diabetes and frequent heartburn during the pregnancy. She lost a few pounds during her first trimester, due to nausea and low appetite; however, she gained weight within the recommended range as her pregnancy progressed. Her pre-existing condition of uterine fibroids caused health issues that resulted in preterm labor. James was born early at 30-weeks' gestation via cesarean section. At birth, he was underweight and jaundiced. His mother was released and sent home three days after the birth. James remained in the neonatal intensive care unit for a week before he was also released to go home, and his mother visited daily until he was released.

James had difficulty latching for breastfeeding. Given this, his mother primarily used a breast pump and bottle-fed James breast milk.

He attained motor developmental milestones within the expected time frames. He was crawling by four months, standing by six months, and walking by eleven months. His language milestones developed at a slower pace. He began saying words at sixteen months and using short sentences at two years old. He was toilet trained by age four.

James has a small frame and a slim build. His mother described him as being a busy kid, stating that he was always on the move and liked to pick things up and put them in his pocket or his mouth. She reported that he had a healthy appetite and ate regular meals. His favorite foods included pizza, spaghetti and meatballs, instant noodles, burgers, soda, and candy. James slept well at night, with rare occasions of difficulty falling asleep. He had nightmares once or twice a year and sleeps in his mother's room after they occur. His nightmare content included monsters and were related to his being afraid of the dark.

Health and Wellness

James received regular physical exams, dental care, eye exams, and hearing tests. He was diagnosed with asthma as a toddler, and occasionally needed to use an inhaler. He was allergic to peanuts and pet dander. James was rarely sick with common illnesses such as colds. He has had a sprained ankle, which occurred while playing kickball. He had occasional stomach aches, usually after eating too many snacks and candy. When sick, James tended to think that he will be sick forever and will not get better despite his mother's assurances that he will get better.

Educational History

James began attending daycare when he was six weeks old. During daycare, he received early learning of language concepts such as colors, body parts, and numbers. He began pre-kindergarten at age four and kindergarten at age five. He developed early reading skills in kindergarten. At age six, James began public elementary school in Georgia. He completed first through third grade there before his family moved to the DMV area. He started the fourth grade in a new elementary school. He has never been skipped or retained within a grade.

James did well with reading, math, and science, but seemed to struggle with writing. More specifically, his handwriting had poor legibility and at times, he struggled with spelling. His teachers noted his tendency to rush through written assignments and quickly become frustrated when prompted to slow down or to re-write an assignment. At home, James did well when an adult sat with him to complete his homework. He was better able to slow down on writing assignments; he had more difficulty with being careful and thorough when he worked on his own. James can become frustrated when given feedback and seemed to feel criticized. For example, when his mother told him that an answer on his homework was incorrect, he became upset and said she was mean to him. His mother admitted that she would become frustrated with him and neither of them handled frustration well. She would sometimes shout at him and use physical discipline such as open hand spanking to get his compliance. After learning about parenting strategies in psychotherapy, James's mother had recently tried to implement more positive parenting strategies, such as giving praise, acknowledging effort, and providing rewards for on-task and compliant behaviors. She had also become more aware of James's emotional responses when frustrated, and she made efforts to support his emotional needs. Once frustrated, he can become withdrawn and go to his room. He sometimes said statements such as "I'm stupid" and seemed to believe he cannot learn like other kids. At other times, particularly when in class, James would refuse to do schoolwork and become disruptive to other students in class by whispering and teasing them.

Social Development

As an infant, James was easily soothed by his mother and maternal grandmother, but fussy when his father was around. Once he became a toddler, he gravitated more to his father. James and his sister generally got along. He enjoyed watching cartoons and playing video games. He had a talent for putting together LEGO building kits. He enjoyed riding his bike in the neighborhood and could do so down his street to a neighbor's house. He played drums, which his maternal grandfather taught him when he was five.

James easily made friends with his peers. He loved sports and often developed friendships with his teammates. He tended to be a follower in groups and will sometimes get into trouble with friends. For example, he and two friends were caught taking money from a tip jar at a neighborhood convenience store. James had been teased by other kids about his dark complexion and his southern accent. He usually teased back and got into two physical scuffles that were sparked by teasing with boys at his school. He was sometimes disciplined due to joking around too much. For example, he would tease his sister to the point that she became frustrated and stormed off or hit him. His mother has talked to him repeatedly about paying attention to when he has taken a joke too far.

Family Background

James's mother was thirty-one and his father was thirty-three when he was born. His mother was an only child and often referred to her close friends as her sisters and brothers. Both James and his sister referred to his mother's friends as aunts and uncles. James's father was the youngest of four children. He was close to one of his brothers. James's parents met while attending a state university in Georgia. They were in a relationship for five years and they did not marry. James's parents lived together until James was three, then they separated.

During the time that James's parents were together, James was present for two incidents of them physically pushing each other, but his mother was uncertain if he understood what was occurring, given that he was a toddler. Once his parents separated, James and his sister spent weekends with his father. His father lived in Georgia and James and his sister visited several times since moving to the DMV area, typically for long weekends and during school breaks. His father used physical discipline more frequently than his mother did. James tended to be better behaved when spending time with his father.

James and his mother were both talkative by nature and liked to watch movies. It has been important to his mother for her children to learn how to cook. James knew how to cook eggs, pancakes, noodles, and grilled cheese sandwiches. James and his sister often got into verbal squabbles and occasionally would get physical and push each other when upset.

James's mother has several friendships that she nurtured to create a community around her and her children. For example, she started a once-a-month potluck with some of their neighbors; they met at a different neighbor's house for dinner on the last Friday of the month.

James's mother has been in a relationship with her boyfriend, whom she met shortly after moving to the DMV area. They have been together for about a year. He sometimes would watch/babysit James and his sister when their mother had to attend work-related events.

Routines in their household frequently included having dinner together, watching TV shows together, having movie nights where one family member got to pick the movie that was watched together with popcorn and candy, and Sunday dinners every few weeks at his maternal grandmother's house.

James's parents have tried to prepare him for what to do if he encounters police. During James's last visitation with his father, his father explained to him that if he ever has an interaction with police officers to say, "Sir" and "Ma'am" and to not make any sudden movements. His father showed him how to respond to what police officers ask him to do, such as put his hands in the air. He explained how to answer questions such as where he lives and what his parents' names are, specifically to say both his parents' first and last names.

Regarding grandparents, James has had a close relationship with his maternal grandparents. They often provided childcare for him while his family lived in Georgia. His paternal grandparents lived in Georgia as well, but were two hours away. He met them on a few occasions. He met his paternal uncles on a few occasions. He grew up looking at his mother's friends as extended family.

Ethnocultural Background

James's mother was born in Georgia, and his father was from North Carolina. His maternal grandparents were born in Georgia, and his paternal grandparents were of Black and Puerto Rican descent, and they moved to Georgia from Florida as young adults. James and his sister spent many weekends at his maternal grandmother's house. Traditions in his family include demonstrating respect for adults by referring to them as Sir and Ma'am, e.g., "Yes Sir," or "Yes Ma'am."

Although James's family genealogy includes African American parents, and African American and Puerto Rican grandparents, he has been exposed to mostly African American family traditions. James and his family members were mostly dark-skinned. He has been teased about his complexion.

Spirituality. James's family attended Baptist churches over his lifetime. They had attended church on Sundays for months at a time, but will sometimes stop attending when life stressors increase. James had participated in the youth choir. Although James's grandmother wanted him to be baptized in the church she attended before the family moved to the DMV area, James's mother wanted to wait until he was older and better able to understand the religious meaning behind the baptism. She wanted to find a new home church in her area and then have him baptized.

James grew up in a family that often prayed, attended church, and expected "Christian-like behavior." A prayer was said before meals and at night before getting into bed. His mother and grandmother used phrases such as "God don't like ugly" to chastise him when he was being mean, and "Don't be hateful, be grateful," when he showed frustration about not getting something he wanted.

Prevention Methods

As discussed in chapters 2 and 4 respectively, addressing child maltreatment involves understanding the types of abuse and neglect that can occur, and utilizing various prevention methods to reduce and/or eliminate maltreatment. There are various forms of child maltreatment—including physical, sexual, psychological abuse, and neglect—and subtypes of maltreatment such as shaken baby syndrome, factitious disorder imposed on another, and substance abuse during pregnancy. In terms of the types of maltreatment that can occur, James experienced sexual abuse, but there are no other reported forms of maltreatment that have been reported.

It is worth considering what prevention methods James was exposed to. As discussed in chapter 4, prevention services are organized into primary, secondary, and tertiary programs, with each tier having different target audiences. Given that primary prevention services are provided to the general population, it is likely that James and his parents previously received some form of prevention about abuse. In other words, it is likely that they have seen or heard of at least one or even more commercials and advertising campaigns about child abuse and neglect. Notably, James's elementary school in Georgia provided a curriculum that discussed safe and unsafe touch, and appropriate social behavior that included respecting other people and their personhood. Such a curriculum would be considered a primary prevention service. As noted in chapter 4, exposure to prevention curriculums provide students and families with a better understanding of the language that can be used to describe touching behavior and help them to understand that they have some degree of control over their body, even at a young age. Such curriculums can also help model for students how adults can help when unsafe touching has occurred, by reinforcing that the student can talk to an adult and the adult will seek to be helpful.

It is not known whether James was exposed to secondary prevention services, which are designed for children and families that are at risk of child maltreatment. However, the services received from CPS are considered tertiary prevention, as these services were provided to reduce and/or eliminate the recurrence of maltreatment. Specifically, the therapy James and his family received included guidance on how to reduce James engaging in inappropriate behaviors.

The behavioral guidance that adults give to children helps to shape the child's understanding of what constitutes appropriate behavior and can contribute to child abuse prevention. Although it is not specifically known what prevention methods were employed within James's family, it is reasonable to expect that James was given some parental guidance on how to be respectful of others, and around what constitutes appropriate behavior. Such behavior guidance is important for a child to receive so that they can conduct themselves in an appropriate manner, but also for the child to recognize when others are engaging in appropriate or inappropriate behavior. Additionally, it is reasonable to presume that, throughout his schooling, James's teachers have provided some guidance regarding appropriate behavior.

Other Relevant Factors

James and his family have had fortunes and challenges through the years. James's mother lost her job when James was two years old. She was out of work for two months and then under-employed for another three months. During that time, they lost their apartment and moved in with his maternal grandmother. When James was four years old, his mother began dating a man, and they cohabitated within about six months. Her boyfriend had two teenage sons also living in his home. When the relationship ended, James, his mother, and his sister moved back with his grandmother. Shortly after, they moved to the DMV.

The employment changes James's mother experienced greatly impacted the financial standing of the family. She received monthly child support contributions from James's father and financial support from his grandparents, all of which helped with their financial standing. The socioeconomic status of James's family is relevant when considering their quality of life and access to resources. Factors such as educational status, employment and income greatly influence socioeconomic status. Both James's parents have undergraduate college degrees. Regarding income, as noted above, James's mother has had challenges with consistent employment that have negatively impacted the family's financial stability, despite financial contributions from James's father and grandparents.

Child Welfare Case

During James's fourth grade school year, he was involved in an incident that caused concern when brought to his teacher's attention. A student in James's class went to the teacher at the end of class and stated that he did not want to go to the bathroom with James. His teacher had a bathroom policy where two students could go to the bathroom at a time. When the student was questioned, he said that he did not like James anymore. When the teacher asked if anything happened, he shook his head vigorously, indicating 'no.' Upon further questioning, he stated that he saw James with another student peeing on a wall. The teacher contacted the parents of James and the other student to report what she heard.

When James got home that day, his mother asked him what happened and let him know that he would not be in trouble no matter what, but that she was worried that something was wrong. After several questions, James said that he and the other student, who is two years younger, were joking around and they decided to see how high on a bathroom wall they could get their stream of urine to land. When the other student performed poorly, James inappropriately touched the student's private parts to aim the urine stream differently. He said the other student became angry and ran out of the bathroom.

James's mother contacted his teacher to discuss what she learned. The teacher then informed the school principal and school counselor, and the decision was made to contact CPS. Additionally, the other student's parents were contacted and informed about what occurred. When the other student's parents inquired further with their son, he explained that the way James grabbed at his private part was "weird" and made him feel uncomfortable. The student became upset and pulled away. The student also said that he and James had played this game before. This student's parents expressed concern about the traumatizing nature of what had occurred.

The CPS investigation led to a substantiated case of child sexual abuse. Further details were learned during the investigation. Specifically, it was revealed that the behavior James exhibited had been done to him on one occasion. The incident occurred when James had to urinate behind a convenience store. He said that a teenage boy, who he did not know, caught him stealing candy and instead of turning him in to the convenience store owner, he said that they could play a game, which involved grabbing private parts to aim urine streams.

Adding to the complexity of this situation, the student who was abused told several peers that "James is a pervert and that they should watch out for him." James's social experiences at school quickly became problematic. He got into two fights with peers after they made comments to him about being a pervert. After a month of social issues, James's mother transferred him to another school so that he could have a fresh start and so that the stigma of his behavior would not cause him further social issues. At the new school, James felt self-conscious. His usual confidence was shaken, and he was more withdrawn. James's mother experienced a strong sense of guilt since she was not aware of what happened to James before this incident came to light. She also felt guilt when she later discovered that James was sexually abused after sneaking out of the home on one of the occasions when he and his sister were left alone for a few hours. James's mother worried that she did not do enough to protect him and worried about the impact the abuse could have on him in the future. She did not feel comfortable asking him questions about any of the things that worried her.

Interventions

James and his family have been provided several intervention services occurring both in home and in treatment centers. More specifically, he received individual counseling subsequent to the child protective case being substantiated. In-home services have been provided over a three-month period, including several home visits by his CPS caseworker. Additionally, his family has had family therapy sessions. His mother attended individual therapy, which included a treatment focused on positive parenting strategies that she has tried to implement. She has expressed feeling guilty that she did not protect James from what happened to him and that she did not know that the incident had occurred.

James's mother made efforts to address the issues that served as interventions. Her decision to transfer James to another school was a means of improving his social experience in school. The negative impact of the stigma and social outcasting that James experienced was taking a toll on him. Transferring to a new school was an opportunity for James to continue his social and academic efforts in a more conducive setting. James's parents have been discussing the possibility of him spending more time, potentially whole summer breaks, with his father. This change in location could create an opportunity for a different household environment and to nurture his relationship with his father. Additionally, spending more time with his father would allow him to have more access to his paternal family as social supports.

James's sister expressed frustration that such a big issue has been made about stuff that "boys do." Her frustration has been discussed in family therapy sessions. Moreover, family therapy has been an opportunity for James, his sister, and mother to build their communication skills with each other and improve the parent-child and sibling dynamics.

Reflections and Considerations

The case of James is multidimensional with many factors to be considered in order to better understand the impact of this abuse, the intersectionality of race, class, and maltreatment, and potential future outcomes. James, like many young Black children, experienced maltreatment and has become involved in the child welfare system. He was able to remain in his home and receive therapeutic interventions to address the abuse he suffered and the subsequent impact of that maltreatment. Additionally, his family also received interventions subsequent to the abuse being discovered, as they too were impacted by the maltreatment. Hopefully, the services received by James and his family helped to reduce or eliminate the likelihood of maltreatment reoccurring.

What else is there to be addressed? As discussed in all previous chapters, the intersection between race, class, and child welfare system involvement has revealed worse outcomes for Black children. In particular, more Black children end up in the child welfare system than any other racial group, and experience longer stays in out-of-home placements. Given this disparity, the details of a maltreatment case involving a Black child warrant a closer look with a question in mind: Was a culturally sensitive lens used at every step of the child welfare process from substantiation of maltreatment to provision of services?

Although all the details involved in James's child welfare case are not known, the information that was provided can be examined through a cultural lens. It is likely that the sexualized behavior that James engaged in with a younger peer, which was revealed to have occurred on more than one occasion, caused a child welfare investigation to be initiated. But how was it determined that this behavior constituted sexual abuse? It is worth considering to what extent was James's race a factor. If James were a White child, might his behavior have been seen in a different, less pathologized light? Determining when experimental sexual behavior of a child becomes abuse is not clearly defined. Additionally, as noted in chapter 4, some aspects of child-to-child sexual abuse remain imprecise. For example, the age difference that constitutes abuse was initially considered to be a two to five-year age difference, but there have since been substantiated cases of sexual abuse between children with a smaller age difference (Collin-Vézina et al., 2013; Mathews & Collin-Vézina, 2019). Additionally, the definition of sexual abuse—any sexual activity perpetrated against a minor by threat, force, intimidation, or manipulation—does not clearly differentiate abuse from normal sexual play and exploration (Collin-Vézina et al., 2013; Mathews & Collin-Vézina, 2019). These unclear aspects of what constitutes child-to-child sexual abuse leaves a great deal of latitude for child welfare caseworkers to determine when such abuse has occurred. These considerations are important to better understand how race impacts how behavior is interpreted, and the question lingers . . . would James's behavior have been seen as abuse or experimentation if he were a White child?

Another question to be pondered is would the intervention services received have been different if James were White? To this end, if race may have affected the decision-making to substantiate a child maltreatment case, then it may also impact all related decision-making, such as interventions deemed necessary, and even the length of time that the child protective case remains open. How are these questions posed and answered in the child welfare process? As discussed in chapter 6, advocacy for child welfare reform is key to ensuring that a culturally attuned lens is used throughout the child welfare system.

In addition to race, the age difference between James and his peer is important to consider. Child development at age seven differs from at age nine. Because James was older than his peer, there is a greater potential for him to control, force, or manipulate this younger peer. Although it is not confirmed in this case, the child that James engaged in sexual behavior with was likely also identified and received intervention services.

Strengths and Protective Factors

This family has many strengths that are notable and can be considered as a protective factor in their recovery from the abuse that occurred. For example, once James's mother was aware that abuse had occurred, she responded to his needs and took actions to provide care and support. She initiated transferring James out of the school where he was being harassed and socially ostracized. She also engaged in psychotherapy for herself and her children, and in doing so, was willing to take the necessary steps to heal from the trauma of abuse. Additionally, James is being raised in a single-parent household, but both of his parents are actively involved in his life, which affords James the benefit of guidance and support from both parents. In fact, this family has multi-generational engagement given that James's grandparents are actively involved in his life, and therefore the familial support is prominent for this family. Also, of note, spirituality and religion are a part of this family's coping and resilience.

It is worth considering what additional tools could be provided to assist this family. First, helping to develop the language of this family related to child maltreatment could be helpful. For example, it could help to provide resources to James's mother so that she can talk with her children about safe and unsafe touch, and how to be assertive and responsive to an adult if inappropriate behavior has occurred. Even if she has already had these conversations, it would be helpful to discuss such issues on an ongoing basis, particularly as her children mature and encounter various life situations.

Second, it could be helpful for James's mother to have ongoing parent-support resources available to her even after the CPS case is closed. As discussed in chapters 4 and 5, providing support for mothers helps to bolster the strength of the family and adds to the protection of the children.

Third, and along the lines of ongoing conversation, it could be helpful for James's parents to discuss the implication of being Black in America in an age-appropriate manner. It could be important to help James understand that his race has implications for how he is seen and how his actions are perceived. Such parental guidance can help him to develop decision-making skills that take race and perception into account. For example, James may learn to make different choices if he understands that he can make the same choice as a White peer, but may be perceived differently, more negatively, because of his race.

Finally, the social implications of James's behavior and the resulting stigma are no small issues. When James's peers learned about his behavior, he was teased and ostracized. This stigma could follow him to into the future as the CPS case is a part of his health record. The question still lingers as to how racial bias contributed to this matter. Interventions that help James understand the social implications of his behavior, and that help build his self-esteem despite being ostracized can help him overcome the stigma of his past behavioral choices.

Closing Summary

When child maltreatment occurs, the child and their family are impacted and the outcomes of the maltreatment can be far-reaching and long lasting. In the case of James, he was a victim of sexual abuse and subsequently engaged in sexualized behaviors with a peer that was considered in the substantiation of a child maltreatment case. As has been noted in chapter 2, there is an association between experiencing and perpetrating abuse, thus James's behavior after being sexually abused is not uncommon. James received prevention services, and once maltreatment was substantiated, he and his family also received intervention services. Providing intervention services when child maltreatment has occurred can be important to mitigate the negative impact of the abuse, and to reduce the potential of abuse reoccurring. Those services should consider a cultural understanding of James and his family. Understanding James's experiences, traditions, and upbringing are important to understanding James, what he needs, and what may work for his family.

In addition to the support that James and his family received, consideration should be given to the impact of the abuse on others. In particular, James's peers likely do not have a full understanding of what occurred or about the nature of child sexual abuse. It may be helpful for a school-wide effort to be developed and implemented to address socially appropriate ways to deal with peers. Notably, the teacher and school counselor who were involved in reporting the child maltreatment may also need support to manage their own reaction to being involved in this case. From a womanist lens, it is important to consider how general sexual attitudes might affect optimal sexual development or lack thereof.

The multi-layered nature of child maltreatment and the actual and potential impact on those directly and indirectly involved warrants several interventions to be employed. In James's case, the maltreatment did not occur in the home and did not warrant removal from the home. In many cases, out-of-home placement becomes another complicating factor in the impact of maltreatment. Ultimately, James's behavior brought to light the abuse he experienced and led to interventions occurring in a timely manner. The hope is that James and all others who have been impacted will receive adequate support to help mitigate potential negative outcomes presently and in the future.

Lastly, James's situation cannot be understood outside of the contextual factors of his life. Many of those have been discussed above, but the impact of his ethnicity, skin color, age, gender, and socioeconomic status cannot be forgotten. Those factors, and many more, influence the way James is perceived by others, including teachers, peers and their parents, child welfare workers, and even the family therapist. These contextual factors influence the type of prevention and intervention services he receives, which can ultimately influence the course and direction of his life. The reader is encouraged to consider the questions that follow in this section to develop a more in-depth understanding of the assessment and management of child maltreatment. In the next chapter, we bring this volume to an end by considering the future of the child welfare system; sharing final insights on Madison, Daniel, Oni, and James; making relevant womanist connections; and providing closing thoughts on this book.

Discussion Questions

CASE DISCUSSION ONE: DEVELOPMENT AND EDUCATION

1. Educational performance can have an impact on a child's development. What learning challenges might James face given his academic strengths and weaknesses?
2. In what ways can his parents and teachers assist and support him with learning?
3. James's mother admitted that she had difficulty managing her own frustration when James becomes frustrated. What suggestions might be helpful to his mother to manage her emotions?

CASE DISCUSSION TWO: SOCIAL DEVELOPMENT

1. In what ways can James be taught more social awareness regarding communication boundaries?
2. In terms of prevention methods, how might social awareness relate to preventing child maltreatment?
3. Should social awareness training be included in prevention programs? Why or why not?

CASE DISCUSSION THREE: FAMILY BACKGROUND

1. As noted in chapter 2, intimate partner violence is associated with child abuse and neglect. What potential impact might witnessing such intimate partner violence have on James?
2. How might discussion about physical discipline be broached with James's parents, in a manner that respects cultural differences and also attends to James's safety?
3. As a means of solidifying the support James receives, what resources would be helpful for his mother to receive given her role as his primary caregiver?
4. What evidence of extended family kinship do you see in James's network?

CASE DISCUSSION FOUR: ETHNOCULTURAL BACKGROUND

1. Why might understanding James's cultural upbringing and family traditions be important for your understanding of his experiences?

2 What strengths do you see in James's family experiences? How might those strengths be used in advocating for him and supporting the family?
3 What may have prevented James's family from adopting the Puerto Rican culture or being multicultural?
4 How might understanding the social implications of skin color in the Black community help with understanding James's experiences?
5 As you reflect on your own socio-cultural background, in what ways might your identity facilitate and/or impede work with this family?

CASE DISCUSSION FIVE: SPIRITUALITY

1 As discussed in chapter 5, religion and spirituality can play a key role in the Black community and Black families. How can the religious and spiritual beliefs of James's family be considered when providing interventions and support to them?
2 What questions can be asked of James and his mother to better understand their spiritual beliefs?
3 How might similarities and differences in the spiritual beliefs of a treatment provider and client impact the services provided?

CASE DISCUSSION SIX: PREVENTION

1 As noted in chapter 4, there are various prevention methods that are associated with reduced child maltreatment. What additional primary prevention methods would be helpful for James to receive?
2 What are some secondary prevention methods that can help to reduce the risk of abuse reoccurring?
3 How might James's awareness of what constitutes child abuse and neglect be determined?

CASE DISCUSSION SEVEN: OTHER RELEVANT FACTORS

1 Should this case have been substantiated as sexual abuse? Why or why not?
2 How might James's parents be encouraged and supported in helping James through the sexual behavior he was exposed to and that he subsequently engaged in?

3 What concerns might there be about the potential of James continuing to engage in sexualized behaviors?
4 What issues should be brought to the attention of a child welfare worker?
5 Where might James's family generally benefit from supportive services? What type of interventions could be helpful?

CASE DISCUSSION EIGHT: INTERVENTIONS

1 How might this situation have been approached differently if James were not Black?
2 What are your thoughts about James's sister's response?
3 What ethnicity do you picture James's younger peer to be?
4 What could be the influence of James and his peer being of different ethnicities?

8

Conclusion

What the Future Should Hold

> Not everything that is faced can be changed; but nothing can be changed until it is faced.
> —James Baldwin, author, playwright, activist

Overview

This chapter summarizes what has been discussed in this book and focuses on what the future should include to ensure the protection of Black children and the reform of the child welfare system. Final thoughts on the cases of Madison, Daniel, Oni, and James are provided, highlighting the ways the child welfare system needs continued monitoring and redress. The potential for the Me Too and Black Lives Matter Movements to address child maltreatment is discussed. Future directions for reducing and eliminating child maltreatment are explored. Finally, the future direction of child protection is reviewed from a global standpoint, including international trends in child protection laws and policies.

Looking across the Chapters

Significant strides have been made in the United States to address child maltreatment comprehensively. There are prevention programs and interventions available for victims of maltreatment, at the national, state, and local levels. Efforts have also been made to identify perpetrators of abuse and reduce their recidivism. However, there is a clear need to consider a family's culture, dynamics, history, and traditions to understand their overall family system and effectively address any occurrences of child maltreatment. Within Black families, the needs of women are essential to prioritize, given their key role as the primary caretakers of Black children. It is also important to understand the complexities of extended kinship networks and others who might be considered as a part of the family. The disproportionate presence of Black children in the child welfare system has a particularly negative impact on the child, the family, and the community as a whole. Prevention that provides targeted information about child maltreatment is helpful, but focusing on the health and wellness of Black children, mothers, and families can address their needs in a more targeted manner. It can also help to promote optimal functioning in the larger Black community. By using advocacy to bolster the voice, power, health, and needs of the Black community, the maltreatment of Black children can be addressed and eventually obviated.

Final Thoughts on Madison, Daniel, Oni, and James

The maltreatment of any child is one child too many. The impact of abuse and neglect can have far-reaching negative effects on the child and their family. Four children—Madison, Daniel, Oni, and James—were discussed throughout this book. Their cases provided an informative view into the effects of child maltreatment, including the benefits and flaws of the child welfare system. In each of these cases, there were events that triggered a report of suspected child maltreatment and a subsequent response from a child welfare agency. Each child and their families received interventions. And while only one of these four children was removed from their home and sent to an out-of-home placement, we know that the statistics of Black children who are removed from their homes are far greater and disproportionate than that.

Each of these cases provided insights about the process involved when child maltreatment is suspected, ranging from the indicators of suspected abuse to the interventions provided once maltreatment is substantiated. There were aspects of each case that highlighted areas of the child protection process that need closer attention for improvement. In Madison's case, the daycare staff's delay in reporting the suspicion of maltreatment to Child Protective Services (CPS) could have been problematic. Once a report was made, the CPS investigation did not substantiate child abuse, but what would the reporting delay have meant if Madison were being abused? She could have been exposed to further abuse if it were occurring. The delay that occurred in this case demonstrated that mandated reporting requirements are subject to individual discretion and may not optimally address child maltreatment. Additionally, how many professionals tasked with mandated reporting fail to make the report despite their suspicion? What does this mean for potentially maltreated children? Madison's case is an example of why continued monitoring and evaluation are necessary for all stages and policies related to child maltreatment, so that problem areas can be identified and remedied.

Across all cases, there was a social impact on the children and their families. James experienced teasing and harassment from peers, which led to his mother deciding to remove him from his school as a protective measure. Daniel's family dynamics were impacted, as was evident through the strained relationship with his father. Oni had evident and problematic social consequences, as she struggled with being separated from her aunt and siblings, and also developed distrust of others. Such separation likely exacerbated feelings of grief and loss that she experienced from the sudden death of her parents. Additionally, Oni's case brought attention to the dangers that can be faced by children in the child welfare system. She experienced sexual abuse while in foster care, which added to the challenges and distress she was already facing. Protecting children by having safeguards in the foster care system that prevent re-exposure to maltreatment is essential.

It is not known what exposure each child had to prevention efforts, but they would have potentially benefited from prevention programming and services. Prevention services such as in-school safe touch/unsafe touch programs could help children learn autonomy, find their voice, and become more familiar with the power they can access, even at their young ages. Additionally, national, state, and local efforts to have primary, secondary, and tertiary prevention programs and services in place are important measures to address maltreatment before it happens as well as after it occurs.

The experiences of James allowed a full circle view of how the victim can become the perpetrator. Given that many perpetrators have a history of experiencing maltreatment themselves, it is not surprising that James's behavior was influenced by the abuse he experienced. It is nonetheless heartbreaking and dismaying to see abused individuals carry on the cycle of abuse. His behavior cannot be adequately addressed without addressing the abuse he experienced. Although the details of the interventions he received are not fully known, it is hoped that helping him heal from the sexual abuse he faced would be a key component to helping him make healthier behavioral choices with his peers. James's history of abuse draws attention to the significant role that a CPS investigation can have in gathering relevant facts and data to assess whether maltreatment occurred. Such agencies also help to determine the needs of the child for intervention and support.

Looking to the Future

As highlighted in chapter 6, advocacy has an important role to play in helping to reduce and eliminate child maltreatment. Historically, social justice movements have provided a powerful advocacy platform to bring light to and affect change for particular groups and causes. Taking a closer look at the movements that have been in the recent spotlight may allow for identifying opportunities for child welfare efforts to be linked to these effective and powerful platforms.

Social Justice Movements

Social justice movements have always necessitated that citizens and lawmakers attend to the issues of people who are marginalized and disadvantaged; Black Lives Matter (BLM) and Me Too movements are two examples of current social justice movements. While these movements are primarily focused on Black rights and sexual harassment, respectively, they are also aligned with womanist tenets, promoting the larger need for all people to have equal access to our most basic human rights. These movements help ensure that the weight of injustices is appropriately seen as broader issues affecting everyone, rather than an issue affecting only those who are victims at a particular moment. As highlighted by the human rights activist, Dr. Martin Luther King, "Injustice anywhere is a threat to justice everywhere. We are caught in an inescapable network of mutuality, tied in a single garment of destiny. Whatever affects one directly, affects all indirectly."

These social justice movements, along with increased media attention, have highlighted the abuses and oppression Black people continue to face in the U.S. In some instances, this media attention has included specific cases where Black children have faced abuse, sometimes fatal, at the hands of people in power (e.g., police officers). As mentioned in chapter 6, one highly publicized case involved the death of a twelve-year-old Black boy in Cleveland, Ohio, named Tamir Rice. He was gunned down by police while he played with a toy gun, alone, in his local park. It was notable that the police shot Tamir within seconds of arriving on the scene (Department of Justice, 2020). The public outcry surrounding his death reverberated from a cross-section of American people, amplifying the importance of widespread citizen involvement in seeking justice and addressing abuse, in this case of a young Black child. Having a media-driven window into the unfair treatment of children can promote awareness of child maltreatment.

The Me Too movement with its focus on the sexual abuse of women and holding men accountable for their abuse of power over women has created a powerful momentum for paternalistic societal patterns to be examined and redefined to promote equal distribution of power (Lee, 2018). As discussed across the chapters of this book, empowering women, who are often the primary caregivers of children, also empowers and protects children. The Me Too movement has primarily brought to light sexual abuse and sexually inappropriate actions against women, which builds toward a culture where disenfranchised groups can be empowered. And where women are strengthened, so are children.

The BLM movement, with its focus on police brutality on Black people, has shed light on the need for citizens of every race to have a stake in addressing the plight of Black people (Hargons et al., 2017). Having a movement that primarily advocates for Black people can become a powerful force in advocating for Black children and their families. The child welfare system, over-saturated with Black children, is a glaring problem that not only impacts Black children but also impacts the families from which they are removed, and the families they will create as they become adults. The needs of Black children necessitate specific, tailored, and ongoing efforts in order to address and eliminate the disparities they face and change the course on the generational strongholds that disadvantage these families. Properly caring for Black children means creating laws and policies specific to Black children, and ongoing efforts to ensure that professionals providing services to Black children have an awareness of their implicit biases, as was discussed in detail in chapter 6 through highlighting the article that proposed an African-American Child Welfare Act. Monitoring of the effectiveness of remediating efforts will also be key to reducing the disparities Black children face and protecting them from maltreatment.

The Power of Feminism in the Charge to End Child Maltreatment

Promoting and establishing equality underpins feminism, womanism, and most other social justice movements. It has been historically evident that equal rights and fair treatment benefit more than the particular individuals or groups who are being advocated for. We all benefit from a society that is free of oppression. In this regard, it is important to continue to ensure that women and children are given the support and resources needed as a key component to preempting and eliminating child maltreatment. There must be multi-layered, concerted efforts to address the needs of children and those who care for children. Too often, the intervention (e.g., solutions to problem) becomes the focus of attention instead of the prevention effort (e.g., what might stop the problem from occurring). To this end, prevention efforts need to be a primary aspect of eliminating child maltreatment. Through a womanist lens, there needs to be an awareness that equal access to power and autonomy is not inherently available to everyone. Therefore, reducing and eliminating child maltreatment requires efforts to protect children and to see them as inherently deserving of access to autonomy and power.

The Next Frontier in Child Welfare

Law and policy have a vital role in continuing the charge to eliminate child maltreatment. It is important to advocate for laws that specifically address the needs and disparities facing Black children. There is inadequate data on whether Black children and families are sufficiently receiving services needed to address the disparities they face; thus, building the available data for such information will inform policy decision-making. Given the disproportionate number of Black children in the child welfare system, it would be important to track, with more specificity, if Black families are receiving the services and support needed to reduce incidents of child maltreatment.

Providing culturally congruent resources to families can also be an effective way to decrease the need to remove children, and to increase the likelihood that they can remain in the home with their family, or in another home with extended family. When children are moved from their home, there should be more stringent oversight of their placements to reduce the risk of them being re-abused while in the welfare system. Efforts need to be made to maintain the integrity of Black families and reduce the unnecessary removal of Black children from their homes.

There is also a need for adequate data about the efficacy of sexual offender programs in reducing and eliminating child maltreatment. Such data will help determine how to improve the efficacy of offender treatment. More robust efficacy data would allow for more strategic building of programs and help with determining how to allocate funding. Additionally, creating policies at agency levels that promote having the child's voice be a part of the decision-making process is important. Furthermore, it is important to ensure that efforts are made to address racial-bias at all levels. This can be accomplished through formal assessments of the biases care providers may have, and by reviewing the decision-making that affects the care and home placement of Black children. Moreover, other efforts are being made across various agencies and levels of society to address inequities which Black people and children stand to benefit from. Agencies such as the National Institutes of Health (NIH) are implementing and promoting the use of frameworks that help to reduce structural racism (National Institutes of Health [NIH], 2021). Public outcry for reform of institutions, most prominently the police force, has brought attention to strategies that could be viable such as defunding the police, and civilianization; that is, hiring more civilians to take on roles and duties in the police department (Blau, 2020). Through sharing power and raising consciousness, these measures hold promise as possible solutions to unequal treatment based on race, which can extend to addressing the maltreatment of Black children.

The means available for communicating and spreading awareness are now expansive, given the current technological age. It is important to embrace the various forms of available communication. Using communication and messages that appeal to all ages and reach all corners of a community and country can offer a bolstered buffer against child maltreatment. Use of technology for advocacy, activism, and continued learning as well as partnering across professions (e.g., medicine/pediatricians, mental health, clergy, community leaders) can create coordinated and comprehensive care for all children, and in particular, Black children.

Finally, we would be remiss if we did not consider the role of research in informing our prevention and intervention efforts. As noted in chapter 6, French et al. (2020) promote a framework which highlights strategies for fostering radical healing in communities of color. Utilizing the tenets of numerous womanist-informed theories (e.g., liberation psychology), these astute scholars argue that "It is important for psychology researchers to push the boundaries of the discipline in innovative ways by developing creative methodologies that inform and inspire new possibilities" (p. 33). They assert that researchers should engage in scholarly efforts that are guided by social justice principles that inform policies and systems-level change. These efforts must include innovative empirical methodologies and epistemologies that accurately and fully capture the unique needs of Black children, families, and communities as we engage in more feminist-centered research (D'Iganzio & Klein, 2020; French et al., 2020). McDonald (2021) provides guidance on how to share power with the communities we study. The days of using White children as the comparison norm must cease if we are truly committed to freeing our Black communities of oppressive and damaging research practices.

The Global Perspective

Troubling child maltreatment trends do not only exist in the U.S. but can also be seen across the globe. As shown in a study that spanned more than eighty countries, child abuse occurs in most parts of the world, with corporal punishment and sexual abuse being common types of the maltreatment (International Society for the Prevention of Child Abuse & Neglect [ISPCAN], 2018). The World Health Organization (World Health Organization [WHO], 2020) and United Nations Children's Fund (United Nations Children's Fund [UNICEF], 2012) report staggering numbers of child maltreatment with prevalence across all societies. The WHO notes the importance of breaking the generational cycle of abused children growing up to abuse others, and of abused children having compromised mental and physical health. Importantly, both WHO and UNICEF endorse support for parents as an effective prevention method, as well as policy changes as important for interventions.

Again, as highlighted throughout this volume, it is important to examine and address structural issues that contribute to the overrepresentation of certain communities within the child welfare system. For example, Canada has recently started exploring racial disparities in their child welfare system. Specifically, Antwi-Boasiako et al. (2020) examined the incidence data of White and Black families in Ontario, Canada across twenty years from 1993 to 2013 and found disparate representation of Black families in the child welfare system across five distinct cycles. Their analysis revealed that Black families "were generally more likely to be investigated for child maltreatment, to have child maltreatment investigations substantiated, to be transferred to ongoing services, to have a child placed in out-of-home care during the investigation, and to be referred to other services" (p. 8). They conjectured these outcomes were due to several factors, including a reduced social safety net, redefined thresholds for risk of harm, and structural racism within the child welfare system and in broader society.

King et al. (2017) conducted a similar study involving 5,625 children and found comparable results when investigating population and decision-based disparities. Namely, they found Black families were overrepresented in Ontario's child welfare system; however, they asserted that race alone did not seem to play the only role in deciding to substantiate the abuse or move these families into ongoing services. The researchers detected notable trends with Black families that were transferred for ongoing services. Specifically, they observed that older Black children were more likely to be transferred, with females having the highest odds of transfer. Additionally, attachment concerns, involving the quality of relationship between the child and primary caregiver, was associated with much greater odds of being transferred. Finally, financial challenges tripled the odds of being transferred to additional services.

Notably, King et al. (2017) highlighted broader social concerns that may influence the overrepresentation of Black families. For example, they considered the racialization of poverty created and maintained by residential segregation, inept labor practices, and problematic immigration policies. They asserted that these troubling factors contribute to these disparities and compromise the overall well-being of Black families, as they were likely to experience higher levels of unemployment and poverty. Both studies conclude that race matters and collaborative steps involving key stakeholders, like Black families, need to be taken to address the specific relational, familial, and community concerns of the Black community in Canada and promote their well-being.

As highlighted above, the U.S. is not unique in having issues with an uneven distribution of power and oppression of some members of its society. Specifically, the U.S. is also not an anomaly, regarding women and children being oppressed subgroups of society. This country's efforts to address child maltreatment can be informed by what other countries have employed to address problems of maltreatment. For example, Iceland, Switzerland, and Finland rank highest regarding children having guaranteed rights, whereas the instability in countries such as Venezuela has caused concerns about the safety of children within these nations (KidsRights, 2019). Interestingly, when Sweden banned the use of corporal punishment of children in 1983, the country witnessed several positive outcomes, including an anti-spanking sentiment, a decrease in child maltreatment, a lessening of injuries associated with physical assault, and a decline in juvenile violence and delinquency (Gershoff & Bitensky, 2007).

Although each society has specific challenges, there are adequately shared problems to signal that what one country has found helpful may be beneficial in another. Adopting a cross-cultural stance can help policy makers, researchers, and practitioners identify valuable insights and best practices for addressing child maltreatment in the U.S. and promoting child welfare. Additionally, borrowing from tenets of womanism, we can promote the empowerment of women across the world, while simultaneously safeguarding children by promoting their basic human rights and prioritizing their welfare.

Final Thoughts

The charge to ensure that human rights are accessible to all must continue. Advocacy for the respect of individual rights is key to leveling the field so that there is access for all people. From law and policy makers, law enforcement, and agency staff, to each and every citizen, the voice of the oppressed must be amplified, fought on behalf of, and continue to be an area of future research and policy development in order to sustain progress and gains. Children who experience maltreatment do not exist in a bubble. They are a part of the larger society, and they grow up to be adults that bear the scars of that abuse and neglect on their body, mental health, and in their potential as contributing citizens. Black families need support, advocacy, and nurturing to thrive. Such positive treatment should be present despite the ill-effects of the maltreatment in their past, and may be able to prevent maltreatment in the future.

Closing Summary

The U.S. has undoubtedly made progress with addressing child maltreatment over the past century. Additionally, child maltreatment is more readily recognized as a public health issue that needs addressing at all levels of society. More cultural awareness is needed to understand the culture and traditions of Black families in order to address occurrences of child maltreatment in Black communities effectively. The discussion of Madison, Daniel, Oni, and James provided key lessons and salient insights throughout this book about the circumstances and processes involved when a Black child enters the child welfare system and the resulting impact on these children and their families. These cases illustrate what happens to a Black child in the system and emphasized why they need protecting. It is essential that a culturally informed lens that is cognizant of relevant worldviews and implicit biases is used when maintaining the safety and well-being of Black children, so that their unique needs are accounted for and they are afforded the protections received by children from other racial groups. Black children are inherently equal and unequivocally deserving of care and well-being. Societal protections cannot continue to be race or gender biased. Striving toward equal protection is not idealistic. Rather, it is the bare minimum standard by which to treat all citizens of a society.

Recommended Readings and Resources

Adichie, C. N. (2014). We Should All Be Feminists. Anchor Books.

Anyon, Y. (2011). Reducing racial disparities and disproportionalities in the child welfare system: Policy perspectives about how to serve the best interests of African American youth. *Children and Youth Services Review, 33*, 242–253. https://doi.org:10.1016/j.childyouth.2010.01.003.

Attia, M., & Edge, J. (2017) Be(com)ing a reflexive researcher: A developmental approach to research methodology. *Open Review of Educational Research, 4*(1), 33–45. https://doi.org:10.1080/23265507.2017.1300068.

Berrick, J. D., & Hernandez, J. (2016). Developing consistent and transparent kinship care policy and practice: State mandated, mediated, and independent care. *Children and Youth Services Review, 68*, 24–33.

Black Demographics. (2019). *Poverty in Black America*. Black Demographics. https://blackdemographics.com/households/poverty/.

Bonnar-Kidd, K. K. (2010). Sexual offender laws and prevention of sexual violence or recidivism. *American Journal of Public Health, 100*(3), 412–419. https://doi.org/10.2105/AJPH.2008.153254.

Bornstein, M. H. (2012). Cultural approaches to parenting. *Parenting, 12*(2–3), 212–221.

Boyd, R. (2014). African American disproportionality and disparity in child welfare: Toward a comprehensive conceptual framework. *Child and Youth Services Review, 37*, 15–27. https://doi.org/10.1016/j.childyouth.2013.11.013.

Boyd-Franklin, N. (2010). Incorporating spirituality and religion into the treatment of African American clients. *The Counseling Psychologist, 38*(7), 976–1000. https://doi.org/10.1177/0011000010374881.

Boyd-Franklin, N. (2013). *Black families in therapy: Understanding the African American experience*. Guilford Publications.

Browning, S. L., Miller, R. R., & Spruance, L. M. (2018). Criminal incarceration dividing the ties that bind: Black men and their families.

In impacts of incarceration on the African American family (pp. 87–102). Routledge.
Castro, F. G., Barrera, M., & Holleran Steiker, L. K. (2010). Issues and challenges in the design of culturally adapted evidence-based interventions. *Annual Review of Clinical Psychology, 6*, 213–239. https://doi.org/10.1146/annurev-clinpsy-033109-132032.
Center for Advanced Studies in Child Welfare. (2016). Child Welfare Reform. University of Minnesota, School of Social Work. http://www.cascw.org/wp-content/uploads/2016/05/CW360_Spring2016_WEB.pdf.
Chasnoff, I., Barber, G., Brook, J., & Akin, B. (2018). The Child Abuse Prevention and Treatment Act: Knowledge of healthcare and legal professionals. *Child Welfare, 96*(3).
Child Welfare Information Gateway. (2013). *How the child welfare system works*. U.S. Department of Health & Human Services, Children's Bureau. https://www.childwelfare.gov/pubpdfs/cpswork.pdf.
Child Welfare Information Gateway. (2016). *Mandatory reporters of child abuse and neglect*. U.S. Department of Health & Human Services, Children's Bureau. https://www.childwelfare.gov/topics/systemwide/laws-policies/statutes/manda/.
Child Welfare Information Gateway. (2017). *Child maltreatment prevention: Past, present, and future*. U.S. Department of Health & Human Services, Children's Bureau. https://www.childwelfare.gov/pubPDFs/cm_prevention.pdf.
Clark, R., Anderson, N. B., Clark, V. R., & Williams, D. R. (1999). Racism as a stressor for African Americans: A biopsychosocial model. *American Psychologist, 54*(10), 805–816.
Collin-Vézina, D., Daigneault, I., & Hébert, M. (2013). Lessons learned from child sexual abuse research: Prevalence, outcomes, and preventive strategies. *Child and Adolescent Psychiatry and Mental Health, 7*(22). https://doi.org/10.1186/1753-2000-7-22.
Comas-Díaz, L. (2016). Racial trauma recovery: A race-informed therapeutic approach to racial wounds. In A. N. Alvarez, C.T.H. Liang, & H. A. Neville (Eds.), *Cultural, racial, and ethnic psychology book series. The cost of racism for people of color: Contextualizing experiences of discrimination* (pp. 249–272). American Psychological Association.
Cowan, R., Cole, R. F., & Craigen, L. (2019). School-Based child sexual abuse prevention: Implications for professional school counselors. *Professional Counselor, 9*(3), 200–210.
Dixon, J. (2008). The African-American Child Welfare Act: A legal redress for African-American disproportionality in child protection cases. *Berkeley Journal of African-American Law and Policy, 10*(2), 108–145.
French, B. H., Lewis, J. A., Mosley, D. V., Adames, H. Y., Chavez-Duenas, N. Y., Chen, G. A., & Neville, H. A. (2019). Toward a psychological framework of radical healing in communities of color.

The Counseling Psychologist, 48(1), 14–46. https://doi.org/10.1177/0011000019843506.
Gypen, L., Vanderfaeillie, J., De Maeyer, S., Belenger, L., & Van Holen, F. (2017). Outcomes of children who grew up in foster care: Systematic-review. *Children and Youth Services Review, 76*, 74–83.
Kids Center. (2019). *Safe Touch Curriculum*. https://kidscenter.org/safe-touch-curriculum/.
Longley, R. (2020). Womanist: Definition and examples. https://www.thoughtco.com/womanist-feminism-definition-3528993#:~:text=Robert%20Longley,of%20humanity%2C%20male%20and%20female.
Morin, A. (2018, June 3). *When does discipline become child abuse*? Verywell Family.http://www.verywell.com/when-does-discipline-become-child-abuse-1094826.
Nami, S., Carlson, C., O'Hara, K., Nakuti, J., Bukuluki, P., Lwanyaaga, J., Namakula, S., Nanyunja, B., Wainberg, M., Naker, D., Michau, L. (2017). Towards a feminist understanding of intersecting violence against women and children in the family. *Social Science and Medicine, 184*, 40–48.
Patton, S. (2017). Corporal punishment in black communities: Not an intrinsic cultural tradition but racial trauma. *CYF News*. https://www.apa.org/pi/families/resources/newsletter/2017/04/racial-trauma.
Santhosh, K. R. (2016). A Review on the perpetrators of child abuse. *Review of Social Sciences, 1*(3), 45–52. https://www.socialsciencejournal.org/index.php/site/article/view/25/15.
Smith, B. (2012). The case against spanking. *Monitor on Psychology, 43*(4), 60–63. https://www.apa.org/monitor/2012/04/spanking.
U.S. Department of Health & Human Services. (2018). Discipline versus abuse. *Child Welfare Information Gateway*. https://www.childwelfare.gov/topics/can/defining/disc-abuse/#discipline.
Zeng, Z. (2018). *Jail inmates 2016*. U.S. Department of Justice, Office of Justice Programs Bureau of Justice Statistics.

Resources for Child Welfare Staff

Centers for Disease Control and Prevention: Children's Mental Health Research
https://www.cdc.gov/childrensmentalhealth/research.html
Child Abuse Education & Prevention Resources
https://www.childhelp.org/story-resource-center/child-abuse-education-prevention-resources/
Child maltreatment indicators
https://www.childtrends.org/indicators/child-maltreatment
Child Welfare Information Gateway
https://content.govdelivery.com/accounts/USACFCWIG/bulletins/2c3dab4

Child Welfare League of America
https://www.cwla.org/
Committee for Children: Teaching Touching Safety Rules
https://www.cfchildren.org/blog/2017/08/activity-teaching-touching-safety-rules-safe-and-unsafe-touching/
KidsSafe Foundation
https://kidsafefoundation.org/
National Center on Substance Abuse and Child Welfare
https://ncsacw.samhsa.gov/
Violence and Injury Prevention
https://www.who.int/news-room/fact-sheets/detail/injuries-and-violence

Programs for Children

Boys & Girls Clubs of America
https://www.bgca.org/
Brothers Academy
https://brothersacademy.org/?gclid=Cj0KCQjwmIuDBhDXARIsAFITC_6jreT1UVUpJ1KzrXn_87jnvNe-3mJBokYh7yRWq_F_UjAEWgHbJYwaAhZoEALw_wcB
Center for Effective Discipline
https://www.zeroabuseproject.org/
GirlTrek
https://www.girltrek.org/
Head Start
https://www.acf.hhs.gov/ohs
Kids Center
https://www.kidscenter.org/
Leg Up Farm
https://www.legupfarm.org/services
National Black Child Development Institute
https://www.nbcdi.org/
National Mentoring Resource Center: Mentoring for Black Male Youth
https://nationalmentoringresourcecenter.org/resource/mentoring-for-black-male-youth/
100 Black Men
https://www.100bmla.net/
Save the Children
https://www.savethechildren.org/us/what-we-do/us-programs
Zensational Kids
https://zensationalkids.com/

Programs for Black Children and Families

Center for the Improvement of Child Caring
https://www.effectiveblackparenting.com/about-3
Color of Autism Foundation
https://thecolorofautism.org
Community Healing Network
https://communityhealingnet.org/
Mothers of Sexually Abused Children (MOSAC)
https://www.mosac.net/About.aspx
Progressive Life Center
https://progressivelifecenter.org/about-us/ntu/
Strong African American Families Program
https://cfr.uga.edu/saaf-programs/saaf/

Programs for Black Women

Black Career Women's Network
https://bcwnetwork.com/
Black Girl's Smile
https://www.blackgirlssmile.org/
Black Mammas Matter Alliance
https://blackmamasmatter.org/
Black Mother's Breatfeeding Association
http://blackmothersbreastfeeding.org/
Black Women for Wellness
https://www.bwwla.org/
Center for Black Women's Wellness
https://www.cbww.org/
National Black Women's Justice Institute
https://www.nbwji.org/

Sex Offender Resources

Federal Bureau of Prisons: Sex Offender Custody and Care
https://www.bop.gov/inmates/custody_and_care/sex_offenders.jsp
U.S. Department of Justice
https://www.nsopw.gov/

Sex Abuse Resources

National Human Trafficking Hotline
https://humantraffickinghotline.org/
National Sexual Violence Resource Center
https://www.nsvrc.org/

Sex trafficking survivor support
https://stoppingtraffic.org/
Violence Against Children and Youth Surveys
https://www.cdc.gov/violenceprevention/childabuseandneglect/vacs/index.html

References

Abramson, A. (2020, April 8). How COVID-19 may increase domestic violence and child abuse. American Psychological Association: Psychology Topics. https://www.apa.org/topics/covid-19/domestic-violence-child-abuse.

Administration for Children & Families. (2020, January 15). *Child abuse, neglect data released* [Press release]. https://www.acf.hhs.gov/media/press/2020/2020/child-abuse-neglect-data-released.

Adopt.org. (2020, January 15). *Discrimination in the foster care system*. Adoption Center. http://www.adopt.org/content/discrimination-foster-care-system.

African American Health Program. (2022). *About Us*. http://aahpmontgomerycounty.org/.

Agu, J. C., Hee-Jeon, Y., Steel, A., & Adams, J. (2019). A systematic review of traditional, complementary and alternative medicine use amongst ethnic minority populations: A focus upon prevalence, drivers, integrative use, health outcomes, referrals and use of information sources. *Journal of immigrant and minority health, 21*(5), 1137–1156.

Ahrens, K. R., Garrison, M. M., & Courtney, M. E. (2014). Health outcomes in young adults from foster care and economically diverse backgrounds. *Pediatrics, 134*(6), 1067–1074. https://pediatrics.aappublications.org/content/pediatrics/134/6/1067.full.pdf.

Alaggia, R., Collin-Vezina, D., & Lateef, R. (2017). Facilitators and barriers to child sexual abuse (CSA) disclosures: A research update (2000–2016). *Trauma, Violence, & Abuse, 20*(2), 260–283. https://doi.org//10.1177/1524838017697312.

Ali, R. (2018). Postpartum depression in Pakistan: Current state and future direction. *Global Women's Health, 1*(1), 21–27.

Al-Saadoon, M., Elnour, I., & Ganesh, A. (2011). Shaken Baby Syndrome as a form of abusive head trauma. *Sultan Qaboos University Medical Center, 11*(3), 322–327.

American Association of Neurological Surgeons. (2019). *Shaken Baby Syndrome*. https://www.aans.org/Patients/Neurosurgical-Conditions-and-Treatments/Shaken-Baby-Syndrome.

American Civil Liberties Union. (2018, May 22). *ACLU obtains documents showing widespread abuse of child immigrants in US custody*. https://www.aclu.org/news/aclu-obtains-documents-showing-widespread-abuse-child-immigrants-us-custody.

American Diabetes Association. (2019). *Statistics about diabetes*. http://www.diabetes.org/diabetes-basics/statistics/.

American Psychological Association. (2014). *Resilience Booster: Parent Tip Tool*. https://www.apa.org/topics/parenting/resilience-tip-tool.

American Psychological Association. (2017a). *Program Evaluation Results*. https://www.apa.org/act/about/evaluation.

American Psychological Association. (2017b). *Advocacy*. https://www.apa.org/advocacy.

American Psychological Association. (2019). *Resolution on Physical Discipline of Children by Parents*. https://www.apa.org/about/policy/physical-discipline-children.

American Psychological Association. (2019). *World Day for the Prevention of Child Abuse*. https://www.apa.org/pi/prevent-violence/programs/international-day.

Anderson, M., & López, G. (2018, January 24). *Key facts about black immigrants in the U.S.* Pew Research Center. http://www.pewresearch.org/fact-tank/2018/01/24/key-facts-about-black-immigrants-in-the-u-s/.

Antwi-Boasiako, K., King, B., Fallon, B., Trocmé, N., Fluke, J., Chabot, M., & Esposito, T. (2020). Differences and disparities over time: Black and White families investigated by Ontario's child welfare system. *Child Abuse & Neglect*, *107*, 104618. https://doi.org/10.1016/j.chiabu.2020.104618.

Anyon, Y. (2011). Reducing racial disparities and disproportionalities in the child welfare system: Policy perspectives about how to serve the best interests of African American youth. *Children and Youth Services Review*, *33*(2), 242–253. https://doi.org:10.1016/j.childyouth.2010.01.003.

Armstrong, N. (2012). The importance of extended families in the African American community: A qualitative analysis using social learning theory. Proceedings from NCUR 2012: The National Conference on Undergraduate Research.

Associated Press. (2018). *US senators want investigation of immigration abuse allegations*. https://www.voanews.com/a/us-senators-want-investigation-of-immigrant-abuse-allegations/4506992.html.

Association of American Indian Affairs. (2020). *Indian Child Welfare Act*. https://www.indian-affairs.org/indian-child-welfare-act.html.

Avellar, S. A., & Supplee, L. H. (2013). Effectiveness of home visiting in improving child health and reducing child maltreatment. *Pediatrics*, *132* (Supplement 2), S90–99. https://pediatrics.aappublications.org/content/132/Supplement_2/S90.

Banks, D., & Kyckelhahn, T. (2011). *Characteristics of Suspected Human Trafficking Incidents, 2008–2011*. U.S. Department of Justice, Office of Justice Programs Bureau of Justice Statistics. https://www.bjs.gov/content/pub/pdf/cshti0810.pdf.

Barner, J. C., Bohman, T. M., Brown, C. M., & Richards, K. M. (2010). Use of complementary and alternative medicine for treatment among African-Americans: A multivariate analysis. *Research in Social & Administrative Pharmacy, 6*(3), 196–208. https://doi.org/10.1016/j.sapharm.2009.08.001.

Barnert, E. S., Dudovitz, R., Nelson, B. B., Coker, T. R., Biely, C., Li, N., & Chung, P. J. (2017). How does incarcerating young people affect their adult health outcomes? *Pediatrics, 139*(2), 1–9. https://doi.org/10.1542/peds.2016-2624.

Barth, R. P., Landsverk, J., Chamberlain, P., Reid, J. B., Rolls, J. A., Hurlburt, M. S., Farmer, E. M. Z., James, S., McCabe, K. M., & Kohl, P. L. (2005). Parent-training programs in child welfare services: Planning for a more evidence-based approach to serving biological parents. *Research on Social Work Practice, 15*(5), 353–371.

Baumrind, D. (1966). Effects of authoritative control on child behaviour. *Child Development, 37*, 887–907.

Beach, S. R., Kogan, S. M., Brody, G. H., Chen, Y. F., Lei, M. K., & Murry, V. M. (2008). Change in caregiver depression as a function of the Strong African American Families Program. *Journal of Family Psychology, 22*(2), 241–252.

Behnke, M., & Smith, V. (2013). Prenatal substance abuse: Short- and long-term effects on the exposed fetus. *Pediatrics, 131*(3), 1009–1024. https://doi.org:10.1542/peds.2012-3931.

Beltran, V., & St. Germain, L. (2018, September 4). *Mother of missing 2-year-old Largo boy admits to killing her son in 'moment of frustration,' report says*. ABC Action News: WFTS Tampa Bay. https://www.abcactionnews.com/news/region-north-pinellas/largo/charisse-stinson-mother-of-missing-2-year-old-largo-boy-admits-to-killing-son-in-moment-of-frustration-report-says.

Bennett, R. (2019). *California takes a step toward banning spanking!*. Paces Connection. https://www.acesconnection.com/blog/california-takes-a-step-toward-banning-spanking.

Berkel, C., Mauricio, A. M., Schoenfelder, E., & Sandler, I. N. (2011). Putting the pieces together: An integrated model of program implementation. *Prevention Science: The Official Journal of the Society for Prevention Research, 12*(1), 23–33. https://doi.org/10.1007/s11121-010-0186-1.

Bernstein, K. M., Najdowski, C. J., & Wahrer, K. S. (2020, July 1). Racial stereotyping and misdiagnosis of child abuse. *Monitor on Psychology, 51*(5). https://www.apa.org/monitor/2020/07/jn.

Berrick, J. D., & Boyd, R. (2016). Financial well-being in family-based foster care: Exploring variation in income supports for kin and non-kin caregivers in California. *Children and Youth Services Review, 69*, 166–173.

Berrick, J. D., & Hernandez, J. (2016). Developing consistent and transparent kinship care policy and practice: State mandated, mediated, and independent care. *Children and Youth Services Review, 68*, 24–33.

Berry, J. W. (1997). Immigration, acculturation, and adaptation. *Applied Psychology, 46*(1), 5–34.

Berry, J. W. (2003). Conceptual approaches to acculturation. In K. M. Chun, P. B. Organista, & G. Marin (Eds.), *Acculturation: Advances in Theory, Measurement, and Applied Research* (pp. 17–37). American Psychological Association.

Berry, J. W. (2015). Acculturation. In J. E. Grusec & P. D. Hastings (Eds.), *Handbook of Socialization: Theory and Research* (pp. 520–538). The Guilford Press.

Bhandari, S. (2012). Unusual psychiatric syndromes. *Core Psychiatry, 3*, 349–357. https://doi.org/10.1016/B978-0-7020-3397-1.00023-9.

Black Demographics. (2019). *Poverty in Black America*. https://blackdemographics.com/households/poverty/.

Black Women for Wellness. (2022). *Black Women for Wellness: Program*. https://www.bwwla.org/about-us/.

Blacklivesmatter.com. (2020). *About Black Lives Matter*. https://blacklivesmatter.com/about/.

Blau, R. (2020, June 8). *Unions, Pols Push NYPD to put civilians in more desk jobs currently held by cops, as calls to 'defund' police grow louder*. The City. https://www.thecity.nyc/2020/6/8/21284549/defund-police-push-for-civilians-in-nypd-desk-jobs.

Bonnar-Kidd, K. K. (2010). Sexual offender laws and prevention of sexual violence or recidivism. *American Journal of Public Health, 100*(3), 412–419. https://doi.org/10.2105/AJPH.2008.153254.

Bornstein, M. H. (2012). Cultural approaches to parenting. *Parenting, 12*(2-3), 212–221.

Boyd, R. (2014). African American disproportionality and disparity in child welfare: Toward a comprehensive conceptual framework. *Child and Youth Services Review, 37*, 15–27. https://doi.org/10.1016/j.childyouth.2013.11.013.

Boyd-Franklin, N. (2010). Incorporating spirituality and religion into the treatment of African American clients. *The Counseling Psychologist, 38*(7), 976–1000. https://doi.org/10.1177/0011000010374881.

Boyd-Franklin, N. (2013). *Black families in therapy: Understanding the African American experience*. Guilford Publications.

Braveman, P. (2006). Health disparities and health equity: concepts and measurement. *Annu. Rev. Public Health, 27*, 167–194.

Braveman, P., & Gottlieb, L. (2014). The social determinants of health: It's time to consider the causes of the causes. *Public Health Report, 129*(2), 19–31. https://doi.org/10.1177/00333549141291S206.

Brewer-Smyth, K., & Koenig, H. G. (2014). Could spirituality and religion promote stress resilience in survivors of childhood trauma?. *Issues in*

Mental Health Nursing, *35*(4), 251–256. https://doi.org/10.3109/01612840.2013.873101.

Brinkley-Rubinstein, L. (2013). Incarceration as a catalyst for worsening health. *Health Justice*, *1*(3), 1–17. https://doi.org/10.1186/2194-7899-1-3.

Brody, G. H., Chen, Y. F., Kogan, S. M., Murry, V. M., & Brown, A. C. (2010). Long-term effects of the strong African American families program on youths' alcohol use. *Journal of Consulting and Clinical Psychology*, *78*(2), 281–285.

Brody, G. H., Murry, V. M., Gerrard, M., Gibbons, F. X., Molgaard, V., McNair, L., Brown, A. C., Willis, T. A., Spoth, R. L., Lou, Z., Chen, Y. F., & Neubaum-Carlan, E. (2004). The strong African American families program: Translating research into prevention programming. *Child Development*, *75*(3), 900–917. https://doi.org/10.1111/j.1467-8624.2004.00713.x.

Brooks, F., Michaelson, V., King, N., Inchley, J., & Pickett, W. (2018). Spirituality as a protective health asset for young people: An international comparative analysis from three countries. *International Journal of Public Health*, *63*(3), 387–395. https://doi.org/10.1007/s00038-017-1070-6.

Brown, S. (2019, February 24). *Epidemic of missing Black girls continues to stump authorities, frustrate parents*. Black Press USA. https://www.blackpressusa.com/epidemic-of-missing-black-girls-continues-to-stump-authorities-frustrate-parents/.

Browning, S. L., Miller, R. R., & Spruance, L. M. (2001). Criminal incarceration dividing the ties that bind: Black men and their families. In R. R. Miller (Ed.), *Impacts of Incarceration on the African American Family* (pp. 87–102). Routledge.

Bryant, L. O. (2014). Partnerships and collaborations in promoting health and wellness in minority communities: Lessons learned and future directions. *Literacy and Health Disparities*, *142*, 91–95. https://www.researchgate.net/profile/Esther_Prins/publication/264772944_Literacy_and_Health_Disparities/links/5a724c7145851551207 5e44c/Literacy-and-Health-Disparities.pdf#page=21.

Bryant-Davis, T., Miteria Austria, A., Kawahara, D. M., & Willis, D. J. (Eds.). (2014). *Religion and spirituality for diverse women: Foundations of strength and resilience*. Praeger.

Burley, M., & Halpern, M. (2001). *Educational attainment of foster youth: Achievement and graduation outcomes for children in state care*. Washington State Institute for Public Policy. https://files.eric.ed.gov/fulltext/ED460220.pdf.

Burns, K., Stein Helland, H., Kriz, K., Sanchez-Cabezudo, S., Skivenes, M. & Strompl, J. (2021). Corporal punishment and reporting to child protection authorities: An empirical study of population attitudes in five countries. *Child and Youth Services Review*, *120*. https://doi.org/10.1016/j.childyouth.2020.105749.

Bustnay, T. G. (2020). Group intervention with parents of juvenile sex offenders. *Journal of child sexual abuse, 29*(3), 278–294.
California Evidence-Based Clearinghouse for Child Welfare. (2019). *Child First program description*. https://www.cebc4cw.org/program/child-first/.
Campinha-Bacote, J. (2002). The process of cultural competence in the delivery of healthcare services: A model of care. *Journal of Transcultural Nursing, 13*(3), 181–184.
Campos-Gil, J. A., Ortega-Andeane, P., & Vargas, D. (2020). Children's microsystems and their relationships to stress and executive functioning. *Frontiers in Psychology, 11*, 1–11. https://doi.org/10.3389/fpsyg.2020.00996.
Carolan, M. T., Bagherinia, G., Juhari, R., Himelright, J., & Mouton-Sanders, M. (2000). Contemporary Muslim families: Research and practice. *Contemporary Family Therapy, 22*(1), 67–79.
Carson, E. A. (2018). *Prisoners in 2016*. U.S. Department of Justice, Office of Justice Programs, Bureau of Justice Statistics, NCJ, 247282, 2.
Carson, E. A. (2020). *Prisoners in 2018*. U.S. Department of Justice, Office of Justice Programs, Bureau of Justice Statistics, NCJ, 253516. https://bjs.ojp.gov/content/pub/pdf/p18.pdf.
Casillas, K. L., Fauchier, A., Derkash, B. T., & Garrido, E. F. (2016). Implementation of evidence-based home visiting programs aimed at reducing child maltreatment: A meta-analytic review. *Child Abuse & Neglect, 53*, 64–80.
Castro, F. G., Barrera, M., & Holleran Steiker, L. K. (2010). Issues and Challenges in the design of culturally adapted evidence-based interventions. *Annual Review of Clinical Psychology, 6*, 213–239. https://doi.org/10.1146/annurev-clinpsy-033109-132032.
Center for Advanced Studies in Child Welfare. (2016). *Child Welfare Reform*. University of Minnesota, School of Social Work. http://www.cascw.org/wp-content/uploads/2016/05/CW360_Spring2016_WEB.pdf.
Center for African American Health. (2020). *Programs and Services*. https://caahealth.org/programs-and-services/.
Center for Black Women Wellness. (2022). *CBWW Programs*. https://www.cbww.org/programs/.
Center for Family Research. (2010). *Strong African Americans program*. University of Georgia. https://cfr.uga.edu/saaf-programs/saaf/.
Centers for Disease Control and Prevention. (2018). *HIV and African Americans*. https://www.cdc.gov/hiv/pdf/group/racialethnic/african americans/cdc-hiv-africanamericans.pdf.
Centers for Disease Control and Prevention. (2020a). *CDC COVID data tracker*. https://covid.cdc.gov/covid-data-tracker/#cases_casesper100klast7days.
Centers for Disease Control and Prevention. (2020b, July 24). *Health equity considerations and racial and ethnic minority groups*. https://www.cdc.gov/coronavirus/2019-ncov/community/health-equity/race-ethnicity.html.
Centers for Disease Control and Prevention. (2021). *Racism is a serious threat to the public's health*. https://www.cdc.gov/healthequity/racism-disparities/index.html.

Chasnoff, I., Barber, G., Brook, J., & Akin, B. (2018). The child abuse prevention and treatment act: Knowledge of healthcare and legal professionals. *Child Welfare, 96*(3), 41–58.
Chatterjee, R., & Davis, R. (2018). *Beyond opioids: How a family came together to stay together.* NPR. https://www.npr.org/sections/healthshots/2018/06/19/619243268/an-alternative-to-foster-care-for-babies-born-to-opioid-addicted-moms.
Child and Family Services Reviews. (2018). *Child and Family Services Reviews Information Portal.* https://training.cfsrportal.acf.hhs.gov/section-2-understanding-child-welfare-system/2992.
Child Trends. (2018). *Racial and Ethnic Composition of the Child Population.* https://www.childtrends.org/indicators/racial-and-ethnic-composition-of-the-child-population.
Child Trends. (2019). *Foster Care.* https://www.childtrends.org/indicators/foster-care.
Child Welfare Information Gateway. (2013). *How the Child Welfare System Works.* U.S. Department of Health & Human Services, Children's Bureau. https://www.childwelfare.gov/pubpdfs/cpswork.pdf.
Child Welfare Information Gateway. (2016a). *Mandatory reporters of child abuse and neglect.* U.S. Department of Health & Human Services, Children's Bureau. https://www.childwelfare.gov/topics/systemwide/laws-policies/statutes/manda/.
Child Welfare Information Gateway. (2016b). *Racial disproportionality and disparity in child welfare.* U.S. Department of Health & Human Services, Children's Bureau. https://www.childwelfare.gov/pubPDFs/racial_disproportionality.pdf.
Child Welfare Information Gateway. (2017a). Child maltreatment prevention: Past, present, and future. US Department of Health & Human Services, Children's Bureau. https://www.childwelfare.gov/pubPDFs/cm_prevention.pdf.
Child Welfare Information Gateway. (2017b). *Grounds for involuntary termination of parental rights.* U.S. Department of Health & Human Services, Children's Bureau.
Child Welfare Information Gateway. (2018). *Child abuse and neglect fatalities 2016: Statistics and interventions.* U.S. Department of Health & Human Services, Children's Bureau. https://www.childwelfare.gov/pubPDFs/fatality.pdf.
Child Welfare Information Gateway. (2019a). *What is child abuse and neglect? Recognizing the signs and symptoms. Factsheet, April 2019.* U.S. Department of Health & Human Services, Children's Bureau. https://www.childwelfare.gov/pubpdfs/whatiscan.pdf.
Child Welfare Information Gateway. (2019b). *About CAPTA: A legislative history.* U.S. Department of Health & Human Services, Children's Bureau. https://www.childwelfare.gov/pubPDFs/about.pdf.
Child Welfare Information Gateway. (2019c). *Major federal legislation concerned with child protection, child welfare, and adoption.* U.S.

Department of Health & Human Services, Children's Bureau. https://www.childwelfare.gov/pubPDFs/majorfedlegis.pdf.

Child Welfare Information Gateway. (2020). *Foster care statistics 2018*. U.S. Department of Health & Human Services, Children's Bureau. https://www.childwelfare.gov/pubPDFs/foster.pdf.

Child Welfare Information Gateway. (2021). *Child welfare practice to address racial disproportionality and disparity*. https://www.childwelfare.gov/pubPDFs/racial_disproportionality.pdf.

Children's Bureau. (2019, March). *Child abuse and neglect fatalities 2017: Statistics and interventions* [PDF File]. https://www.childwelfare.gov/pubPDFs/fatality.pdf.

Children's Bureau. (2020). Fact Sheet: How the Child Welfare System Works. https://www.childwelfare.gov/pubpdfs/cpswork.pdf.

Children's Trust Fund. (2020). *Social Media to Prevent Child Abuse and Neglect*. https://www.michigan.gov/ctf/0,4554,7-196-75686_27136-229437—,00.html.

Clark, R., Anderson, N. B., Clark, V. R., & Williams, D. R. (1999). Racism as a stressor for African Americans: A biopsychosocial model. *American Psychologist, 54*(10), 805–816.

Clayton, D. (2018). Black Lives Matter and the civil rights movement: A comparative analysis of two social movements in the United States. *Journal of Black Studies, 49*(5), 448–480. https://doi.org/10.1177/0021934718764099.

Clements, J. M., West, B. T., Yaker, Z., Lauinger, B., McCullers, D., Haubert, J., Ali Tahboub, M., & Everett, G. (2020). Disparities in diabetes-related multiple chronic conditions and mortality: The influence of race. *Diabetes Research and Clinical Practice, 159*, 1–19. https://doi.org/10.1016/j.diabres.2019.107984.

Coakley, T. M. (2008). Examining African American fathers' involvement in permanency planning: An effort to reduce racial disproportionality in the child welfare system. *Children and Youth Services Review, 30*(4), 407–417.

Coakley, T. M. (2013). An appraisal of fathers' perspectives on fatherhood and barriers to their child welfare involvement. *Journal of Human Behavior in the Social Environment, 23*(5), 627–639.

Cohen, E., & Canan, L. (2006). Closer to home: Parent mentors in child welfare. *Child Welfare: Journal of Policy, Practice, and Program, 85*(5), 867–884.

Collins, J. C., & Rocco, T. S. (2014). Disparities in healthcare for racial, ethnic, and sexual minorities. *New Directions for Adult and Continuing Education, 142*, 5–14.

Collin-Vézina, D., Daigneault, I., & Hébert, M. (2013). Lessons learned from child sexual abuse research: Prevalence, outcomes, and preventive strategies. *Child and Adolescent Psychiatry and Mental Health, 7*(22). https://doi.org/10.1186/1753-2000-7-22.

Comas-Díaz, L. (2016). Racial trauma recovery: A race-informed therapeutic approach to racial wounds. In A. N. Alvarez, C.T.H. Liang, & H. A. Neville (Eds.), *Cultural, racial, and ethnic psychology book series. The cost of racism for people of color: Contextualizing experiences of discrimination* (pp. 249–272). American Psychological Association.
Committee for Children. (2017). *Teaching Touching Safety Rules: Safe and Unsafe Touching Activity*. https://www.cfchildren.org/blog/2017/08/activity-teaching-touching-safety-rules-safe-and-unsafe-touching/.
Committee on Child Maltreatment Research, Policy, and Practice for the Next Decade: Phase II. (2014). *New Directions in Child Abuse and Neglect Research*. National Academy Press. https://www.ncbi.nlm.nih.gov/books/NBK195989/.
Conger, R. D., Wallace, L. E., Sun, Y., Simons, R. L., McLoyd, V. C., & Brody, G. H. (2002). Economic pressure in African American families: A replication and extension of the family stress model. *Developmental Psychology, 38*(2), 179–193.
Congress.gov. (2016). *Emmett Till Unsolved Civil Rights Crimes Reauthorization Act of 2016*. https://www.congress.gov/bill/114th-congress/senate-bill/2854.
Congressional Research Service. (2004). Child welfare: Implementation of the Adoption and Safe Families Act. https://www.everycrsreport.com/files/20041108_RL30759_96784ee8d3d99882a9c887e9da08d e67ee99e872.pdf.
Cook, M. (2018, July 22). *County failed to repeatedly stop sexual abuse of foster children, lawsuit alleges*. The San Diego Union Tribune. http://www.sandiegouniontribune.com/news/watchdog/sd-me-foster-care-20180722-story.html.
Cooney, V. (2019). *Expanded bill aims to address racial disparities in state's child protection system through sweeping change*. Minnesota House of Representatives. https://www.house.leg.state.mn.us/SessionDaily/Story/13704#:~:text=The%20bill%20%E2%80%94%20also%20known%20as%20the%20African,Rep.%20Rena%20Moran%20%28DFL-St.%20Paul%29%2C%20the%20bill%20sponsor.
Corley, L. & Crenshaw, W. (2018). Mother of infant found dead charged with cruelty. https://www.macon.com/news/local/crime/article215090735.html.
Coulter, M. L., & Mercado-Crespo, M. C. (2015). Co-occurrence of intimate partner violence and child maltreatment: Service providers' perceptions. *Journal of Family Violence, 30*(2), 255–262.
Courtney, M. E. (2013). Child welfare: History and policy framework. *Encyclopedia of Social Work*. https://doi.org/10.1093/acrefore/9780199975839.013.530.
Courtney, M. E., & Zinn, A. (2009). Predictors of running away from out-of-home care. *Children and Youth Services Review, 31*(12), 1298–1306.
Cowan, R., Cole, R. F., & Craigen, L. (2019). School-based child sexual abuse prevention: Implications for professional school counselors. *Professional Counselor, 9*(3), 200–210.

Craissati, J., McClurg, G., & Browne, K. (2002). Characteristics of perpetrators of child sexual abuse who have been sexually abused as children. *Sexual Abuse: A Journal of Research and Treatment, 14*(3), 221–235.

Cunningham, T. J., Croft, J. B., Liu, Y., Lu, H., Eke, P. I., & Giles, W. H. (2017). Vital signs: racial disparities in age-specific mortality among Blacks or African Americans in the Unites States, 1999–2015. *Morbidity and Mortality Weekly Report, 66*(17), 444–456. https://doi.org/10.15585/mmwr.mm6617e1.

Dargis, M., & Koenigs, M. (2018). Two subtypes of psychopathic criminals differ in negative affect and history of childhood abuse. *Psychological Trauma: Theory, Research, Practice, and Policy, 10*(4), 444–451. https://doi.org/10.1037/tra0000328.

Darkness to Light. (2021). *Our Approach.* https://www.d2l.org/our-work/our-approach/.

DeAngelis, T. (2014). Building resilience among Black boys. *Monitor on Psychology, 45*(9). https://www.apa.org/monitor/2014/10/cover-resilience.

DePanfilis, D. (2018). *Child Protective Services: A guide for caseworkers.* Child Welfare.gov. https://www.childwelfare.gov/pubPDFs/cps2018.pdf.

Department of Justice. (2020). *Justice department announces closing the investigation into 2014 office involved shooting in Cleveland, Ohio.* https://www.justice.gov/opa/pr/justice-department-announces-closing-investigation-2014-officer-involved-shooting-cleveland.

Derose, K. P., Williams, M. V., Branch, C., Florez, K. R., Hawes-Dawson, J., Mata M. A., Oden, C. W., & Wong, E. C. (2019). A community-partnered approach to developing interventions to reduce health disparities among African Americans and Latinos. *Journal of Racial Ethnic and Health Disparities, 6*(2), 254–264. https://www.ncbi.nlm.nih.gov/pmc/articles/PMC6378139/pdf/nihms-1504059.pdf.

D'Ignacio, C., & Klein, L. (2020). *Data Feminism.* https://data-feminism.mitpress.mit.edu/.

Division of Reproductive Health. (2018). *Pregnancy Mortality Surveillance System.* National Center for Chronic Disease Prevention and Health Promotion. https://www.cdc.gov/reproductivehealth/maternalinfanthealth/pregnancy-mortality-surveillance-system.htm?CDC_AA_refVal=https%3A%2F%2Fwww.cdc.gov%2Freproductivehealth%2Fmaternalinfanthealth%2Fpmss.html.

Dixon, J. (2008). The African-American Child Welfare Act: A legal redress for African-American disproportionality in child protection cases. *Berkeley Journal of African-American Law and Policy, 10*(2), 108–145.

Dixon, S. V., Graber, J. A., & Brooks-Gunn, J. (2008). The roles of respect for parental authority and parenting practices in parent-child conflict among African American, Latino, and European American families. *Journal of Family Psychology, 22*(1), 1–10.

Drake, B., Moon Lee, S., & Jonson-Reid, M. (2008). Race and child maltreatment: Are Blacks overrepresented?. *Child and Youth Services Review, 31*(3), 309–316.

DuMonthier, A., Childers, C., & Milli, J. (2017). *The status of Black women in the United States*. Report from the Institute of Women's Policy Research. https://iwpr.org/wp-content/uploads/2017/06/The-Status-of-Black-Women-6.26.17.pdf.

Eiserer, T. (2017, December 12). *Munchausen by Proxy: Mom arrested after son has 323 hospital visits, 13 surgeries*. https://www.wfaa.com/article/news/munchausen-by-proxy- mom-arrested-after-son-has-323-hospital-visits-13-surgeries/287-499020336.

Elliott, K., & Urquiza, A. (2006). Ethnicity, culture and child maltreatment. *Journal of Social Issues, 63*(4), 787–809.

Family and Children Services Division. (1995). *Orphanages: An historical overview*. Minnesota Department of Human Services. https://www.leg.state.mn.us/docs/pre2003/other/950265.pdf.

Farrell, C., Fleegler, E., Monuteaux, M., Wilson, C., Christian, C., & Lee, L. (2017). Community poverty and child abuse fatalities in the United States. *American Academy of Pediatrics, 139*(5), 1–11. http://pediatrics.aappublications.org/content/early/2017/04/20/peds.2016-1616.

Federal Bureau of Investigation. (2014). *2014 Crime in the United States: Arrests by race*. Federal Bureau of Investigation, Criminal Justice Information Services Division. https://ucr.fbi.gov/crime-in-the-u.s/2014/crime-in-the-u.s.-2014/tables/table-43.

Feldman, N., & Pattani, A. (2019). Black mothers get less treatment for their postpartum depression. *NPR news*. https://www.wbur.org/npr/760231688/black-mothers-get-less-treatment-for-their-postpartum-depression.

Feletti, V., J., Anda, R. F., Nordernberg, D., Williamson, D. F., Spitz, A. M., Edwards, V., Koss, M., & Marks, J. S. (1998). Relationship of childhood abuse and household dysfunction to many of the leading causes of death in adults: The adverse childhood experiences (ACE) study. *American Journal of Preventative Medicine, 14*(4). https://www.ajpmonline.org/article/S0749-3797(98)00017-8/pdf.

Felix Aaron, K., Levine, D., & Burstin, H. R. (2003). African American church participation and health care practices. *Journal of General Internal Medicine, 18*(11), 908–913.

Fluke, J., Jones Harden, B., Jenkins, M., & Ruehrdanz, A. (2011). A research synthesis of child welfare disproportionality and disparities. Papers from a research symposium of the Center for the Study of Social Policy and The Alliance for Race Equity in Child Welfare. https://casala.org/wp-content/uploads/2015/12/Disparities-and-Disproportionality-in-Child-Welfare_An-Analysis-of-the-Research-December-2011-1.pdf.

Forray, A. (2016). Substance use during pregnancy. *F1000Research, 5*, F1000 Faculty Rev-887. https://doi.org/10.12688/f1000research.7645.1.

Foster, E. M., Hillemeier, M. M., & Bai, Y. (2011). Explaining the disparity in placement instability among African-American and White children in child welfare: A Blinder–Oaxaca decomposition. *Children and Youth Services Review, 33*(1), 118–125.

Frazier, E. F. (1939). *The Negro Family in United States.* University of Chicago Press.
French, B. H., Lewis, J. A., Mosley, D. V., Adames, H. Y., Chavez-Dueñas, N. Y., Chen, G. A., & Neville, H. A. (2020). Toward a psychological framework of radical healing in communities of color. *The Counseling Psychologist, 48*(1), 14–46. https://doi.org/10.1177/0011000019843506.
Fryar, C. D., Carroll, M. D., & Ogden, C. (2018). Prevalence of overweight, obesity, and severe obesity among adults age 20 and over: United States, 1960–1962 through 2015–2016. Centers for Disease Control and Prevention. https://www.cdc.gov/nchs/data/hestat/obesity_adult_15_16/obesity_adult_15_16.htm.
Fryda, C., & Hulme, P. (2014). School-based childhood sexual abuse prevention programs: An integrative review. *Journal of School Nursing, 31*(3), 167–182. https://doi.org/10.1177/1059840514544125.
Gallup, G., & Newport, F. (2006). *Religion most important to Blacks, women and older Americans.* http://www.gallup.com/poll/25585/Religion- Most-Important-Blacks-Women-Older-Americans.aspx.
Gaylord-Harden, N. K., & Cunningham, J. A. (2009). The impact of racial discrimination and coping strategies on internalizing symptoms in African American youth. *Journal of Youth and Adolescence, 38*(4), 532–543.
George, R. M., Bilaver, L., Lee, B. J., Needell, B., Brookhart, A., & Jackman, W. (2002). *Employment outcomes for youth aging out of foster care 3/1/2002.* U.S. Department of Health & Human Services. Office of the Assistant Secretary for Planning and Evaluation. http://aspe.hhs.gov/hsp/fostercare-agingout02/.
Gershoff, E. T., & Bitensky, S. H. (2007). The case against corporal punishment of children: Converging evidence from social science research and international human rights law and implications for U.S. public policy. *Psychology, Public Policy, and Law, 13*(4), 231–272. https://doi.org/10.1037/1076-8971.13.4.231.
Glosser, A., Gardiner, K., & Fishman, M. (2004*). Statutory rape: A guide to state laws and reporting requirements.* Office of the Assistant Secretary for Planning and Evaluation, Department of Health & Human Services. https://aspe.hhs.gov/system/files/pdf/75531/report.pdf.
Gonzalez, D., Bethencourt M. A., & McCall J. D. (2021). *Child Abuse and Neglect.* https://www.ncbi.nlm.nih.gov/books/NBK459146/.
Goodman, L., Liang, B., Helms, J., Latta, R., Sparks, E., & Weintraub, S. (2004). Training Counseling Psychologists as Social Justice Agents. *The Counseling Psychologist, 32*(6), 793–836. https://doi.org/10.1177/0011000004268802
Gramlich, J. (2020). Black imprisonment rate in the U.S. has fallen by a third since 2006. Pew Research Center. https//www.pewresearch.org/fact-tank/2020/05/06/share-of-black-white-hispanic-americans-in-prison-2018-vs-2006/.

Gramlich, J. (2021). America's incarceration rate falls to lowest level since 1995. Pew Research Center. https://www.pewresearch.org/fact-tank/2021/08/16/americas-incarceration-rate-lowest-since-1995/.

Gramlich, J., & Funk, C. (2020, June 4). *Black Americans face higher COVID-19 risks, are more hesitant to trust medical scientists, get vaccinated.* Pew Research Center: FactTank News in the Numbers. https://www.pewresearch.org/fact-tank/2020/06/04/black-americans-face-higher-covid-19-risks-are-more-hesitant-to-trust-medical-scientists-get-vaccinated/.

Greenbaum, V. J. (2017). Child sex trafficking in the United States: Challenges for the healthcare provider. *PLoS Medicine, 14*(11), 1–8. https://doi.org/10.1371/journal.pmed.1002439.

Greene-Moton, E., & Minkler, M. (2019). Cultural competence or cultural humility? Moving beyond the debate. *Health Promotion Practice, 21*(1), 142–145. https://journals.sagepub.com/doi/full/10.1177/1524839919884912.

Guedes, A., Bott, S., Garcia-Moreno, C., & Colombini, M. (2016). Bridging the gaps: A global review of intersections of violence against women and violence against children. *Global Health Action, 9*(1), 1–15.

Gypen, L., Vanderfaeillie, J., De Maeyer, S., Belenger, L., & Van Holen, F. (2017). Outcomes of children who grew up in foster care: Systematic-review. *Children and Youth Services Review, 76*, 74–83.

Hardeberg Bach, M., & Demuth, C. (2018). Therapists' experiences in their work with sex offenders and people with pedophilia: A literature review. *Europe's Journal of Psychology, 14*(2), 498–514. https://doi.org/10.5964/ejop.v14i2.1493.

Hargons, C., Mosley, D., & Falconer, J. (2017). Black Lives Matter: A call to action for counseling psychology leaders. *The Counseling Psychologist, 46*(6), 873–901. https://journals.sagepub.com/doi/full/10.1177/0011000017733048.

Harris, M. S., & Hackett, W. (2008). Decision points in child welfare: An action research model to address disproportionality. *Children and Youth Services Review, 30*(2), 199–215. https://doi.org/10.1016/j.childyouth.2007.09.006.

Haselgruber, A., Knefel, M., Sölva, K., & Lueger-Schuster, B. (2021). Foster children's complex psychopathology in the context of cumulative childhood trauma: The interplay of ICD-11 complex PTSD, dissociation, depression, and emotion regulation. *Journal of affective disorders, 282*, 372–380.

Health Resource & Service Administrator. (2020). *Home visiting.* U.S., Department of Health & Human Services. https://mchb.hrsa.gov/maternal-child-health-initiatives/home-visiting-overview.

Heard-Garris, N. J., Cale, M., Camaj, L., Hamati, M. C., & Dominguez, T. P. (2018). Transmitting trauma: A systematic review of vicarious racism and child health. *Social Science & Medicine, 199*, 230–240. https://doi.org/10.1016/j.socscimed.2017.04.018.

Herman-Davis, L. (2012). Investigating child sexual abuse: A feminist perspective. [Bachelor's degree thesis], Florida Atlantic University, USA. https://aus.libguides.com/apa/apa-theses.

Herman, E. (2011). *Adoption history in brief.* Social Welfare History Project. https://socialwelfare.library.vcu.edu/programs/child-welfarechild-labor/adoption/.

Hernandez, D. (2012). *Changing demography and circumstances for young Black children in African and Caribbean immigrant families.* Migration Policy Institute. https://www.migrationpolicy.org/research/CBI-changing-demography-black-immigrant-children.

Herrenkohl, T., Leeb, R., & Higgins, D. (2016). The public health model of child maltreatment prevention. *Trauma, Violence & Abuse, 17*(4), 363–365.

Hill, R. B. (1998). Understanding Black family functioning: A holistic perspective. *Journal of Comparative Family Studies*, 15–25.

Hill, R. B. (2004). Institutional racism in child welfare. In J. E. Everett, S. P. Chipungu, & B. R. Leashore (Eds.), *Child welfare revisited: An acrocentric perspective* (pp. 57–76). Rutgers University Press.

Hill, R. B. (2006). *Synthesis of research on disproportionality in child welfare: An update.* Casey-CSSP Alliance for Racial Equity in Child Welfare (p. 60).

Hines, P. M., & Boyd-Franklin, N. (2005). African American families. In M. McGoldrick, J. Giordano, & N. Garcia-Preto (Eds.), *Ethnicity and family therapy* (3rd ed., pp. 87–100). Guildford.

Hodge, D. R. (2020). Religious congregations: An important vehicle for alleviating human suffering and fostering wellness. *Journal of Religion & Spirituality in Social Work: Social Thought, 39*(2), 119–137. https://doi.org/10.1080/15426432.2020.1728604.

Horn, I. B., Joseph, J. G., & Cheng, T. L. (2004). Nonabusive physical punishment and child behavior among African-American children: A systematic review, *Journal of the National Medical Association, 96*(9), 1162–1168.

Hostinar, C. E., Stellern, S. A., Schaefer, C., Carlson, S. M., & Gunnar, M. R. (2012). Associations between early life adversity and executive function in children adopted internationally from orphanages. *Proceedings of the National Academy of Sciences of the United States of America, 109* (Suppl 2), 17208–17212. https://doi.org/10.1073/pnas.1121246109.

Hughes, D., Rodriguez, J., Smith, E. P., Johnson, D. J., Stevenson, H. C., & Spicer, P. (2006). Parents' ethnic-racial socialization practices: A review of research and directions for future study. *Developmental Psychology, 42*(5), 747–770.

Hurd, E. P., Moore, C., & Rogers, R. (1995). Quiet success: Parenting strengths among African Americans. *Families in Society, 76*(7), 434–443.

Hussey, J. M., Chang, J. J., & Kotch, J. B. (2006). Child Maltreatment in the United States. *Pediatrics, 118*(3), 933–942.

Iati, M. (2019, June 11). *Alabama approves 'chemical castration' bill for some sex offenders.* Washington Post. https://www.washingtonpost.com/health/2019/06/11/alabama-chemical-castration-bill/.

Illinois African American Family Commission Act, Title 20 ILCS 3903. (2015). http://il.elaws.us/law/20ilcs3903.

International Society for the Prevention of Child Abuse and Neglect. (2018). World Perspectives on Child Abuse 2018. https://www.ispcan.org/wp-content/uploads/2018/10/World-Perspectives-on-Child-Abuse-2018_13th-Edition_Interactive.pdf.

Jason, L. A., Glantsman, O., O'Brien, J. F., & Ramian, K. N. (Eds.). (2019). Introduction to community psychology: Becoming an agent of change. *College of Science and Health Full Text Publications*. https://via.library.depaul.edu/cshtextbooks/1.

Jonson-Reid, M., Kohl, P., & Drake, B. (2012). Child and adult outcomes of chronic child maltreatment. *Pediatrics, 129*(5), 839–845. https://doi.org/10.1542/peds.2011-2529.

Jorm, A. F., Patten, S. B., Brugha, T. S., & Mojtabai, R. (2017). Has increased provision of treatment reduced the prevalence of common mental disorder? Review of the evidence from our countries. *World Psychiatry, 16*(1), 90–99. https://onlinelibrary.wiley.com/doi/full/10.1002/wps.20388.

Joyce T., & Huecker, M. R. (2019). *Pediatric abusive head trauma (Shaken baby syndrome)*. StatPearls Publishing. https://www.ncbi.nlm.nih.gov/books/NBK499836/.

Kahan, M. (2006). "Put up" on platforms: A history of twentieth century adoption policy in the United States. *The Journal of Sociology & Social Welfare, 33*(3), 51–72. https://scholarworks.wmich.edu/jssw/vol33/iss3/4.

Kajstura, A. (2018). States of women's incarceration: The global context 2018. Prison Policy Initiative. https://www.prisonpolicy.org/global/women/2018.html.

Kamo, Y. (2000). Racial and ethnic differences in extended family households. *Sociological Perspectives, 43*(2), 211–229.

Kane, C. M. (2000). African American family dynamics as perceived by family members. *Journal of Black Studies, 30*(5), 691–702.

Karenga, M. (1988). *The African American holiday of Kwanzaa. A celebration of family, community and culture*. University of Sankore Press.

Keller, T. E., Salazar, A. M., & Courtney, M. E. (2011). Prevalence and timing of diagnosable mental health, alcohol, and substance use problems among older adolescents in the child welfare system. *Child Youth Services Review, 32*(4). 626–634. https://www.ncbi.nlm.nih.gov/pmc/articles/PMC2840264/.

KIDS Center. (2019). *Safe Touch Curriculum*. https://kidscenter.org/safe-touch-curriculum/.

KidsRights. (2019). *KidsRights Index*. https://kidsrights.org/research/kidsrights-index/?gclid=Cj0KCQiA4feBBhC9ARIsABp_nbXEyfwEXJ-oVfrqsTqaAuxPPot_YBCqh856LaKZyfnDxISvVG-URekaApZmEALw_wcBTheInternational.

Kim, B.S.K. (2007). Acculturation and enculturation. In F.T.L. Leong, A. G. Inman, A. Ebreo, L. Yang, L. Kinoshita, & M. Fu (Eds.), *Handbook of Asian American psychology* (2nd ed., pp. 141–158). Sage.

King, B., Fallon, B., Boyd, R., Black, T., Antwi-Boasiako, K., & O'Connor, C. (2017). Factors associated with racial differences in child welfare investigative decision-making in Ontario, Canada. *Child abuse & neglect, 73*, 89–105. https://doi.org/10.1016/j.chiabu.2017.09.027.

King, C. (2004). Race and cultural identity: Playing the race game inside football. *Leisure Stuies, 23*(1), 19–30.

Kizgin, H., Jamal, A., Dey, B. L., & Rana, N. P. (2018). The impact of social media on consumers' acculturation and purchase intentions. *Information Systems Frontier, 20*(3), 503–514. https://doi.org/10.1007/s10796-017-9817-4.

Knott, T., & Donovan, K. (2010). Disproportionate representation of African-American children in foster care: Secondary analysis of the National Child Abuse and Neglect Data System, 2005. *Child and Youth Services Review, 32*, 679–684. https://doi.org/10.1016/j.childyouth.2010.01.003.

Kohl, P. L., Jonson-Reid, M., & Drake, B. (2011). Maternal mental illness and the safety and stability of maltreated children. *Child Abuse & Neglect, 35*(5), 309–318. https://doi.org/10.1016/j.chiabu.2011.01.006.

Krause, N. (2006). Exploring the stress-buffering effects of church-based and secular social support on self-rated health in late life. *The Journals of Gerontology Series B: Psychological Sciences and Social Sciences, 61*(1), S35–S43.

Kuang, X., Aratani, Y., & Li, G. (2018). Association between emergency department utilization and the risk of child maltreatment in young children. *Injury Epidemiology, 5*(1), 1–8. https://www.ncbi.nlm.nih.gov/pmc/articles/PMC6300447/.

Kumpfer, K. L., Alvarado, R., Smith, P., & Bellamy, N. (2002). Cultural sensitivity and adaptation in family-based prevention interventions. *Prevention Science, 3*(3), 241–246.

Kumpfer, K. L., Scheier, L. M., & Brown, J. (2020). Strategies to avoid replication failure with evidence-based prevention interventions: Case examples from the Strengthening Families Program. *Evaluation & the Health Professions, 43*(2), 75–89.

Lagaay, M., & Courtney, L. (2013). *Time to listen: Independent advocacy within the child protection process*. The National Children's Bureau: Working with children, for children. https://www.basw.co.uk/system/files/resources/basw_122703-5_0.pdf.

Lash, D. (2013). Race and class in the U.S. foster care system. *International Socialist Review*. https://isreview.org/issue/91/race-and-class-U.S.-foster-care-system.

Lating, J. M., Barnett, J. E., & Horowitz, M. (2009). Increasing advocacy awareness within professional psychology training programs: The 2005 National Council of Schools and Programs of Professional Psychology Self-Study. *Training and Education in Professional Psychology, 3*(2), 106–110.

Lau, A. S. (2006). Making the case for selective and directed cultural adaptations of evidence-based treatments: Examples from parent training. *Clinical psychology: Science and practice, 13*(4), 295–310.

Lau, K., Krase, K., & Morse, R. (2009). *Mandating reporting of child abuse and neglect: A practical guide for social workers.* Spring Publishing Company.
Lee, B. (2018). #Me Too Movement: It is time that we all act and participate in transformation. *Psychiatric Investigation, 15*(5). https://doi.org/10.30773/pi.2018.04.30.
Lee, J. Y., & Cho, K. S. (2013). Chemical castration for sexual offenders: Physicians' views. *Journal of Korean medical science, 28*(2), 171–172. https://doi.org/10.3346/jkms.2013.28.2.171.
Leeb, R. T., Paulozzi, L., Melanson, C., Simon, T., & Arias, I. (2008). *Child maltreatment surveillance: Uniform definitions for public health and recommended data elements, Version 1.0.* Centers for Disease Control and Prevention, National Center for Injury Prevention and Control. https://www.cdc.gov/violenceprevention/pdf/CM_Surveillance-a.pdf.
Leeb, R., & Fluke, J. (2015). Child maltreatment surveillance: enumeration, monitoring, evaluation and insight. *Health Promotion and Chronic Disease Prevention in Canada, 35*(8–9), 138–140. https://www.ncbi.nlm.nih.gov/pmc/articles/PMC4911133/.
Leg Up Farm. (2020). *Services.* https://www.legupfarm.org/services.
Letourneau, E. J., Henggeler, S. W., Borduin, C. M., Schewe, P. A., McCart, M. R., Chapman, J. E., & Saldana, L. (2009). Multisystemic therapy for juvenile sexual offenders: 1-year results from a randomized effectiveness trial. *Journal of Family Psychology, 23*(1), 89–102. https://doi.org/10.1037/a0014352.
Lindquist, M. J., & Santavirta, T. (2014). Does placing children in foster care increase their adult criminality?. *Labour Economics, 31*, 72–83.
Linehan, M. (2015). DBT Skills Training Manual (2nd Ed.). Guilford Press.
Littlejohn-Blake, S. M., & Darling, C. A. (1993). Understanding the strengths of African Amercan families. *Journal of Black Studies, 23*(4), 460–471.
Liu, W., Liu, R. Z., Garrison, Y. L., Kim, J.Y.C., Chan, L., Ho, Y.C.S., & Yueng, C. W. (2019). Racial trauma, microaggressions, and becoming racially innocuous: The role of acculturation and White supremacist ideology. *American Psychologist, 74*(1), 143–155. https://psycnet.apa.org/fulltext/2019-01033-012.pdf.
Livingston, G. (2018). *About one-third of U.S. children are living with an unmarried parent.* Pew Research Center. https://www.pewresearch.org/fact- tank/2018/04/27/about-one-third-of-u-s-children-are-living-with-an-unmarried-parent/.
Lobanov-Rostovsky, C. (2017). *Sex offender management strategies.* Office of Sex Offender Sentencing, Monitoring, Apprehending, Registering, and Tracking. https://smart.ojp.gov/somapi/chapter-8-sex-offender-management-strategies.
Lozada, F. T., Jagers, R. J., Smith, C. D., Bañales, J., & Hope, E. C. (2017). Prosocial behaviors of Black adolescent boys: An application of a

sociopolitical development theory. *Journal of Black Psychology, 43*(5), 493–516.
MacKay, J. M., Steel, A., Samuel, E., Creppy, T., & Green, A. (2016). *The rise of medicine in the home: Implications for today's children, March 2016*. Safe Kids Worldwide. https://www.poison.org/~/media/files/pdf-for-article-dowloads-and-refs/safekids-medicine-safety-2016.pdf?la=en.
Mancini, C. (2018). The media, public opinion and sex offender policy in the US. In. P. Lussier & E. Beauregard (Eds.), *Sexual offending: A criminological perspective*, 116–137. Routledge.
Mantwill, S., Monestel-Umana, S., & Schulz, P. J. (2015). The relationship between health literacy and health disparities: A systematic review. *PLOS ONE, 10*(12). https://doi.org/10.1371/journal.pone.0145455.
Martin, E. (2017, March 1). *Hidden consequences: The impact of incarceration on dependent children*. National Institute of Justice. https://www.nij.gov/journals/278/Pages/impact-of-incarceration-on-dependentchildren.aspx.
Mathews, B., & Collin-Vézina, D. (2019). Child sexual abuse: Toward a conceptual model and definition. *Trauma, Violence, & Abuse, 20*(2), 131–148.
Mattis, J. S., & Jagers, R. J. (2001). A relational framework for the study of religiosity and spirituality in the lives of African Americans. *Journal of Community Psychology, 29*(5), 519–539.
Maxwell, C., & Solomon, D. (2018). *Mass incarceration, stress, and Black infant mortality*. Center for American Progress. https://www.americanprogress.org/issues/race/reports/2018/06/05/451647/mass-incarceration-stress-black-infant-mortality/.
McCallum, C. M. (2016). "Mom made me do it": The role of family in African Americans' decisions to enroll in doctoral education. *Journal of Diversity in Higher Education, 9*(1), 50–63.
McCartney, G., Popham, F., McMaster, R., & Cumbers, A. (2019). Defining health and health inequalities. *Public Health, 172*, 22–30. https://doi.org/10.1016/j.puhe.2019.03.023.
McDaniel, M., Simms, M., Monson, W., & Fortuny, K. (2013). Imprisonment and disenfranchisement of disconnected low-income men. *Race, Place, and Poverty, 4*, 1–10. https://aspe.hhs.gov/system/files/pdf/56191/rpt_imprisonment.pdf.
McDonald, B. (2021). Professional power struggles in participatory research. *Journal of Participatory Research Methods, 2*(1), 1–7. https://doi.org/10.35844/001c.18692.
McGuire, T., & Miranda, J. (2008). Racial and ethnic disparities in mental health care: Evidence and policy implications. *Health Affairs (Project Hope), 27*(2), 393–403. https://doi.org/10.1377/hlthaff.27.2.393.
McLoyd, V. C., Cauce, A. M., Takeuchi, D., & Wilson, L. (2000). Marital processes and parental socialization in families of color: A decade review of research. *Journal of Marriage and Family, 62*(4), 1070–1093.

Mehta, N., Elo, I. T., Ford, N. D., & Siegel, K. R. (2015). Obesity among U.S.- and foreign-born Blacks by region of birth. *American Journal of Preventive Medicine, 49*(2), 269–273. https://doi.org/10.1016/j.amepre.2015.02.014Get.

Mersky, J., Topitzes, J., & Reynolds, A. (2012). Unsafe at any age: Linking childhood and adolescent maltreatment to delinquency and crime. *Journal of Research in Crime and Delinquency, 49*(2), 295–318. https://doi.org/10.1177/0022427811415284.

Mikton, C., & Butchart, A. (2009). Child maltreatment prevention: A systematic review of reviews. *Bulletin of the World Health Organization, 87*(5), 353–361. https://doi.org/10.2471/blt.08.057075.

Miller, M. C. (2018). Destroyed by slavery? Slavery and African American family formation following emancipation. *Demography, 55*(5), 1587–1609. https://doi.org/10.1007/s13524-018-0711-6.

Morin, A. (2018, June 3). *When does discipline become child abuse?*. Verywell Family. http://www.verywell.com/when-does-discipline-become-child-abuse-1094826.

Mosley-Howard, G. S., & Evans, C. B. (2000). Relationships and contemporary experiences of the African American family: An ethnographic case study. *Journal of Black Studies, 30*(3), 428–452.

Mothers of Sexually Abused Children. (2020). *About MOSAC*. https://www.mosac.net/About.aspx.

Muvuka, B., Combs, R. M., Ayangeakaa, S. D., Ali, N. M., Wendel, M. L., & Jackson, T. (2020). Health literacy in African-American communities: Barriers and strategies. *HLRP: Health Literacy Research and Practice, 4*(3), e138–e143. https://doi.org/10.3928/24748307-20200617-01.

Myers, L. J. (1992). *Understanding an Afrocentric world view: Introduction to an optimal psychology*. Kendall/Hunt.

Myers, L. J., & Speight, S. L. (2010). Reframing mental health and psychological well-being among persons of African descent: Africana/Black psychology meeting the challenges of fractured social and cultural realities. *The Journal of Pan African Studies, 3*(8), 66–82.

Nami, S., Carlson, C., O'Hara, K., Nakuti, J., Bukuluki, P., Lwanyaaga, J., Namakula, S., Nanyunja, B., Wainberg, M., Naker, D., & Michau, L. (2017). Towards a feminist understanding of intersecting violence against women and children in the family. *Social Science and Medicine, 184*, 40–48.

National Association of School Nurses. (2018). *Prevention and intervention of child maltreatment—The role of the school nurse (Position Statement)*. https://www.nasn.org/advocacy/professional-practice-documents/position-statements/ps-child-maltreatment.

National Center for Chronic Disease Prevention and Health Promotion. (2019). *Infant Mortality*. Division of Reproductive Health, National Center for Chronic Disease Prevention and Health Promotion, Centers for Disease Control and Prevention. https://www.cdc.gov/reproductivehealth/maternalinfanthealth/infantmortality.htm.

National Center for Health Statistics. (2015). *Health, United States, 2015: With Special Feature on Racial and Ethnic Health Disparities.* https://www.ncbi.nlm.nih.gov/books/NBK367643/#highlights.s1.

National Center for Innovation and Excellence. (2020). *Bring C.A.R.E.S. To Your Community.* https://ncfie.org/cares-replication/.

National Center on Shaken Baby Syndrome. (2019). *Facts and Information.* https://www.dontshake.org/learn-more/itemlist/category/13-facts-info.

National Coalition for Child Protection Reform. (2015). *Foster care vs. family preservation: The track record on safety and well-being.* https://drive.google.com/file/d/0B291mw_hLAJsV1NUVGRVUmdyb28/view.

National Conference of State Legislators. (2020, April 1). *Family First Prevention Services Act.* https://www.ncsl.org/research/human-services/family-first-prevention-services-act-ffpsa.aspx.

National Conference of State Legislatures. (2021, January 26). *Disproportionality and Race Equity in Child Welfare.* https://www.ncsl.org/research/human-services/disproportionality-and-race-equity-in-child-welfare.aspx.

National Indian Law Library. (2020). *Topic 13. Termination of parental rights.* https://narf.org/nill/documents/icwa/faq/termination.html

National Institute on Drug Addiction. (2019). *Dramatic Increase in Maternal Opioid Use and Neonatal Abstinence Syndrome.* https://www.drugabuse.gov/related-topics/trends-statistics/infographics/dramatic-increases-in-maternal-opioid-use-neonatal-abstinence-syndrome.

National Institutes of Health. (2006). *World Day for the Prevention of Child Abuse.* https://www.nichd.nih.gov/newsroom/resources/spotlight/112006_child_abuse_prevention.

National Institutes of Health. (2021). *Ending Structural Racism.* https://www.nih.gov/ending-structural-racism.

National Kids Count. (2019). Children in single-parent families by race in the United States. The Annie E. Casey Foundation. Kids Count Data Center.

National Partnership for Women & Families. (2018). Black women's maternal health: A multifaceted approach to addressing persistent and dire health disparities. https://www.nationalpartnership.org/our-work/health/reports/black-womens-maternal-health.html.

New York Society for the Prevention of Cruelty to Children. (n.d). *History.* https://nyspcc.org/about-the-new-york-society-for-the-prevention-of-cruelty-to-children/history/.

Newkirk II, V. R. (2016, June 17). *A generation of bad blood.* The Atlantic. https://www.theatlantic.com/politics/archive/2016/06/tuskegee-study-medical-distrust-research/487439/.

Norman, R., Byambaa, M., De, R., Butchart, A., Scott, J., & Vos, T. (2012). The long-term health consequences of child physical abuse, emotional abuse, and neglect: A systematic review and meta-analysis. *PLOS Medicine, 9*(11), 1–31.

ObamaWhiteHouse. (2017). *Let's move!: America's move to raise a healthier generation of kids.* https://letsmove.obamawhitehouse.archives.gov/.

Office of Sex Offender Sentencing, Monitoring, Apprehending, Registering and Tracking. (2020). *Legislative History of Federal Sex Offender Registration and Notification*. https://smart.ojp.gov/sorna-archived/legislative-history-federal-sex-offender-registration-and-notification.

Office on Women's Health. (2019). *Relationships and safety*. U.S. Department of Health & Human Services. https://www.womenshealth.gov/relationships-and-safety.

O'Hara, M., & McCabe, J. (2013). Postpartum depression: Current status and future directions. *Annual Review of Clinical Psychology*, *9*, 379–407. https://www.annualreviews.org/doi/abs/10.1146/annurev-clinpsy-050212-185612.

Okamoto, S. K., Kulis, S., Marsiglia, F. F., Steiker, L.K.H., & Dustman, P. (2014). A continuum of approaches toward developing culturally focused prevention interventions: From adaptation to grounding. *The Journal of Primary Prevention*, *35*(2), 103–112.

Pager, D., & Shepherd, H. (2008). The sociology of discrimination: Racial discrimination in employment, housing, credit, and consumer markets. *Annual Review of Sociology*, *34*, 181–209.

Paradies, Y., Ben, J., Denson, N., Elias, A., Priest, N., Pieterse, A., Gupta, A., Kelaher, M., & Gee, G. (2015). Racism as a determinant of health: A systematic review and meta-analysis. *PLOS One*. https://doi.org/10.1371/journal.pone.0138511.

Patton, S. (2017, April). Corporal punishment in black communities: Not an intrinsic cultural tradition but racial trauma. *CYF News*. https://www.apa.org/pi/families/resources/newsletter/2017/04/racial-trauma.

Peacock, S., Konrad, S., Watson, E., Nickel, D., & Muhajarine, N. (2013). Effectiveness of home visiting programs on child outcomes: A systematic review. *BMC Public Health*, *17*, 1–14. https://doi.org/10.1186/1471-2458-13-17.

Pearson, S. M., & Bieschke, K. J. (2001). Succeeding against the odds: An examination of familial influences on the career development of professional African American women. *Journal of Counseling Psychology*, *48*(3), 301–309.

Pecora, P. J. (2012). Maximizing educational achievement of youth in foster care and alumni: Factors associated with success. *Children and Youth Services Review*, *34*(6), 1121–1129.

Pennsylvania Department of Human Services. (2017). *Keep kids safe. Suspect shild abuse? Report it.* [Video]. http://keepkidssafe.pa.gov/media/index.htm.

Petersen, A. C., Joseph, J., & Feit, M. (2014). *New directions in child abuse and neglect research. Child abuse and neglect policy*. National Academies Press. https://www.ncbi.nlm.nih.gov/books/NBK195993/.

Pollock, E. D., Kazman, J. B., & Deuster, P. (2015). Family functioning and stress in African American families: A strength-based approach. *Journal of Black Psychology*, *41*(2), 144–169.

Prince, Z. (2016). *Census Bureau: Higher percentage of Black children live with single mothers*. AFR. https://afro.com/census-bureau-higher-percentage-black-children-live-single-mothers/.

Prins, E., & Mooney, A. (2014). *Literacy and health disparity*. https://www.researchgate.net/profile/Esther_Prins/publication/264772944_Literacy_and_Health_Disparities/links/5a724c71458515512075e44c/Literacy-and-Health-Disparities.pdf#page=21.

Progressive Life Center. (2016). *The uniqueness of PLC's NTU approach*. https://progressivelifecenter.org/about-us/ntu/.

Przybylski, R. (2017). *Effectiveness of treatment for adult sex offenders. Sex offender management assessment and planning initiative*. Office of Sex Offender Sentencing, Monitoring, Apprehending, Registering, and Tracking. https://smart.ojp.gov/somapi/chapter-7-effectiveness-treatment-adult-sex-offenders.

Raz, M., Dettlaff, A., & Edwards, F. (2021). The perils of child "protection" for children of color: Lessons from history. *Pediatrics, 148*(1), e2021050237. https://www.publications.aap.org/pediatrics/article-abstract/148/1/e2021050237/180165/The-Perils-of-Child-Protection-for-Children-of?redirectedFrom=fulltext.

Redfield, R., Linton, R., & Herskovits, M. J. (1936). Memorandum for the study of acculturation. *American Anthropologist, 38*(1), 149–152.

Reupert, A. E., Maybery, D. J., & Kowalenko, N. M. (2013). Children whose parents have a mental illness: Prevalence, need and treatment. *The Medical Journal of Australia, 199*(3), 7–9. https://doi.org/10.5694/mja11.11200.

Robinson, L. (2012). *Psychology for social workers: Black perspectives on human development and behavior* (2nd ed.). Routledge.

Roopnarine, J. L., Krishnakumar, A., Metindogan, A., & Evans, M. (2006). Links between parenting styles, parent-child academic interaction, parent-school interaction, and early academic skills and social behaviors in young children of English-speaking Caribbean immigrants. *Early Childhood Research Quarterly, 21*(2), 238–252.

Rowland, M. L., & Isaac-Savage, P. (2014). The Black church: Promoting health, fighting disparities. *New Direction for Adults and Continuing Education, 142*, 15–24. https://doi.org/10.1002/ace.20091.

Safe & Together Institute. (2020). *Concrete strategies. Meaningful tools. Real change*. https://safeandtogetherinstitute.com/about-us/about-the-model/.

Sahgal, N., & Smith, G. (2009, January 30). A religious portrait of African Americans. Pew Research Center. http://www.pewforum.org/2009/01/30/a-religious-portrait-of-african-americans/#section-i-religious-affiliation-and-demographics.

Samuels, J. (2018). *A mother and child fled the Congo, only to be cruelly separated by the US government*. ACLU. https://www.aclu.org/blog/immigrants-rights/deportation-and-due-process/mother-and-child-fled-congo-only-be-cruelly.

Santhosh, K. R. (2016). A review on the perpetrators of child abuse. *Review of Social Sciences, 1*(3), 45–52. https://www.socialsciencejournal.org/index.php/site/article/view/25/15.

Sattler, K. M., Font, S. A., & Gershoff, E. T. (2018). Age-specific risk factors associated with placement instability among foster children. *Child Abuse & Neglect, 84*, 157–169.
Saunders, S. (2007). What you need to know about child abuse: A cautionary tale from Bedford Hills. *New York Teacher*. NYSU.
Sauter, J., Turner, D., Briken, P., & Rettenberger, M. (2020). Testosterone-lowering medication and its association with recidivism risk in individuals convicted of sexual offenses. *Sexual Abuse*, 1–26
Schwartz, S. J., Unger, J. B., Zamboanga, B. L., & Szapocznik, J. (2010). Rethinking the concept of acculturation: Implications for theory and research. *American Psychologist, 65*(4), 237–251.
Sedlak, A. J., Mettenberg, J., Basena, M., Petta, I., McPherson, K., Green, A., & Li, S. (2010). *Fourth national incidence study of child abuse and neglect (NIS-4). Report to Congress, Executive Summary*. U.S Department of Health & Human Services, Administration for Children and Families. https://cap.law.harvard.edu/wp-content/uploads/2015/07/sedlaknis.pdf.
Shapiro, E. (2018, September 26). *5-month-old drowns in bathtub while dad plays video games*. ABC News. https://abcnews.go.com/U.S./month-drowns-bathtub-dad-plays-video-games-police/story?id=58091687.
Shehadeh, M. H., Heim, E., Chowdhary, N., Maercker, A., & Albanese, E. (2016). Cultural adaptation of minimally guided interventions for common mental disorders: a systematic review and meta-analysis. *JMIR mental health, 3*(3), e5776.
Smith, B. (2012). The case against spanking. *Monitor on Psychology, 43*(4), 60–63. https://www.apa.org/monitor/2012/04/spanking.
Sood, Turner B., Delaney-Black, V., Covington, C., Nordstrom-Klee, B., Ager, J., Templin, T., Janisse, J., Martier, S., & Sokol, R. (2001). Prenatal alcohol exposure and childhood behavior at age 6 to 7: I. Dose-response effect. *Pediatrics, 108*(2), 1–9.
St. Petersburg-USA Orphanage Research Team. (2008). The effects of early social-emotional and relationship experience on the development of young orphanage children. *Monographs of the Society for Research in Child Development, 73*(3), vii–295. https://doi.org/10.1111/j.1540-5834.2008.00483.x.
STATIC99 Clearinghouse. (2020). Static-99/Static99R Overview. http://www.static99.org/.
Statista Research Department. (2019a). Child abuse rates in the U.S. in 2017, by race/ethnicity of the victim. Statista. https://www.statista.com/statistics/254857/child-abuse-rate-in-the-us-by-race-ethnicity/.
Statista Research Department. (2019b). Total lifetime costs of fatal and non-fatal child maltreatment in the U.S. as of 2010, by source of cost (in million U.S. dollars). Statista. https://www.statista.com/statistics/255199/total-lifetime-costs-of-fatal-and-nonfatal-child-maltreatment-in-the-us/.
Substance Abuse and Mental Health Services Administration (U.S.), & Office of the Surgeon General (U.S.). (2016). *Facing Addiction in*

America: The Surgeon General's Report on Alcohol, Drugs, and Health [Internet]. U.S. Department of Health & Human Services.

Szilagyi, M. A., Rosen, D. S., Rubin, D., & Zlotnik, S. (2015). The Council on Foster Care, Adoption, and Kinship Care, The Committee on Adolescence, & The Council on Early Childhood. Health care issues for children and adolescents in foster care and kinship care. *Pediatrics, 134*(4), 1142–1166. https://doi.org/10.1542/peds.2015-2656.

Taveras, E. M., Gillman, M. W., Kleinman, K. P., Rich-Edwards, J. W., & Rifas-Shiman, S. L. (2013). Reducing racial/ethnic disparities in childhood obesity: The role of early life risk factors. *JAMA Pediatrics, 167*(8), 731–738. https://doi.org/10.1001/jamapediatrics.2013.85.

Taylor, C. R., Lee, J. Y., & Stern, B. B. (1995). Portrayals of African, Hispanic, and Asian Americans in magazine advertising. *American Behavioral Scientist, 38*(4), 608–621.

Taylor, E. (2017, March 22). *Arrests made in West Memphis shaken baby case.* News Channel 3 WREG Memphis. https://wreg.com/2017/03/22/arrests-made-in-west-memphis-shaken-baby-case/.

Taylor, R. J., Chatters, L. M., & Celious, A. (2003). Extended family households among Black Americans. *African American Research Perspectives, 9*(1), 133–151.

Taylor, R. J., Chatters, L. M., & Jackson, J. S. (2007). Religious and spiritual involvement among older African Americans, Caribbean Blacks, and non-Hispanic Whites: Findings from the National Survey of American Life. *The Journals of Gerontology Series B: Psychological Sciences and Social Sciences, 62*(4), 238–250.

Taylor, R. J., Chatters, L. M., Woodward, A. T., & Brown, E. (2013). Racial and ethnic differences in extended family, friendship, fictive kin, and congregational informal support networks. *Family relations, 62*(4), 609–624.

Taylor, R. J., Forsythe-Brown, I., Taylor, H. O., & Chatters, L. M. (2014). Patterns of emotional social support and negative interactions among African American and Black Caribbean extended families. *Journal of African American Studies, 18*(2), 147–163.

Taylor, R., Chatters, L., & Cross, C. J., (2021). Fictive kin networks among African Americans, Black Caribbeans, and Non-Latino Whites. *Journal of Family Issues, 43*(1), 20–46.

Thomas, S. (2019). *Statistics on drug addiction*. American Addiction Center. https://americanaddictioncenters.org/rehab-guide/addiction-statistics.

Turner, D., & Briken, P. (2018). Treatment of paraphilic disorders in sexual offenders or men with a risk of sexual offending with Luteinizing hormone-releasing hormone agonists: An updated systemic review. *Journal of Sexual Medicine, 15*, 77–93.

Turner, S., Taillieu, T., Cheung, K., & Afifi, T. (2017). The relationship between child sexual abuse and mental health outcomes among males: Results from a nationally represented United States sample. *Child Abuse and Neglect*, 66, 64–72. https://doi.org/10.1016/j.chiabu.2017.01.018.

United Nations Children's Fund. (2012). *Child maltreatment: Prevalence, incidences, and consequences, in the East Asia and Pacific Regions*. https://www.unicef.org/eap/media/2916/file/maltreatment.pdf.

United Nations Children's Fund. (2020). *End Violence campaign*. https://www.unicef.org/end-violence.

U.S. Census Bureau. (2018). *Child population by race in the United States*. Kid Count Data Center, Population Division, U.S. Census Bureau.

U.S. Department of Commerce. (2017). *Quick facts: United States*. United State Census Bureau. https://www.census.gov/quickfacts/fact/table/U.S./PST045217.

U.S. Department of Education. (2016). *Status and trends in the education of racial and ethnic groups 2016*. https://nces.ed.gov/pubs2016/2016007.pdf.

U.S. Department of Health & Human Services. (2018a). *Discipline versus abuse*. Child Welfare Information Gateway. https://www.childwelfare.gov/topics/can/defining/disc-abuse/#discipline.

U.S. Department of Health & Human Services, Administration for Children and Families, Administration on Children, Youth and Families, Children's Bureau. (2020). *Child Maltreatment 2018*. https://www.acf.hhs.gov/cb/research-data-technology/statistics-research/child-maltreatment.

U.S. Department of Health & Human Services, Administration for Children and Families, Administration on Children, Youth and Families, Children's Bureau. (2021). *Child Maltreatment 2019*. https://www.acf.hhs.gov/cb/research-data-technology/statistics-research/child-maltreatment.

U.S. Department of Health & Human Services. (2001). *Mental health: Culture, race, and ethnicity—A supplement to mental health: A report of the surgeon general*. U.S. Department of Health and Human Services, Substance Abuse and Mental Health Services Administration, Center for Mental Health Services.

U.S. Department of Health & Human Services. (2018b). *The Child Abuse Prevention and Treatment Act*. https://www.acf.hhs.gov/sites/default/files/cb/capta.pdf.

U.S. Department of Labor. (1965). *The Negro family: The case for national action*. U.S. Government Printing Office.

U.S. Preventative Services Task Force. (2019). Interventions to prevent child maltreatment: Recommendation statement. *American Family Physician, 100*(2), 110–112.

United States Department of Justice. (2020). *National Sex Offender Public Website*. https://www.nsopw.gov/.

van der Put, C. E., Assink, M., Gubbels, J., & van Solinge, N.F.B. (2018). Identifying effective components of child maltreatment interventions: A meta-analysis. *Clinical Child and Family Psychology Review, 21*(2), 171–202.

Van Mourik, K., Crone, M. R., De Wolff, M. S., & Reis, R. (2017). Parent training programs for ethnic minorities: A meta-analysis of adaptations and effect. *Prevention Science, 18*(1), 95–105.

Vidal, S., Prince, D., Connell, C., Caron, C., Kaufman, J., & Tebes, J. (2017). Maltreatment, family environment, and social risk factors: Determinants of the child welfare to juvenile justice transition among maltreated children and adolescents. https://www.ncbi.nlm.nih.gov/pmc/articles/PMC5283859/.

Waid, J., & Choy-Brown, M. (2021). Moving upstream: The Family First Prevention Services Act and re-imagining opportunities for prevention in child welfare practice. *Children and Youth Services Review*, 127, 106098.

Wallace, K. (2014, July 21). *Mom arrested for leaving 9-year-old alone at the park*. CNN. https://www.cnn.com/2014/07/21/living/mom-arrested-left-girl-park-parents/index.html.

Walsh, K., Zwi, K., Woolfenden, S., & Shlonsky, A. (2015). School-based education programmes for the prevention of child sexual abuse (review). *The Cochrane Library, 4*, 1–121.

Walsh, K., Zwi, K., Woolfenden, S., & Shlonsky, A. (2018). School-based education programs for the prevention of child sexual abuse: A Cochrane systematic review and meta-analysis. *Research on social work practice, 28*(1), 33–55

Ward, C., & Geeraert, N. (2016). Advancing acculturation theory and research: The acculturation process in its ecological context. *Current Opinion in Psychology, 8*, 98–104.

Watkins, S. (1990). The Mary Ellen Myth: Correcting Child Welfare History. *Social Work, 35*(6), 500–503. www.jstor.org/stable/23715954.

Watt, T., & Kim, S. (2019). Race/ethnicity and foster youth outcomes: An examination of disproportionality using the national youth in transition database. *Children and Youth Services Review, 102*, 251–258. https://10.1016/j.childyouth.2019.05.017.

Wexler, R. (2017). Abuse in foster care: Research vs child welfare alternative facts. https://youthtoday.org/2017/09/abuse-in-foster-care-research-vs-the-child-welfare-systems-alternative-facts/.

Wildeman, C., & Waldfogel, J. (2014). Somebody's children or nobody's children? How the sociological perspective could enliven research on foster care. *Annual Review of Sociology, 40*, 599–618. https://doi.org/10.1146/annurev-soc-071913-043358.

Wildeman, C., Goldman, A.W., & Turney, K. (2018). Parental incarceration and child health in the United States. *Epidemiological Reviews, 40*(1), 146–156. https://doi.org/10.1093/epirev/mxx013.

Wilson, M. N. (1986). The Black extended family: An analytical consideration. *Developmental Psychology, 22*(2), 246–258.

Wilson, M. N., Woods, L. N., & Hijjawi, G. R. (2004). African American families in context. Child welfare revisited: An Africentric perspective. In J. E. Everett, S. P. Chipungu, & B. R. Leashore (Eds.), *Child Welfare Revisited* (pp. 124–144). Rutgers University Press.

Wong, R. J., Chou, C., & Ahmed, A. (2014). Long term trends and racial/ethnic disparities in the prevalence of obesity. *Journal of Community Health, 39*(6), 1150–1160. https://doi.org/10.1007/s10900-014-9870-6.

World Health Organization. (2002). *World report on violence and health: Summary*. https://www.who.int/violence_injury_prevention/violence.

World Health Organization. (2020). *Child Maltreatment*. https://www.who.int/news-room/fact-sheets/detail/child-maltreatment#:~:text=Child%20maltreatment%20is%20the%20abuse%20and%20neglect%20that,occurs%20to%20children%20under%2018%20years%20of%20age.

Yampolskaya, S., Greenbuam, P., & Berson, I. (2009). Profiles of child maltreatment perpetrators and risk for fatal assault: A latent class analysis. *Journal of Family Violence, 24*(5), 337–348. https://doi.org/10.1007/s10896-009-9233-8.

Zeng, Z. (2018). *Jail inmates 2016*. U.S. Department of Justice, Office of Justice Programs Bureau of Justice Statistics.

Zensationalkids.com. (2017). The Science Behind the Practices. https://zensationalkids.com/.

Zinn, H. (1980). *A people's history of the United States: 1492-present*. HarperCollins Publisher.

Index

About the Authors

MELISSA PHILLIPS, PhD, is a mid-career psychologist in clinical practice. She identifies as a bi-cultural Black American woman who is a second-generation Caribbean immigrant, all of which have shaped her professional development in clinical practice, teaching, and research. She is an advocate for diversity, social justice, gender equity, and immigrant issues.

SHAVONNE J. MOORE-LOBBAN, PhD, ABPP, is an African American woman, raised in a womanist-value driven family, who identifies as spiritual, and whose experiences are influenced by the intersection of these identities. She is an early career psychologist who specializes in trauma, promotes social justice, and advocates for mental health care in communities of color.

MILTON A. FUENTES, PhD, is a professor of psychology at Montclair State University in Montclair, New Jersey, and a licensed psychologist in New Jersey and New York. His scholarship focuses on equity, diversity, and inclusion, and he has authored several peer-reviewed articles, book chapters, and books in this area. Fuentes also coauthored a manual with Julia Silva for facilitators of the ACT Raising Safe Kids Program, an international parenting program housed at the American Psychological Association. In this manual, he applies the principles of motivational interviewing to the program's parenting sessions, promoting child welfare and discouraging child maltreatment.

THE PREVENTING CHILD MALTREATMENT COLLECTION

PREVENTING CHILD MALTREATMENT IN THE U.S.: MULTICULTURAL CONSIDERATIONS
Milton A. Fuentes, Rachel R. Singer, and Renee L. DeBoard-Lucas
9781978822573 Paper
9781978822580 Cloth

PREVENTING CHILD MALTREATMENT IN THE U.S.: THE LATINX COMMUNITY PERSPECTIVE
Esther J. Calzada, Monica Faulkner, Catherine LaBrenz, and Milton A. Fuentes
9781978822887 Paper
9781978822894 Cloth

PREVENTING CHILD MALTREATMENT IN THE U.S.: AMERICAN INDIAN AND ALASKA NATIVE PERSPECTIVES
Royleen J. Ross, Julii M. Green, and Milton A. Fuentes
9781978821101 Paper
9781978821118 Cloth

PREVENTING CHILD MALTREATMENT IN THE U.S.: THE BLACK COMMUNITY PERSPECTIVE
Melissa Phillips, Shavonne J. Moore-Lobban, and Milton A. Fuentes
9781978820630 Paper
9781978820647 Cloth

The Preventing Child Maltreatment collection is a four-book miniseries within the Violence Against Women and Children series at Rutgers University Press. This collection, curated by Milton A. Fuentes from Montclair State University, is devoted to advancing an understanding of the dynamics of child maltreatment across ethnically diverse populations. Starting with *Preventing Child Maltreatment in the U.S.: Multicultural Considerations*, which provides a general examination of child maltreatment through the interaction of feminist, multicultural, and social justice lenses, the rest of the series takes a closer look at Native American/Alaska Native, Black, and Latinx communities in order to provide insight for social workers who may encounter those populations within their scope of treatment. Policymakers, practitioners, graduate students, and social workers of all kinds will find this collection of great interest.

RUTGERSUNIVERSITY**PRESS**
rutgersuniversitypress.org